> "America's leading source of self-help legal information." ★★★★
> —YAHOO!

LEGAL INFORMATION ONLINE ANYTIME

24 hours a day

www.nolo.com

AT THE NOLO.COM SELF-HELP LAW CENTER, YOU'LL FIND

- Nolo's comprehensive Legal Encyclopedia filled with plain-English information on a variety of legal topics
- Nolo's Law Dictionary—legal terms <u>without</u> the legalese
- Auntie Nolo—if you've got questions, Auntie's got answers
- The Law Store—over 250 self-help legal products including: Downloadable Software, Books, Form Kits and eGuides
- Legal and product updates
- Frequently Asked Questions
- NoloBriefs, our free monthly email newsletter
- Legal Research Center, for access to state and federal statutes
- Our ever-popular lawyer jokes

Quality LAW BOOKS & SOFTWARE FOR EVERYONE

Nolo's user-friendly products are consistently first-rate. Here's why:

- A dozen in-house legal editors, working with highly skilled authors, ensure that our products are accurate, up-to-date and easy to use
- We continually update every book and software program to keep up with changes in the law
- Our commitment to a more democratic legal system informs all of our work
- We appreciate & listen to your feedback. Please fill out and return the card at the back of this book.

OUR "NO-HASSLE" GUARANTEE

Return anything you buy directly from Nolo for any reason and we'll cheerfully refund your purchase price. No ifs, ands or buts.

Read This First

The information in this book is as up to date and accurate as we can make it. But it's important to realize that the law changes frequently, as do fees, forms, and procedures. If you handle your own legal matters, it's up to you to be sure that all information you use—including the information in this book—is accurate. Here are some suggestions to help you:

First, make sure you've got the most recent edition of this book. To learn whether a later edition is available, check the edition number on the book's spine and then go to Nolo's online Law Store at www.nolo.com or call Nolo's Customer Service Department at 800-728-3555.

Next, even if you have a current edition, you need to be sure it's fully up to date. The law can change overnight. At www.nolo.com, we post notices of major legal and practical changes that affect the latest edition of a book. To check for updates, find your book in the Law Store on Nolo's website (you can use the "A to Z Product List" and click the book's title). If you see an "Updates" link on the left side of the page, click it. If you don't see a link, that means we haven't posted any updates. (But check back regularly.)

Finally, we believe accurate and current legal information should help you solve many of your own legal problems on a cost-efficient basis. But this text is not a substitute for personalized advice from a knowledgeable lawyer. If you want the help of a trained professional, consult an attorney licensed to practice in your state.

1st edition

Patenting Art & Entertainment

New Strategies for Protecting Creative Ideas

by Gregory Aharonian
& Attorney Richard Stim

First Edition	JUNE 2004
Editor	LISA GUERIN
Cover Design	TERRI HEARSH
Book Design	TERRI HEARSH
Proofreading	ROBERT WELLS
Index	ELLEN DAVENPORT
Printing	CONSOLIDATED PRINTERS, INC.

Aharonian, Gregory, 1958-
    Patenting art and entertainment/written by Gregory Aharonian and Richard
Stim.--1st ed.
        p. cm.
    ISBN 1-4133-0032-4 (alk. paper)
    1. Art--United States--Patents--Popular works. 2. Performing arts--United
States--Patents--Popular works. I. Stim, Richard. II. Title.

KF3133.A38A79 2004
346.7304'86--dc22

                          2004041474

Quantity sales: For information on bulk purchases or corporate premium sales, please contact the Special Sales department. For academic sales or textbook adoptions, ask for Academic Sales, 800-955-4775. Nolo, 950 Parker St., Berkeley, CA 94710.

Acknowledgments—Greg Aharonian

If I am a farmer of artistic ideas, I owe it all to my mother. If I can account for these ideas for the benefit of the community, I owe it all to my father. This book is in honor of them, though my niece and nephews are a better honor. And to all my friends, thanks for your encouragement—donuts on me.

Acknowledgments—Rich Stim

Thanks to:

Greg A. for instigation and good ideas

Lisa G. for keeping things on track with her editorial GPS

Terri H. for finishing the great layout and cover before Prague

Drea S. for taking my calls

This book is for my Dad, Joe Stim, a great artist and lawyer.

Table of Contents

Theory

3 Design Patents for Art & Entertainment

4 Traditional Protection for Art & Entertainment

5 Should You Apply for a Patent?

Practice

Appendixes

A How the USPTO Handles Patent Applications

B Art & Entertainment Classifications

Index

Theory

Introduction

*A*s far as we can tell, this is the first book about patenting art and entertainment. Being first doesn't get us a patent. There's nothing in this book that's particularly novel (one requirement of patentability) and much of what we write will probably be obvious to others in the field.

But we do attempt to do something new here: To consider art and entertainment patents as a family, much like pharmacology, software, and business methods patents are currently categorized. We explain—through lots of examples—what kinds of art and entertainment innovations have been granted patents, and how to decide whether your idea might be patentable.

Our challenge when deciding how to present this information was whether to create a theoretical book that explores the need for a separate art and entertainment patent category or to write a practical book that explains how to identify and protect patentable art and entertainment subject matter. We opted to do both, dividing the book into Part One (theoretical) and Part Two (practical).

Don't be afraid of Part One. We're not pushing a doctrine nor speculating on the future. We're just taking a closer look at patents for art and entertainment. In doing so, we define our terms and survey innovations that have received patents. We also look at copyright and other types of intellectual property protection, and help you decide which provides the best protection for your idea.

In Part Two, we speak directly to artists, entertainers, and other innovators and at-tempt to make the world of patent procedures more accessible. We explain patent searching, invention documentation, and patent application procedures.

This emphasis on the "how-to" may disappoint those seeking an academic treatise or exploration of moral issues ("Will patenting art stifle creativity?" "Does art serve a purpose?"). Of course, if interest in patenting art grows (as we believe it will), others will explore these ideas and many more. For now, we hope this book serves as an introduction to the concept and the process of protecting art and entertainment innovations.

Chapter 1 sets the stage by defining some key terms and providing important basic information on patent law.

A. The Nutty Professor as a Paradigm

In Jerry Lewis's film *The Nutty Professor*, mild-mannered scientist Professor Julius Ferris invents a serum that allows him to moonlight as suave entertainer Buddy Love. None of the film's characters suspect that the urbane Love and the nerdy inventor are one and the same. After all, artists and inventors are two distinct breeds.

But are they? This book argues a different view—that art and invention have been intertwined throughout history; the artist's studio is also the inventor's laboratory; and the chasm separating Buddy Love and Professor Ferris is dissolving (if it ever existed at all).

Need proof that Buddy Love and Dr. Ferris are the same? Look no farther than the Nutty Professor himself:

Jerry Lewis had a problem as director of the film, *The Bellboy*; he couldn't view his scenes through the camera while acting. So, he mounted a video camera on the motion picture camera which allowed him to simultaneously watch each scene (as a director) and participate (as an actor). Lewis's "Video Assist" system was a hit with most directors and became a mainstay of film production (though some directors despised the video monitor for turning actors into "directors," eager to give opinions and "collaborate" on decisions).

Jerry Lewis got a patent for his innovation, a rarity for artists. This award allowed Lewis (or whoever he assigned the patent to) to control who made, sold, used, or offered the Video Assist system for sale for approximately 17 years.

In this book we argue that Lewis is not alone. Arts and entertainment are the breeding grounds for many patentable ideas. What's more, patent law provides advantages for artists that other forms of intellectual property protection, such as copyrights and trademarks, don't necessarily offer. (This is not to say that all works of art and entertainment qualify for patent protection or that patent protection, by itself, guarantees commercial success.) But the use of patents to protect arts and entertainment is likely to increase in coming years, for two reasons:

- **Art and technology are intertwined.** Much like alchemy evolved into the science of chemistry, the creation of arts and entertainment have evolved into formal sciences. Technology and process are as important as content when it comes to today's art and entertainment, from video games to raves, flash animation, hip-hop, MP3s, and computerized animation.

- **Patent law is expanding.** As the arts are changing, patent law is growing to include methods and processes that would have been considered unpatentable just 20 years ago. In recent years, for example, the United States Patent and Trademark office (USPTO) granted patents for:
  - a method for creating an antigravity illusion (U.S. Pat. 5,255,452)
  - a system that provides financial incentives for citizens to view political messages on the Internet (U.S. Pat. 5,855008)
  - a method of exercising a cat (U.S. Pat. 5,443,036)
  - a system for automating airline seat upgrades (U.S. Pat. 6,246,998), and
  - an online dating service (U.S. Pat. 5,884,272).

If patents like these are being issued why not patents for a "Method of Deceiving an Audience as to Presence of a Weapon," a "System for Accomplishing a Falling Stunt," or "A Process for Eliciting Laughter"?

Much of what we discuss here is still evolving. For example, controversy still exists over what constitutes a patentable business method, whether international law will conform to changes in United States law, and what kinds of art and entertainment will be subject to patent protection. Also, many people continue to resist the idea of merging the arts and science. Jerry Lewis remains bitter over the lack of respect he got for the Video Assist. As he told a writer for the *Society of Camera Operators Magazine*, "They [the film community] haven't appreciated the work of an innovator because he's a pratfall comic so I won't dignify them with any further comment about my device."

B. Art and Entertainment

For the purposes of this book, "art and entertainment" refers to a wide range of tools and works that inspire, provoke, amuse, distract, and divert humans. These include media and processes like film, music, video, painting, graphic art, and writing. In the following sections, we'll look at the distinctions between tools of art and works of art and the differences between art and entertainment.

1. Tools and Works

In 1841, John Rand invented a method of storing oil paint using a tin tube closed at each end with a pincer and solder. With his patented invention—known as the collapsible tube—artists could, for the first time, squeeze paint out in increments and then reseal the tube. Compared to the previous method—stuffing oil paint in an animal bladder (known as a "skin bag") and then jabbing the bag with a bone—Rand's invention was a quantum leap forward. Colors could be squeezed when needed, stored for long periods, and applied

in any order or in any amount. In short, artists could paint with more spontaneity.

What was especially remarkable about Rand's invention was that it didn't just change the way paint was stored: it also changed the way artists painted. "Without paints in tubes," remarked Pierre-Auguste Renoir, "there would have been no Cezanne, no Monet, no Sisley, or Pissarro, nothing of what the journalists were later to call Impressionism."

John Rand created a tool for artists—a functional method that changed the methodology of an art form. Rand also created works of art—he was a well-respected portrait painter. Although there is a fundamental difference between a tool and a work of art, *both* tools of art and works of art are potentially patentable subject matter. We group them together for several reasons:

- It is sometimes difficult to separate tools from works, ideas from expression, and function from aesthetics—for example in a *Playstation* game, where does the tool (the software and game play choices) end, and where does the art or entertainment (the sound and visuals) begin? Similarly, when you choose a pop song to serve as the "ringer" for your cell phone—one of the fastest-growing sources of music revenue—is the song functional or artistic?

- Patent law protects both tools and works. "Utility patents" are granted for useful inventions (tools) and "design patents" are granted for aesthetic or ornamental designs (works). Many inventions trigger both forms of protection—for example, the Mickey Mouse telephone.

- The boundaries of protection in patent law are changing. The explosion of new technology patents, particularly business-method patents, has redefined what is patentable. Some invented concepts—the structure for a romance novel or the construction of a heavy metal ballad, for example—do not fall neatly into either the tools or works categories.

2. The Fusion of Art and Entertainment

Without getting too deeply into the territory of philosophies or art critics, it's safe to say that there's entertainment in virtually every art work, and vice versa (see "Killing the Clown on Stilts," below). Both art and entertainment are human expressions that require organization, arrangement, and an audience—and historically, these two categories have overlapped and intertwined. In this book, we use the term, "arts," to refer to both categories.

We're not alone in grouping these two concepts together—just look at the "Arts & Entertainment" cable channel or the ubiquitous "arts and entertainment" supplement in every local newspaper. Nowadays, these two categories seem to be permanently fused. The marketing of any venture today—whether it is the soft news known as infotainment or the placement of computer product references in hip-hop songs—requires some element of distraction, recreation, or diversion that merges art and entertainment. The public, unaware

that the message of art has been replaced by the message of commerce, no longer sees any distinction between art and entertainment in these marketing ventures.

The distinction between art and entertainment has only one minor impact on our analysis of patents. Patents only protect useful inventions. What's useful? Legally speaking, providing entertainment is considered a useful activity. On the other hand, beauty, the provocation of thought or inspiration—things accomplished by art—are not considered useful. For that reason, you cannot patent Picasso's *Guernica* but you can patent a musical condom that plays "Happy Birthday to You."

In practical terms, the applicant for a patent can establish that an invention is useful simply by demonstrating any functionality that has a legitimate use for humans. And that covers a broad range of art and entertainment expressions.

C. What Is an Invention?

Patents are granted only to new inventions, but the term "invention" is much more elastic than you might think. When most people think of an invention, they think of a "thing"—for example, the collapsible tube or the Video Assist camera and monitor. But Jerry Lewis and John Rand didn't set out to invent a "thing"; instead they wanted to invent a method of doing something—a method of storing paint and a method of using a closed-circuit

Killing the Clown on Stilts

Though we group art and entertainment together, there is a historical difference. Comedian Marc Maron tells the story of walking in Montreal, where he sees a clown on stilts juggling for an ecstatic, adoring crowd. Unimpressed—"It's just a clown," thinks Maron—he walks down the block, where a saxophone player is blowing a brilliant composition to an audience of one homeless person. Maron tells the sax player he likes the song. Turns out it's an original featured on the sax player's new CD—the song title: "Killing the Clown on Stilts."

Art, as exemplified by the saxophone player's purposeful composition, is infused with intention. The artist intends to communicate something, whether it is an aesthetic, a thought, or emotion. For that reason, art is also sometimes determined by the public's reaction—that is, whether it instigates thought, appreciation, or inspiration.

Entertainment, like the juggling clown's performance, isn't infused with any meaningful intention other than the desire to … well, entertain. The customer is amused or pleased. Instead of provoking thought or conveying an aesthetic, the clown diverts and distracts.

In the real world, of course, the separation between art and entertainment is not always so clear. Some clowns, such as Emmet Kelly's "Weary Willy" character, provoke thought, appreciation, even sadness. And some saxophone players, for example Boots "Yakety Sax" Randolph, are quite content to entertain.

camera. They used "things" to accomplish their goals.

An invention, for patent purposes, typically develops in two stages: first as a brainstorm or "Eureka moment," and second as a physical manifestation of the idea—for example, a prototype or a writing that explains how to make and use the idea. The brainstorm, is known in patent law as "conception." The embodiment of the idea—that is, when the inventor shows how to make and use the invention—is known as "reduction to practice."

EXAMPLE: **Da Vinci invents *sfumato*.** Artists had difficulty representing atmospheric conditions in paintings until Leonardo da Vinci had an idea —to blur shadows and objects using minute transitions between color areas. He showed how to do this (in other words, reduced it to practice) in his 1485 painting *Virgin of the Rocks*, and again, in the delicate, smoky, mountainous landscape that forms the background of the *Mona Lisa*. Like many great art inventions, da Vinci's innovative process, known as *sfumato,* transcended its technique and, as one writer put it, created an emotional effect on viewers—a "willingness to embrace uncertainty."

Today, the definition of invention is so broad and all-encompassing that it includes virtually anything under the sun that can be made by humans. Curiously, this broad definition of invention is not far from the thinking of Aristotle and Plato, both of whom grouped art and invention into one category.

Aristotle categorized as *poiesis,* the making, producing, or performing of something. Plato considered both to be *operative* ventures—the transforming of natural objects into man-made things.

D. What Is a Patent?

In the 15th century, architect Filippo Brunelleschi was commissioned to build a cathedral with a massive dome (a "cupola"). While attempting this task, he made a brilliant architectural breakthrough: he discovered that curves in the cupola could be constructed without a supporting framework. Bruneleschi's idea led to the popularization of Renaissance architecture. But this innovation might never have happened if Brunelleschi had not solved a more practical problem—how to haul large stones to the cathedral construction site. To accomplish this task, Brunelleschi devised a unique boat capable of moving heavy loads upriver. For his efforts, he was granted the exclusive right to haul heavy loads on the river using his boat. With this monopoly over the use of his invention, Brunelleschi became the first recipient of a "patent grant."

The government rewards innovators today with a more sophisticated patent arrangement. In the United States, an inventor who creates a new, useful, nonobvious invention gets the exclusive right to make use, sell, or offer the invention for sale for a period of approximately 17 to 18 years.

Of course, there are some strings attached: The patent will be denied unless the inventor files the patent application within a fixed period of time and meets rigorous standards at the USPTO. Even if you are granted a patent, the rights it confers are purely offensive. It does not give you a right to prevent others form stealing your innovention (called "infringing your patent"), but it gives you a right to sue the infringer. (This is why author/attorney David Pressman refers to a patent as an inventor's hunting license.) If you don't take action to stop infringers, your patent will become worthless.

The USPTO grants three types of patents: utility, design, and plant patents. A utility patent, the most common type, covers inventions that function in a unique manner to produce a useful result. Unless we say otherwise, whenever we refer to a patent in this book, we're referring to a utility patent.

A design patent is granted for product designs—for example, an Eames chair, Keith Haring wallpaper, or a Nike shoe. You can even get a design patent for a computer screen icon. There are strings attached to a design patent, too. The design must be ornamental or aesthetic; it can't be functional. You can enforce your design patent for only 14 years after it's issued. (For more information on design patents, see Chapters 3 and 8.) The USPTO also issues patents for plants. Because they're unlikely to fit into the art and entertainment premise of this book, however, we do not discuss them here.

Patents aren't renewable. Once the patent expires, others have the right to use your idea (and you can't repatent an invention, either). Patent rights extend throughout the entire United States, its territories, and possessions. Under international treaties, the owner of a United States patent can acquire patent rights in other countries by filing corresponding patent applications abroad. However, there are strict time limits for filing such foreign applications.

Finally, a patent is a form of personal property. It can be sold outright for a lump sum, or its owner can give anyone permission to use the invention ("license it") in return for royalty payments to the patent owner. A patent can also be transferred by gift, will, or descent (under the state's intestate succession [no-will] laws). In subsequent chapters we'll discuss patent standards in more detail, including what you have to do to get a patent.

E. Patent Requirements— Prior Art, Novelty, and Nonobviousness

No introduction to patents would be complete without an explanation of several patent concepts: "prior art," "novelty," and "nonobviousness." These three terms all speak to the "newness" of the invention. Patents are granted only to inventions that differ from those that preceded it. If the invention was already in use, or if it would have been obvious to those in the field of the invention—for example, if paint tubes already

were available or obvious to painters—then the inventor cannot get a patent.

1. Prior Art

To be patentable, an invention must be distinguishable from the hundreds of thousands of innovations that preceded it. Or, as the writer André Malraux wrote (referring to art and literature), "The convincing force of a work … lies in the difference between it and the works that preceded it." These previous innovations are referred to, coincidentally for our purposes, as "prior art." They include:

- any invention in public use or on sale in the United States for more than one year before the filing date of your patent application
- anything that was publicly known or used by others in the United States before the date of invention
- anything that was made or built in the United States by another person before the date of invention
- any work that was the subject of a prior patent, issued more than one year before the filing date of your patent or any time before the date you created the invention, or
- any work that was published more than one year before the filing date of your patent or any time before your date of invention.

Prior art is used to gauge two patent standards, novelty and nonobviousness.

2. Novelty

An invention is novel if it differs in some way from the prior art. The most common way to establish novelty is to create an invention that physically differs from past ideas—for example, Rand was the first person to conceive of storing paint in extruded tin, rather than in an animal skin. Novelty can also be established by creating a new combination of existing elements. For example, Richard Hollingshead, Jr., combined two existing inventions—movies and automobiles—and patented the drive-in movie theater in 1933.

3. Nonobviousness

In order to obtain a patent, the difference between the invention and the prior art must not be obvious to someone with ordinary skill in the field. Or as it is sometimes put, the invention must yield one or more new and unexpected results. For example, even though John Rand's collapsible tube had been around for 50 years, it wasn't until 1892 that a dentist came up with the idea of filling it with toothpaste, eliminating the communal toothpaste jar. The fact that it took 50 years for someone to realize that toothpaste could be put in tubes demonstrates that it wasn't obvious to those working in the field of oral hygiene.

Nonobviousness is always measured against a person having ordinary skill in the field of the invention. The law considers a person having "ordinary skill in the art" to be a worker in the field of the invention who has ordinary skill, but who also knows about all of the prior art in the field. Of course, this is a legal fantasy—no such person ever lived (or ever will), but there's just no other realistic way to set an objective standard for determining nonobviousness. Instead, the PTO creates a hypothetical person and tries to weigh the obviousness of the invention against the knowledge this hypothetical person would possess. To determine nonobviousness, courts go through these steps.

- determine the scope and content of the prior art
- determine the novelty of the invention
- determine the level of skill of artisans in the pertinent art and consider secondary and objective factors, such as commercial success, long-felt but unsolved need, and failure of others
- against this background, determine whether the invention is obvious or nonobvious.

In light of these standards, consider the invention of the printing press in 1452. The screw-type wine (or olive) press had already been in existence for centuries. Block-print technology, oil-based inks, and mass-produced paper production had also been around for a few hundred years. Yet none of the people involved with paper, movable block texts, or wine presses had the flash of brilliance that Gutenberg had when he converted his wine press to hold metal type blocks and reproduce text on pages of paper. The rapid success and popularity of the press, and the fact that it solved a long-perceived need to disseminate textual information demonstrated that Gutenberg's invention was nonobvious.

To paraphrase Albert Szent-Gyorgyi, Gutenberg "saw what everybody had seen and thought what nobody had thought." Judge Learned Hand echoed this when he stated, "Many great inventions are of this character, and the reason why the ordinary man does not discover them although they are so plain when some one else has done so is that habit has limited his power to see what he has not been accustomed to see, and his selective attention is fast bound by his past experience."

Two mainstays of the 20th century—radio commercials and supermarkets—both seem obvious to us in hindsight, but were actually nonobvious inventions. Initially, radio stations were created as a means of selling radios— stations that played music, for example, increased sales. It wasn't until August 1922 that radio station owners realized they could earn money directly from the new medium when WEAF in New York created the first "commercial" broadcasting, a paid advertisement for the rental of nearby apartment buildings.

Prior to 1916, whenever a customer wanted an item at a retail store, a clerk fetched it and brought it to the cash register. Clarence Saunders realized that the customer could do the fetching when he invented and patented the supermarket—a place where customers perused aisles of products, made their choice, and carried it to the cash register.

Beating the Clock: The One-Year Rule

Under the "one-year rule," an inventor must file a patent application within one year after the inventor first sells, offers for sale, or commercially or publicly uses or describes the invention. An inventor who fails to file within this year cannot get a patent. After one year has passed following a sale, offer for sale, public or commercial use, or public knowledge about an invention, the USPTO will no longer consider that invention novel. If the USPTO is unaware of the public sale or use and issues a patent, the patent will be declared invalid if it is later shown that the invention was publicly shown or sold more than a year before the patent issued.

Icons Used in This Book

To aid you in using this book, we use the following icons:

 The caution icon warns you of potential problems.

 This icon indicates that the information is a useful tip.

 This icon refers you to helpful books or other resources.

 This icon refers you to a further discussion of the topic elsewhere in this book.

From Paint to Transgenic Bunnies

In order to give you some historic perspective, we've borrowed portions of a timeline of important innovations in art and entertainment from the Patenting Art and Entertainment website (www.patenting-art.com). We chose these innovations because, within their time, they probably met our modern patent standards of usefulness, novelty, and nonobviousness. (The dates of invention are, in many cases, approximate.) You can find other examples of patentable art and entertainment in Chapters 2 and 3.

350,000 BCE	African tribes invent paint, as evidenced by pigments and paint-grinding equipment found in a cave at Twin Rivers, near Lusaka, Zambia.
31,000 BCE	Representational painting is invented, as evidenced by the murals of stampeding bulls, cantering horses, red bears, and woolly rhinoceros found in the Chauvet cavern in the Ardeche region of France. (Nearby paintings from 15,000 BCE are found in the Lascaux caves.)
22,000 BCE	Paleolithic tribes invent sculpture, as evidenced by the Venus of Willendorf statuette, a female figure carved in porous oolitic limestone measuring 11 centimeters in length and found about 30 meters above the Danube near the town of Willendorf in Austria.
4000 BCE	Egyptians invent papyrus, the precursor of paper, by pounding flat woven mats of reeds.
2500 BCE	Egyptian chemists invent the synthetic color pigment, Egyptian blue, a mixture of limestone (calcium oxide), malachite (copper oxide), and quartz (silica), fired to a temperature of 800 to 900 degrees Celsius.
2500 BCE	Egyptian priests invent theater, with their annual ritual, the Abydos Passion Play, about the god Osiris. Evidence of this is found on the Ikhernofret hieroglyphic stone dating from 1868 BCE. The stone is an account of one Ikhernofret, who was a participant. The stone lists eight acts from the play.
2200 BCE	Sumerian priests invent mythic storytelling, a story about the flooding of the earth involving many gods and a pious king Ziusdra. (Around 1800 BCE, the Babylonians invent the "derivative work" when they adapt and expand the flood story in their Epic of Gilgamesh, involving the pious king Atrahasis. Around 500 BCE, Hebrew priests in Babylonia take the regionally popular flood story, reduce the gods to one, and demote the king to a commoner named Noah.)

From Paint to Transgenic Bunnies (continued)

1950 BCE	Egyptian authors invent the novel, in the form of a narrative, *Story of Sinuhe*, about a prince of Egypt who flees after a court killing, is saved in the desert by a Bedouin tribe, and later marries the eldest daughter of a king. (Some believe this to be the precursor of the Biblical story of Moses.)
675 BCE	Stesichorus of Sicily invents the heroic ballad.
600 BCE	The Cretan poet and prophet Epimenides invents the Liar's Paradox with his phrase "Cretans are ever liars."
570 BCE	Musicians in India invent the first stringed instrument, the vina, which consists of two hollow gourds connected by strings and a bamboo reed.
500 BCE	Greek artists invent encaustic paints, where color pigments are embedded in wax.
450 BCE	Greek artists invent three-dimensional painting, or chiaroscuro, by using highlighting and shadowing.
450 BCE	Sophron of Syracuse invents mime.
250 BCE	Syrian craftsmen in Babylonia invent glassblowing.
105	Chinese court official Ts'ai Lun invents paper.
553	Procopius invents scandal literature, in his story *Anecdota* about the Romans Justinian, Theodora, and Belisarius.
619	The Chinese royal courts invent orchestras, comprising hundreds of instruments and musicians.
650	Chinese artists in the Tang Dynasty invent porcelain, a fired mixture of kaolin (a clay) and petuntse (a feldspar).
808	The Chinese invent the printed book with their seven-page scroll, *The Diamond Sutra*, printed with woodblocks on paper.
855	Polyphonic music is invented.
910	The musician Hucbaldus invents the musical score, in which groups of musical parts are written together. He also invented a staff consisting of an indefinite number of lines.
1022	Murasaki Shikibu (a young noblewoman in Kyoto, Japan) invents the (romance) novel, the story *Genji the Shining One*.

From Paint to Transgenic Bunnies (continued)

1025	Guido of Arezzo invents musical notes, naming them UT, RE, MI, FA, SO, LA (in the 1500s UT is changed to DO, and TI is added), as well as lines/staves to space printed notes.
1030	Guido of Arezzo invents *solfege*, a system for learning music by ear. In the 19th century, *solfege* evolves into the tonic sol-fa system used today.
1225	English monk John of Fornsete invents rounds (songs sung in harmony) with his song *Sumer is icumen in*.
1306	Giotto di Bondone uses depth, perspective, and temporal realism—that is, the conveyance of a single moment in time versus the telling of an event—to end thousands of years of Oriental/Egyptian/early Christian painting in which narratives were conveyed without depth and by completely showing every figure.
1420	Italian artist Masaccio (Tommaso di Giovanni) invents the use in paintings of a single consistent source of light and the three-dimensional portrayal of humans (as demonstrated in his 1427 painting *Tribute Money*).
1430	Leon Battista Alberti introduces the painting concepts of perspective and special precision.
1494	Venetian printer Aldus Manutius invents the textbook, small printed books, octavo sized (6 by 9 inches), for students.
1503	Flemish artist Hieronymus Bosch invents Surrealism in his triptych *Garden of Earthly Delights*. (Surrealism was popularized 400 years later by Henri Rousseau, in his 1897 painting *The Sleeping Gypsy*.)
1597	Jacopo Peri invents opera with his *Dafne*.
1607	Claudio Monteverdi's *Orfeo*, considered to be the first opera masterpiece, revolutionizes music by establishing a tonal system and giving the recitative a more flexible accompaniment.
1610	Italian artist Artemisia Gentileschi invents feminist "revenge" art, painting women who wreak violence against men who have wronged them (for example, in her 1614-1620 painting *Judith Slaying Holofernes*).
1650	Italians Antonio Maria Abbatini and Marco Marazzoli invent the comic opera with their *Dal Male du Violon*, performed in Rome in 1653.

From Paint to Transgenic Bunnies (continued)

1657	Savinien Cyrano de Bergerac invents science fiction with his story about a trip to the moon, *Les Etats et empires de la lune*.
1663	A German publisher invents the magazine, with his *Erbauliche Monaths-Unterredungen* (Edifying Monthly Discussions). In 1731, the first modern magazine, *The Gentleman's Magazine*, is published in England.
1696	French music master Etienne Loulie invents the first metronome, a device for beating time. (Nicolaus Winkler's compact design for the modern metronome was later stolen in 1812 by a German technician who patented and commercialized the idea.)
1730	English artist William Hogarth invents political cartoon by painting sequences of anecdotal pictures that poked fun at aristocracy, corrupt politicians, and the foibles of the day.
1774	Josiah Wedgwood invents Jasperware, a dense vitreous pottery that could be turned on a lathe.
1780	Spanish dancer Sebastiano Carezo invents the bolero dance.
1787	Amadeus Mozart invents algorithmic music with his *Musikalisches Wurfelspiel*, a musical composition dice game where dice are used to choose and combine pre-written measures of music.
1816	Mary Shelley invents literary horror in her story *Frankenstein*.
1816	Joseph-Nicéphore Niepce invents the first photograph, using paper coated with silver chloride that was "fixed" with nitric acid. He later partners with Louis-Jacques-Mandé Daguerre, for whom the Daguerreotype (the first modern form of photography) was named.
1816	Jean-Auguste-Dominique Ingres invents the technique of resolution contrast, by which human faces in drawings or paintings are done in high resolution with the rest of the image in lower resolution (as for example, in his drawing *Mrs. Charles Badham*).
1816	David Brewster invents the kaleidoscope, a tube with mirrors, lenses, and loose pieces of glass.
1829	The Austrian Damian invents the accordion, a portable reed instrument.

From Paint to Transgenic Bunnies (continued)

1830	Painter, art professor, and design engineer Samuel Morse invents the telegraph.
1833	Thomas Dartmouth "Daddy" Rice invents minstrel shows, where white men painted in black perform comedy and sing black songs and spirituals that have been turned into formal compositions. (Minstrel shows popularize the banjo, the Americanized version of the African banza/banshaw/banjar.)
1835	Richard Adams Locke, reporter for the *New York Sun* daily newspaper, invents tabloid journalism when, in a series of stories over the course of a few weeks, he reports that famed astronomer John Herschel, using his powerful telescope, had discovered life on the moon. Locke makes up stories about bipedal beavers, man-bats, and small buffalo all living together on the moon.
1837	German scientist Friedrich Froebel invents kindergarten—structured educational entertainment for children. (One student of Froebel's kindergartens was Piet Mondrian, who started the De Stijl style of art with Theo van Doesburg in 1917.)
1841	Belgian instrument maker Adolphe Sax invents the saxophone.
1843	Edgar Allan Poe invents the mystery novel, with his book *The Gold Bug*.
1843	Anna Atkins invents the photographically illustrated book, with her book *British Algae: Cyanotype Impressions*.
1843	W&SB Ives Company invents the first modern board game, *The Mansion of Happiness*.
1857	Gustave Flaubert publishes *Madame Bovary*, in which he conceals his personal perspective and uses multiple points of view.
1861	Physicist James Clerk Maxwell invents the color photograph.
1862	Edouard Manet invents nonlinear alignment, using no horizontal or vertical lines but rather using curved or askew edges, in his painting *Music in the Tuileries* (an outdoor party scene in the woods).
1863	Edouard Manet invents multiple subject painting, rejecting 1,000 years of artistic custom requiring that art have a consistent subject depicted, in his painting *Le Dejeuner sur l'herbe*. The painting has four disconnected subjects (not looking at each other), as well as a disconnected background-to-foreground perspective (eliminating the middle ground, and subjects are lighted in the painting from different directions.

From Paint to Transgenic Bunnies (continued)

1865 — Jules Chéret in Paris invents chromolithographs, printing multicolor posters using stones. An example is the 1866 poster *Bubbles* by the painter Sir John Millais, of a young boy blowing bubbles, used to advertise soap.

1865 — Lewis Carroll invents the literary use of distorted space and time in his story *Alice in Wonderland*.

1872 — Photographers Eadweard Muybridge and Etienne-Jules Marey invent serial photo-montages, the precursors to motion pictures, when they use multiple cameras to prepare photographs of moving objects,.

1873 — Edouard Manet invents the use of nonlinear horizon lines, by slightly bending the primal horizon line, eliminating the horizon line in his 1874 painting *Boating*.

1880 — Argentinians invent the tango dance and music, that combines African, Indian, and Spanish rhythms. The first forms of the tango dance are based on the "acting out" of the relationship between prostitutes and pimps.

1882 — Edouard Manet invents the use of multiple time depiction, in his *A Bar at the Folies-Bergere*, which depicts a bar scene from two points in space at two different moments in time.

1884 — Georges Seurat invents pointillism, creating a painting by juxtaposing small dots/dabs of pure unmixed color over the whole canvas.

1886 — American painter William Michael Harnett invents *trompe l'oeil*, microscopically accurate paintings of ordinary objects as depicted in his painting *Still Life—Violin & Music*.

1887 — Linguistic researchers invent a new human language, Esperanto.

1888 — Paul Cezanne invents the technique of universal perspective, in his *Still Life with Fruit Basket*, portraying objects from various perspectives. Cezanne also invents the technique of object distortion, by elongating objects in his paintings (later taken to the extreme in Alberto Giacometti's 1947 sculpture *Man Pointing*).

1890 — Emile Jaques Dalcroze invents eurhythmics, a system of musical training through physical movement.

From Paint to Transgenic Bunnies (continued)

1891 — Claude Monet invents the technique of unfreezing time in images by painting the entrance to the cathedral in Rouen at 40 different times of the day (similarly painting the same haystack at 20 moments in a year), a technique inspired by Katsushika Hokusai's 1820's paintings of Mount Fuji from 36 points of view.

1895 — Publisher Joseph Pulitzer invents the first serial comic strip, *The Yellow Kid*, in the *New York World* newspaper. In 1897, Rudolph Dirks invents the comic strip, *Katzenjammer Kids*.

1895 — Auguste and Louis Lumière offer the first for-pay public movie in Paris. They also invent the first newsreel and documentary.

1902 — Paul Cezanne invents the technique of indeterminate time, as used in in his painting *Mont Sainte-Victorie*, painted so that the sources and direction of light in the painting are not discernible, which made it impossible to determine time of day.

1902 — Morris and Rose Michtom invent the teddy bear toy, based on a cartoon of a bear saved by United States President Theodore Roosevelt.

1903 — Auguste and Louis Lumiere invent the three-dimensional movie with their one minute film, *L'Arrivée du Train*. The early 1950s has Hollywood pushing 3-D movies as the next big fad, making 65 films from 1952 to 1954. One of the best was the 1953 *House of Wax*, directed by Andre de Toth.

1904 — Henri Matisse, Maurice de Vlaminck, André Derain, and others invent *Fauvism*, the use of vibrant colors in paintings without reference to actual appearance, as seen in Derain's 1905 painting *Big Ben*.

1905 — Buddy Bolden and Jelly Roll Morton combine ragtime, the blues, and spirituals to invent what later becomes known as jazz.

1907 — Georges Méliès, in his film *Tunneling the English Channel*, invents a variety of special effects: stop-motion photography, split-screen photography, stop action animation, and live action combined with full-scale mechanical backgrounds.

1915 — Cartoonist W. E. Hill invents the multistable image with his drawing *My Wife and My Mother-in-Law*, an image that can appear to depict either a young woman or an old woman.

	From Paint to Transgenic Bunnies (continued)
1917	Piet Mondrian and Theo van Doesburg invent the De Stijl art style, a style based on the use of pure geometry, often intersecting horizontal and vertical black lines, forming rectangles (some of which are colored with pure red, blue, and yellow).
1919	Lev Theremin invents the first electronic music instrument, the theremin, played by moving hands near an antenna.
1920	Ford Motors invents product placement in movies, by donating Model T Fords to be used in the comedy movies of Mark Sennett.
1922	Brig. General George Owen Squier invents *Muzak,* the concept of engineered music that has no vocals, no tempo changes, and no brass instruments.
1922	Radio station WGY in Schenectady, New York, invents radio drama by broadcasting Eugene Walter's play *The Wolf.* The station later created the radio show *The WGY Players,* which presented radio adaptations of popular stage plays.
1923	Charles Francis Jenkins invents broadcast television, by transmitting the first synchronized transmission of pictures and sound using the U.S. Navy station NOF in Anacostia (Washington, D.C.), broadcasting a ten-minute film of a miniature windmill in motion.
1926	Fritz Lang invents science fiction movies—incorporating dynamic visual and special effects—with his movie *Metropolis.* (In 1902, Georges Méliès films the first science fiction movie, *A Trip to the Moon.*)
1928	General Electric invents broadcast drama, broadcasting *The Queen's Messenger* from station WGY in New York.
1929	Director Josef von Sternberg invents film noir in his movie, *Thunderbolt.*
1930	Coca-Cola invents Santa Claus as a jolly figure in order to bolster winter sales of soft drinks.
1932	Alexander Calder invents mobiles, where he suspends sheets of metal painted black, white, and primary colors, from wires and rods. (His inspiration was seeing the colored rectangles covering the walls of Mondrian's studio.)
1935	Technicolor releases *Becky Sharp,* the first movie using a three-color process.

From Paint to Transgenic Bunnies (continued)

1936	Walt Disney invents a device (U.S. Pat. 2,201,689) which greatly speeds up the process of making cartoons with more realistic shading, demonstrated in the 1937 classic *Snow White and the Seven Dwarfs*.
1946	The DuMont network invents the television soap opera, with the debut of *Faraway Hill*.
1947	NBC invents the news show, with *Meet the Press*.
1953	Bill Haley invents rock and roll music, combining guitars, saxophones, piano, bass, and snare drums in his song, *Crazy Man Crazy*.
1957	Scientists at the University of Illinois in Urbana invent computer-assisted musical composition, completing their work titled the *Illiac Suite for String Quartet*.
1962	Students at MIT, using a PDP-1 computer, invent the first graphical computer game, *Spacewar*. (In 1958, Willy Higginbotham at Brookhaven National Laboratory had invented an electronic circuit, with pushbutton input and oscilloscope output, to let two people play a simple game of tennis.)
1979	Sylvia Robinson invents the rap record business when she produces and markets the first rap song, *Rapper's Delight*, at what is to become Sugar Hill Studio in Englewood, New Jersey. (The opening line of the song, "I said a hip hop, the hippie the hippie, to the hip hip hop, and you don't stop" is used to name the genre.)
1979	Daniel Okrent invents fantasy sports leagues by developing rules for a game based on baseball. (In 1984 a rule book is published, *Rotisserie Baseball*.)
1987	Nadia and Daniel Thalmann produce the first movie using computer-generated celebrities, *Rendez-vous a Montreal*, a seven-minute film with a synthetic Marilyn Monroe and Humphrey Bogart.
2000	Eduardo Kac invents transgenic animal art when he creates the GFP Bunny, a transgenic rabbit whose cells are augmented with the Green Fluorescent Protein gene, which causes the rabbit to glow under a black light.

Chapter 2

Utility Patents for Art & Entertainment

*M*arshall McLuhan, the author and media critic, wrote that "art is anything you can get away with." The same may also be said for the granting of utility patents by the USPTO. Assuming you can convince a patent examiner that you've come up with something new, useful, and not obvious to others in your field, you can get a patent for just about anything … including any artistic method, process, or tool.

In this chapter, we'll shine a light on a variety of art and entertainment patents to show the range and somewhat elastic boundaries of patent law. Our purpose here is to give you an idea of the extent of patent possibilities and to help you consider your own innovations within this domain.

Keep in mind that the boundary of what is patentable is always expanding, never retracting. Gene sequences, software innovations, and business methods are just a few examples of inventions that were once perceived as unpatentable. When deciding whether to pursue an art or entertainment-related patent, past performance at the USPTO is no guarantee of future results.

Sometimes it's not worth the effort to pursue a patent. The real issue may not be whether you qualify for a patent, but whether acquiring the patent is in your best business interest. Can you afford to file it? Does it have a chance for commercial success? Can you afford to enforce it? We discuss some of these questions in more detail in Chapter 5.

Always Check for Prior Art

One thing you will notice when examining the patents in this chapter is the importance of prior art. As discussed in Chapter 1, prior art is any published information available before you created your invention, including previously issued patents. If someone else described your invention prior to your date of invention, you won't be entitled to a patent. In Chapter 6 we discuss the basics of patent searching.

To get a better idea of the expansive world of art and entertainment patents, you can review Greg Aharonian's online database of art and entertainment patents (www .patenting-art.com/database/dbase1-e.htm).

A. Patent Drawings, Abstracts, and Claims

This chapter includes excerpted sections from art and entertainment patents to help demonstrate what makes an artistic or entertaining invention patentable. In order to best describe the strengths (or weaknesses) of these innovations, we sometimes reproduce drawings, an abstract, or a string of instructions known as patent claims. A patent include many more sections (and we discuss these briefly in Chapter 9) but for our purposes here, the drawings, abstract, and claims are the most illustrative segments.

1. Drawings

We've included patent drawings for some of the patents described in this chapter. (The term "drawing" has a broad meaning in patent law and may include illustrations, schematics, flowcharts, and other visual indicia necessary to understand an invention.) The typical patent application includes several drawings, usually of different views of the invention. Due to space limitations, when we include a drawing for an invention in this chapter, we usually only include one view. If you would like to see other views of an invention described here, search for the patent at the USPTO website.

If you have access to the Internet, you can easily view any of the patents discussed in this book. Visit the USPTO website (www.uspto .gov) and under the heading "Patents" click "Search" on the home page. If you know the patent number, you can plug it in and immediately view the invention. If you don't know the number you can use the basic or advanced searching techniques described in more detail in Chapter 6.

2. The Abstract

The abstract is a concise, one-paragraph summary of the structure, nature, and purpose of the invention. It is used by the USPTO and the public to quickly determine the gist of what is being disclosed.

Below is the abstract for a patent entitled "Entertainment device and system" (U.S. Pat. 6,513,173). This patent, issued in 2003, is for a device that apparently elevates bathroom art to new levels—a sensor in a urinal triggers a display above the urinal that provides "entertainment and/or education."

U.S. Pat. 6,513,173

Abstract:

A facility for use as entertainment and/or education wherein there is provided at least one sensor on or adjacent to a surface of the facility that is in connection with a visual display. The condition of the display changes in response to the activation of the sensor. In one embodiment, the facility is a urinal. An alternate embodiment includes a video or electronic message display mounted in conjunction with the urinal to be viewed that may or may not be activated by a sensor.

3. Patent Claims

Patent claims establish the protectible scope of an invention. They are the standard by which patent rights are measured. In other words, when a patent owner sues for infringement, it is because someone has made, used, or sold an invention that has all of the elements in one of the claims (or that closely fits the description in the claims). In this manner, claims function like the boundaries in a deed for real estate.

You will note that some claims are easier to read than others—a result of many factors including the nature of the invention, the writing skills and style of the person drafting the patent, and your familiarity with the area of invention. You may have to read some claims a few times to figure out what's being described. The more you read patent claims, the easier they will be to understand what is claimed.

By law, patent claims must be specific enough to distinguish the invention from prior art. They must also be clear, logical, and precise (see 35 U.S.C. § 112(2)). Nonetheless, claims are often the hardest part of the patent to decipher. One reason is that claims have to follow strict grammatical requirements: they must be sentence fragments; they must always start with an initial capital letter; and must contain one period and no quotation marks or parentheses (except in mathematical or chemical formulas). The claims also tend to contain obtuse terminology (although this is not a legal requirement!).

EXAMPLE: Patent attorney David Pressman, in *Patent It Yourself,* drafted sample claims for the most basic tool of artistic expression—the wooden pencil.

A hand-held writing instrument comprising:

   a. elongated core-element means that will leave a marking line if moved across paper or other similar surface, and

   b. an elongated holder surrounding and encasing said elongated core-element means, one portion of said holder being removable from an end thereof to expose an end of said core-element means so as to enable said core-element means to be exposed for writing, whereby said holder protects said core-element means from breakage and provides an enlarged means for holding said core-element means conveniently.

B. Painting Patents

In the 1964 comedy, *What a Way to Go,* a bohemian expatriate painter played by Paul Newman devises a mechanical method of creating modern art works by connecting multiple paint brushes to his record player. The works are a great commercial success, but in the heat of inspiration, the machine causes the artist's demise. The film's painting machine satirized the common public perceptions of modern art—that is, the works required no skill, lacked human emotion, and could be created just as competently by a machine.

In truth, Hollywood's invention wasn't far from reality. In the 1950s and 1960s, Swiss artist Jean Tinguely designed machines that could randomly create works of art. His devices, known as Meta-Matic #9 and Meta-Matic #17, featured motor-driven pens that automated the process of creating abstract art. Today, consumers are still fascinated by mechanical art-making devices, including spin-art machines that sell for a few hundred dollars and feature a rotating canvas on which paint is dropped. (If you can't afford a spin-art machine, apparently salad spinners and similar devices will work as well.)

New techniques for creating paintings and new inventions that assist painters are constantly being created. Below, we provide some details about two painting patents— U.S. Pat. 4,490,413, "Method for producing a painting," and U.S. Pat. 6,565,059, "Hand rest for an artist's easel."

1. The Floating Painting Process: U.S. Pat. 4,490,413

Like Jean Tinguely, discussed above, Frank Stimson came up with a new way of creating paintings. Though Stimson's method did not use motor-driven devices, it did rely, to some extent, on happenstance, as bits of paint randomly formed together while suspended in water.

Stimson's patent, issued in 1984 (see Illustration 2-1), has since expired. Today, anyone is free to use his process for creating "floating ink" paintings. But during the period of patent protection, Mr. Stimson effectively controlled the right of any artist to use his patented process in the United States.

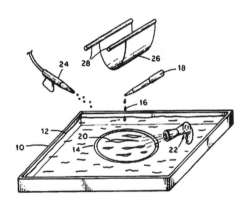

Illustration 2-1

Like all of the patents discussed in this chapter, Mr. Stimson's rights were not tied to a specific artwork. If he saw a work for sale and that work had been made using his method, Mr. Stimson could sue the retailer for

offering it for sale, the distributor for selling it, and the artist for making it or importing it to this country. Unlike a copyright, which gives the holder the right to sue someone who copies a unique design, a patent allows the holder to sue anyone who uses the patented method. This is a much broader right, and one the advantages of seeking patent protection for your invention.

The patent includes the following abstract and claim:

Abstract:

A method for producing a painting using a flotation process in which a floating elongate member is placed in a shallow pan of water and one or more oil based litho inks having different viscosities are placed on the surface of the water within the closed shape of the elongate member. Using an external force such as an air stream, the litho ink is formed into a desired pattern on the surface of the water and it is allowed to float undisturbed by external forces for a time lapse of about six to fourteen hours to form a textured pattern having finer and more textured paint globules than when the paint was first blown into a desired pattern. The paint pattern is lifted off of the surface of the water and onto a flexible sheet, and after the paint is at least partially dried, artist's non-oil base ink is applied to the flexible sheet within the closed shape of the painting to areas of the sheet on which paint is not present. A sufficient quantity of ink is used to flow the ink to the edge of the oil pattern and to stop the ink substantially without flowing ink onto the oil pattern.

What is claimed is:

1. *A method for producing a painting using printers litho oil ink,*

   a shallow pan, water, and a flexible sheet comprising:

   partially filling the shallow pan with water;

   introducing a litho oil ink onto the surface of the water, said ink being capable of forming globules when contacting said surface;

   forming a desired pattern in the litho oil ink as it floats on the surface of the water;

   allowing the litho oil ink to float undisturbed by external forces on the surface of the water for a time lapse such that the ink has formed into a desired globule pattern, whereby the ink forms a pattern on the water having a textured appearance of depth;

   after the time lapse, lowering the flexible sheet in a limp condition onto the surface of the water over the ink with a central portion of the sheet being first lowered onto the water surface; and

   lifting the flexible sheet from the water to lift the litho oil ink pattern from the water onto the sheet corresponding to the pattern previously formed on the water's surface.

2. Hand Rest for an Artist's Easel: U.S. Pat. 6,565,059

Like John Rand's collapsible tube, (discussed in Chapter 1), new inventions are constantly being created to assist painters in their traditional tasks. For example, Russell Swonger invented a novel method for stretching canvas, and was awarded a patent for his "Stretcher frame for an artist's canvas" (U.S. Pat. 4,432,150). Milton Kalish invented an innovative "Portable easel system" (U.S. Pat. 5,337,996).

Many artists and inventors have tried to solve a basic painting dilemma—how to maintain a steady brush stroke. Oil and water-color artists, particularly amateurs, lack a steady hand to perform delicate brush strokes. For centuries, the most widely known device used for this purpose was the maulstick, a long wooden stick with a soft leather or padded end, used as a support to keep the hand that holds the brush from touching the painting surface.

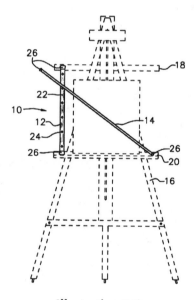

Illustration 2-2

One problem with the maulstick is that the padded end must touch Ç;% work surface and might damage the artwork. Also using a maulstick takes some getting used to—as well as sufficient arm strength to hold it firmly while painting.

The USPTO has approved patents for several devices that steady the painter's hand—Marion E. Hoyt (U.S. Pat. 5,141,198), Angelo J. Cortimilia (U.S. Pat. 3,815,856), Raymond R. Givonetti (U.S. Pat. 5,765,791), Michael S. Weber (U.S. Pat. 5,299,772), and Acop J. Amirian (U.S. Pat. 5,172,883) all patented hand-steadying devices. A recent entry in this crowded field is Leonard Falconer's "Hand rest for an artist's easel" (U.S. Pat. 6,565,059).

Falconer claims that his invention "substantially departs from the conventional concepts and designs of the prior art" (see Illustration 2-2). Below are the abstract and first claim.

Abstract:
Hand rests are desirable to the artist for steadying the hand when performing delicate brush strokes. The use of this invention provides added control to both the oil and watercolor artist. The hand rest is a welcome addition to the recreational artist because it can help him complete more difficult brush strokes with a steadier hand. Additionally, the hand rest is lightweight and easy to install on either an easel or canvas, making it readily portable. The hand rest for an artist's easel consists of a peg assembly and a hand rest. The peg assembly consists of a lightweight aluminum rod with pegs incorporated along its length and is positioned vertically on the left or right side of the easel depending upon which hand the artist uses to paint. The hand rest consists of a cylindrical birch wood rod with end caps, one end of which is positioned upon one of the pegs and the other end of which is supported by the artist's free hand. Positioning is easily changed by moving the hand rest rod to another peg.

I claim:
1. *A hand rest for an artist's easel comprising:*
   a vertical support having a top, a central portion with a front and a back, and a bottom and having a length wherein said top of said support reaches at least to an upper horizontal member of an artist's easel when said bottom of said support is rested on a lower horizontal member of an artist's easel and formed with a plurality of pegs extending perpendicularly from said front of said central portion wherein each said peg extends from said front of said central portion in a direction parallel to each said other peg and said pegs are arranged along a line which is parallel to a longitudinal axis of said front surface of said central portion;
   a first end cap connected to said top of said support;
   a second end cap connected to said bottom of said support; and
   a rod having a first end and a second end and having a length sufficient to reach diagonally from said upper horizontal member of an artist's easel to said lower horizontal member of an artist's easel and removably connected to said vertical support wherein said first end of said rod is placed between two of said pegs and said second end of said rod rests on said lower horizontal member of an artist's easel.

C. Drawing Patents

Of all forms of art and entertainment, drawing requires the fewest tools—all you need is a two-dimensional surface (such as paper) and a drawing utensil (such as a pencil). Because of its simplicity, drawing has been a preferred method for creating visual records and has been instrumental in the advancement of medicine, architecture, and other practical professions. With pen and paper, a competent draftsman can render views of an image—for example, a patent drawing—that are often more informative and more useful than a photograph. In addition, drawings—like Leonardo da Vinci's imagery of a helicopter—can show us things that exist only in our imaginations.

Drawing was not popular until after the 15th century. Prior to that time, two limitations hindered its use. First, paper—the material on which drawing was usually accomplished—was a rare commodity. This hurdle was quickly resolved after the Great Plague, when tons of cloth from victims' garments became available for conversion to paper (in those days paper was made from cloth).

The second and bigger hurdle in the popularization of drawing was that handmade sketches did not always look "real." Leonardo da Vinci solved this second problem when he perfected his theories of perspective. The artist/inventor distinguished the three ways that we visualize objects as they recede into the distance: changes in size (linearity), changes in hue (color), and blurring. He realized that creating perspective on paper was also a geometric matter; the artist need only extend lines from each object, forming a pyramid as they converged to a single point. Da Vinci's theories helped to popularize drawing as a tool in art and the sciences, and his concepts remain a staple of art classes 500 years later.

Considering da Vinci's classic breakthrough, as well as the myriad styles and systems that have since been perfected for drawing, is there anything novel and nonobvious left to create for those who draw? The two patents below, one for a method for creating perspective, and the other for a system for drawing circles, demonstrate that there is always room for innovation.

1. Patenting Perspective: U.S. Pat. 6,002,405

Leonardo da Vinci did not have the last word on perspective. Centuries after he provided his theories, new innovations for creating perspective—particularly in relation to computer-generated imagery—continue to appear. In 1999, for example, Abelardo Berroteran received U.S. Pat. 6,002,405 for a "Method for creating a graphic work using a five point perspective system and a graphic work produced by the method." The effect of Berroteran's method is visually similar to the software used in photo manipulation programs such as Adobe Photoshop which allow the user to create bulges, tunnels, or similar funhouse effects.

Berroteran's abstract states:

A method is set forth for fashioning graphic works with perspective based upon five perspective points. The method includes selecting axes X, Y which extend to vanishing points A-D and cross at a fifth reference point Z. By using lines extending to the vanishing points A-D and the center point Z a perspective grid can be fashioned the spacing of the points and reference lines of the grid defined by the five points of the perspective. The grid can be fashioned to provide a "bulging" perspective or a "tunnel" perspective. Also set forth are works produced by the method.

Below we provide the first claim for Mr. Berroteran's patent (filed in 1996). As noted in Section A, patent claims establish the boundaries for the innovation—what it is that the inventor can stop anyone from making, using or selling. (If Berroteran's description is not clear, it you may get a better sense of what he meant by viewing the figures in the published patent (see Illustration 2-3).)

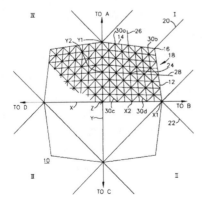

Illustration 2-3

I claim:

1. *A method for fashioning a two-dimensional graphic work with perspective comprising:*

   (A) *fashioning the work to have its perspective elements conform to reference lines of a grid; and*

   (B) *providing said grid by the steps of,*

   (i) *defining orthogonal axes X, Y crossing at a center point Z, said axes directed to at least to vanishing points A,B,*

   (ii) *selecting at least two points X1, Y1 equidistant from the center Z along the X and Y axes respectively, said points selected to define the outer bounds for the grid;*

   (iii) *establishing additional points along the X and Y axes by,*

   (a) *from each of the points X1, Y1 directing reference lines (12, 14) to each vanishing point A,B, said reference lines crossing at a point (16), said points Y1, (16), X1, Z defining a reference box;*

   (b) *extending a diagonal line (20) from point Z through point (16) and from Point X1 to point Y1, said diagonal lines crossing at a reference point (24),*

   (c) *extending reference lines through the reference point (24) to vanishing points A,B, said lines intersecting the X and Y axes to establish points X2,Y2 thereon and define four reference sub-boxes,*

   (d) *repeating steps (b)-(c) to define additional points along the X and Y axes, said points along the X and Y axes and the reference lines extending therefrom to the vanishing points A,B defining said grid.*

2. Drawing Circles: U.S. Pat. 4,589,210

One important skill required for drawing, particularly technical drawing, is the ability to create circles. Draftsmen do this with the aid of a template—a plastic sheet with precut circles—or with a compass. Drawing circles becomes more complicated when the artist must create a series of circles with a common center (known as concentric circles).

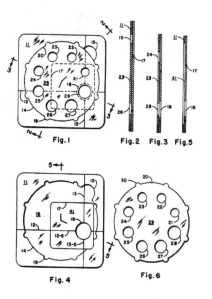

Fig. 1   Fig. 2   Fig. 3   Fig. 5

Fig. 4   Fig. 6

Illustration 2-4

If you use a compass to create concentric circles, you may damage the paper with a series of compass piercing points. To avoid

this, some draftsmen affix a small piece of plastic to the paper, then balance the compass point on that. But this can cause problems if the plastic slips, or if the compass point doesn't always engage exactly the same position.

Using a template for concentric circles can be tricky, too. A draftsman can never be sure that each succeeding circle is precisely aligned, not to mention that the range of sizes available with templates is restricted.

In response to these problems, Joseph Konrad patented a "Method and means for centerless circle construction" (see Illustration 2-4) in 1986. Using his template-within-a-template approach, Konrad claims to have solved the concentricity issue.

Below we provide the abstract and first claim for his invention.

Abstract:

A template set for inscribing a plurality of curvilinear figures with pencil, inking pen or other marking means is disclosed. The invention comprises a two-part unit for small circles, or a three-part unit for larger circles, enabling an individual circle or family of circles to be drawn without a compass, where such circles have a common center. The device can further be used to draw ellipses of varying size, the ellipses having varying sizes and degrees of eccentricity, and having common foci. The device consists of an exterior holder, an interior holder, a large-circle guide portion and a small-circle guide portion. In the embodiment for drawing large circles, a shim is used to maintain the large-circle guide portion in spaced relationship from the drafting medium.

I claim:

1. *A template set for constructing curvilinear figures consisting of an exterior holder with a cavity defining an interior conformation and a recess extending through the holder; a large-circle guide portion adapted to fit into said cavity of said exterior holder and a shim with an exterior perimeter adapted to fit into said recess, said large-circle guide portion being complementary in size and shape with said interior conformation of said exterior holder and including a plurality of curvilinear cutouts, the exterior perimeter of said shim being complementary in size and shape with said recess of said exterior holder; said shim including at least one opening, whereby, when one of said curvilinear cutouts of said large-circle guide portion is aligned with said opening of said shim, a user can construct a curvilinear figure.*

D. Graphic Art

Graphic art is a form of commerce—it's art that's used to sell products and services and to communicate the message of business. Unlike fine art paintings or sculptures, the works of graphic artists are prized for their ability to sell, persuade, and entertain. By merging multiple media—for example photographs, drawings, and text—illustrators and graphic designers create the look of websites, books, posters, sale displays, product trade dress, and other two-dimensional surfaces (such as limited-edition lithographs or silk screens).

Because graphic art is crucial for communicating corporate messages, it's no surprise that American business has tried to enhance the graphic art skills of its artistically challenged corporate executives. The first shot across the bow occurred in April 1987, when a product entitled Forethought Presenter was offered for sale for use on Macintosh computers. The program enabled users to generate black and white text and graphic overhead transparencies —a boon to those who wanted to make graphic business presentations. Microsoft acquired the rights for $14 million and in February 1988 offered a Macintosh and PC version of the program entitled PowerPoint 1.0. The rest, as anyone who has ever attended a corporate event can tell you, is history.

Today, PowerPoint software can be found on over 250 million computers around the world. According to Microsoft, users of the program generate over 30 million PowerPoint presentations every day. With its wealth of clip art, preset background templates, customizable typefaces, slick transitions, and slide show format, PowerPoint is the technology that empowers corporate workers with graphic artist tools. (Unfortunately, PowerPoint does not give those same works graphic art skills. As one writer states, the program often simply "turns mediocre presenters into lousy presenters," because it fails to offer guidelines in the use of imagery, color, content, or pacing.)

Below we examine two graphic art patents. One of these—the LZW compression algorithm —was instrumental in popularizing visual images on the Web but reviled by graphic artists. The other patent is for a more traditional tool, a tape device that applies register marks, allowing for the reproduction of color separations.

1. LZW Compression (The GIF Patent): U.S. Pat. 4,558,302

The Internet exploded once it became a visual medium; graphic art was what attracted millions of Web surfers. In a sense, what really enabled the rapid growth of the Internet was a particular innovation—a method of compressing image files so that they could be stored on servers and quickly reproduced on personal computer screens. On midnight on June 19, 2003, the patent for this innovation expired and many graphic artists and software engineers were happy to see it die.

U.S. Pat 4,558,302, a method of compressing data in digital images, was created by Abraham Lempel, Jacob Ziv, and Terry Welch. (Welch alone is listed as the inventor on patent 4,558,302, though this work was derived from an earlier patent that names Lempel and Ziv as well.) The algorithm, also known as LZW compression, was patented in 1985 and owned by Unisys.

Because the LZW technology had been reproduced in so many articles and magazines, many people believed that it was in the public domain, including engineers at CompuServe. In the late 1980s, these engineers used LZW to create the GIF (Graphic Interchange Format) image file format. Unisys didn't seem bothered by the use of LZW in GIFs, never hassled CompuServe over its use, and did not object when CompuServe published the LZW standard and offered it as an open specification—making it, by 1994, the Internet standard for digital graphic artists.

In 1994, Unisys shocked programmers by announcing that this "open standard" was actually patented. Unisys, which had worked out an arrangement with CompuServe, said it would begin collecting royalty fees in 1995 from businesses that used the formulas in their reader/writer programs—software that enabled users to create or convert into GIF format. Some programmers referred to the Unisys announcement as "the online communications community's equivalent of the sneak attack at Pearl Harbor."

Other compression standards existed at the time, notably JPEG (Joint Photographic Experts Group). However, JPEG wasn't a true substitute for GIF because JPEG was a "lossy" format (in other words, it slightly altered compressed images) and because, at the time, JPEG did not support palette-based images. (The TIFF (Tagged Image File Format) format, also in existence, used LZW technology and software companies paid royalties for the right to include the technology.)

Initially it looked like freeware (software given for free) and related public domain software would be exempt from royalties. But as Unisys changed its course, programmers decided to take things into their own hands and developed an open-source, freely usable version of compression that could be substituted for LZW, known as Portable Networks Graphics (PNG). The result, many programmers believed, was an improved standard— and one directly inspired by Unisys' handling of the LZW patent.

Improved or not, PNG never became as universally popular as GIFs. Unisys created more controversy in 1999, when it demanded that website owners using GIF images (including noncommercial sites) pay the company a onetime license fee of $5,000. Many switched formats instead.

 The LZW patent provides a few lessons for those involved in arts-related patents. It's possible, for example, for a patent owner to selectively enforce a patent. That is, Unisys's failure to enforce its patent against certain users, or for a period of time, did not prevent it from later seeking royalties. However, if a patent owner deliberately misled a user into believing that no royalty would be charged, the owner may later be prevented from seeking royalties. In addition, it demonstrates the concept of "reverse licensing." That is, a patent owner can legitimize an illegal user by turning the illegal use into a license via the payment of a royalty.

In addition, it's interesting to note that Unisys was apparently unaware of the financial potential of its own patent. According to some reports, it was only after a foreign company approached Unisys for permission to incorporate LZW in a graphics program that Unisys became aware of the truly widespread use of its patented technology.

Below are the abstract and claims for the patent for LZW compression which brought graphic art to the Web.

Abstract:

A data compressor compresses an input stream of data character signals by storing in a string table strings of data character signals encountered in the input stream. The compressor searches the input stream to determine the longest match to a stored string. Each stored string comprises a prefix string and an extension character where the extension character is the last character in the string and the prefix string comprises all but the extension character. Each string has a code signal associated therewith and a string is stored in the string table by, at least implicitly, storing the code signal for the string, the code signal for the string prefix and the extension character. When the longest match between the input data character stream and the stored strings is determined, the code signal for the longest match is transmitted as the compressed code signal for the encountered string of characters and an extension string is stored in the string table. The prefix of the extended string is the longest match and the extension character of the extended string is the next input data character signal following the longest match. Searching through the string table and entering extended strings therein is effected by a limited search hashing procedure. Decompression is effected by a decompressor that receives the compressed code signals and generates a string table similar to that constructed by the compressor to effect lookup of received code signals so as to recover the data character signals comprising a stored string. The decompressor string table is updated by storing a string having a prefix in accordance with a prior received code signal and an extension character in accordance with the first character of the currently recovered string.

I claim:

1. *In a data compression and data decompression system, compression apparatus for compressing a stream of data character signals into a compressed stream of code signals, said compression apparatus comprising*

    storage means for storing strings of data character signals encountered in said stream of data character signals, said stored strings having code signals associated therewith, respectively,

    means for searching said stream of data character signals by comparing said stream to said stored strings to determine the longest match therewith,

    means for inserting into said storage means, for storage therein, an extended string comprising said longest match with said stream of data character signals extended by the next data character signal following said longest match,

    means for assigning a code signal corresponding to said stored extended string, and

    means for providing the code signal associated with said longest match so as to provide said compressed stream of code signals.

2. Multi-Layer Graphic Arts Tape System: U.S. Pat. 4,223,055

In order to reproduce a color picture on paper, (in a magazine, for example), the printer uses four colors of ink: cyan, magenta, yellow, and black (known as CMYK colors). By overlaying these four ink layers, all of the colors seen in nature can be reproduced. To guarantee the correct color printing, a graphic artist submits artwork to production "separated" into these four colors. Although software has simplified this process somewhat, it is still often done the old fashioned way, by preparing separate translucent sheets for each color. The challenge is getting the four overlapping color images to land in precisely the same spot and to avoid the defective appearance of a bad separation (when one of the colors bleeds). To properly align the color sheets, graphic artists use register marks consisting of a circle with two perpendicular diameters.

A graphic artist who uses a computer program can insert these register marks electronically. But in the manual world, register marks must be pulled from a roll of register tape and taped to the color separated sheet. The artist has to make sure that the register marks applied to each sheet are aligned so that the printer will get a perfect four-color image. This is usually time-consuming and a bit tricky.

In 1980, two inventors from New York patented a process for applying register marks. In their "Multilayer graphic arts tape system," two separate aligned markings tapes are held together by a weak adhesive, and the outer surfaces of the two tapes are coated with a strong adhesive. The user cuts the tape, places it between two sheets, and applies pressure to the top sheet. Then, each tape adheres to its respective sheet and the tapes are aligned. Below is the abstract and first claim for this patent.

Abstract:

There is disclosed a multilayer tape system, of the type disclosed in Castelluzzo application Ser. No. 930,700, U.S. Pat. 4,182,789, for applying register marks or other symbols to aligned artwork sheets used in the graphic arts field. In a two-layer system, each of two super-imposed tapes has aligned markings thereon. A weak adhesive secures the two tapes together, and the two outer surfaces are coated with a strong adhesive. In a four-layer system, a separator is disposed between a pair of two-layer systems; the separator has holes therein so that the two tape systems can adhere to each other and remain in alignment, contact being made in the regions of the holes. The relative adhesive strengths maintain the system integrity prior to use while also permitting tape separation during use. Instead of using clear tapes and printed markings as in the Castelluzzo system, opaque or colored tapes with punched markings are employed. This greatly simplifies manufacture because there is no need to align pre-marked tapes during the lamination step; the registration markings are punched after lamination. Color contrast is achieved by use of the opaque or colored tapes.

What we claim is:

1. A multilayer graphic arts tape system comprising a first opaque tape having an adhesive coating on a first surface thereof, a second opaque tape having a first surface in facing relationship with the second surface of said first tape and having an adhesive coating on the second surface thereof, a separator strip having a first surface in facing relationship with said second surface of said second tape, a third opaque tape having an adhesive coating on a first surface thereof in facing relationship with the second surface of said separator strip, said separator strip containing holes therein for allowing said adhesive coatings on said second surface of said second tape and said first surface of said third tape to adhere to each other in the regions of said holes, an adhesive disposed between said second surface of said first tape and said first surface of said second tape and having a bonding force which is less than that provided by the adhesive coating on each of said first and second tapes when each of said tapes is applied to an application surface, and a plurality of punched-out markings extending through said first, second and third tapes and said separator strip.

E. Music/Songwriting

Ten years ago, a musician who wanted to release an album would have had to hire a recording studio, pay several thousand dollars (or more) for a master recording, and then pay additional thousands to create artwork and make vinyl or compact disc copies. If an arrangement were needed, a professional arranger would have had to be hired to draft sheet music. Today, all of this—the recording, the sheet music, the artwork, and the pressings—can be accomplished with a ten-pound laptop computer, a few software programs, and some blank compact discs.

3-D Pie Charts: A Questionable Graphic-Art Patent

Because graphic art is so important to effective business communications, traditional spreadsheet programs such as *Excel* and *Quattro Pro* now enable the user to present data in graphic art formats with 3-D effects and multiple colors. A graphic-art patent filed in 1992 (U.S. Pat. 5,491,779) includes the following first claim:

We claim:

1. In a data processing system, a method of graphically displaying

data in a pie figure comprising:

defining at least first and second data sets relative to plural identities, the second data set including at least one value which is unequal to at least one other value of the second data set;

defining the angles of plural pie slices, each pie slice corresponding to an identity, such that the angles are proportional to data of the first data set, the angles totaling 360 degrees;

defining a second dimension of each pie slice such that the second dimensions are proportional to data of the second data

set; and generating a three-dimensional display of the plural pie slices in a circular arrangement as a single pie figure, each pie slice having the defined angle and the defined second dimension.

If you haven't guessed already, this is a patent for 3-D pie charts, a computer graphics technique actually invented in the 1970s. (Of course, the chart is not actually in three dimensions; it simply appears that way thanks to clever use of perspective and graphics.)

There is sometimes a big difference between what can be patented and what should be patented. If the prior art for a patent has not been thoroughly analyzed, approval by the USPTO—even for the most well-written claims—may prove worthless.

Enforcing this patent may prove difficult, particularly if the defendant in an infringement lawsuit does some basic prior art searching. This type of claim drafting is illustrative of a principle you see in many patents: If you can't dazzle them with brilliance, baffle them with baloney.

Innovations such as of Digidesign's *Pro Tools* and Sonic Foundry's *Acid* software allow musicians to create professional-studio-quality recordings at home, using standard Macintosh and PC home computers. While these inventions have led to the demise of many recording studios, they have also leveled the playing field for musicians. Below we discuss three music-related patents: Dr. Harold Hildebrand's remarkable Auto-Tuner, guitarist Tom Scholz's beloved Rockman personal amplifier, and the Freehand MusicPad Pro.

1. Pitch Detection and Intonation Correction Apparatus and Method: U.S. Pat. 5,973,252

Oh, how embarrassing it used to be at the karaoke bar, when your vocal interpretation of "Like a Virgin" went suddenly and badly out of tune. But then one day, something magical seemed to happen; when you sang into the microphone, you hit every note just as originally performed by Ms. Ciccone. That's because the owner of the club installed a piece of hardware known as the ATR-1, a device that automatically "tunes" your performance to the accompanying music.

The ATR-1 (short for "auto-tune rack") was initially developed by Dr. Harold (Andy) Hildebrand as Auto-Tune, a software product that, when used in conjunction with digital recording programs such as *Pro Tools*, could guarantee correct intonation for a vocal or instrumental performance. The product was addictive. It quickly became one of the best-selling music software programs (though

purists claimed the "perfection" of recorded intonation dehumanized the art and added to the generic fungibility of pop music.)

Auto-tuning wasn't Dr. Hildebrand's only musical innovation. He also perfected a method of producing seamless loops of digitally sampled music (known as the commercial product "Infinity"). In 1999, he introduced a revolutionary software product that enabled the user of an inexpensive microphone to simulate the qualities of an expensive microphone (the "Microphone Modeler"). These innovations seem all the more remarkable when you consider that prior to entering the music software business, Dr. Andy, as he likes to be known, wasn't even on the fringes of the music world—he worked for 13 years developing stand-alone seismic data interpretation workstations for geophysical companies. Below is the abstract and first claim for the Auto-Tune innovation.

Abstract:

A device and method is disclosed to correct intonation errors and generate vibrato in solo instruments and vocal performances in real time. The device determines the pitch of a musical note produced by voice or instrument and shifts the pitch of that note to produce a very high quality, high fidelity output. The device includes a pitch detector that automatically recognizes the pitch of musical notes quickly. The detected pitch is then used as an input to a pitch corrector that converts the pitch of the input to an output with a desired pitch. The corrected musical note is then in tune with the pitch standard. The device and method employ a microprocessor that samples the signal from a musical instrument or voice at regular intervals using an analog-to-digital converter and then utilizes data derived from an auto-correlation function of the waveform to continuously determine the period of the waveform. The period of the waveform is then compared to a desired period or periods (such as found in a scale). The ratio of the waveform period and the desired period is computed to re-sample the waveform. This ratio is smoothed over time to remove instantaneous output pitch changes. The ratio is used to resample the input waveform. The resulting output waveform is processed through a digital-to-analog converter and output through audio interfaces.

2. The Bass Rockman: U.S. Pat. 4,683,589

As big bands grew in size in the 1930s and 1940s, audiences found it harder and harder to hear the guitarist. Then, Les Paul wired and amplified his guitar. Les Paul's perfection of the electric guitar was, ironically, one of the factors in the demise of big bands because it helped to popularize rock and roll. Making the guitar louder also jeopardized the relationship between parents and children—after all, where was a budding electric guitarist going to practice without disturbing Mom, Dad, and the neighbors?

Tom Scholz came to the rescue in the early 1980s, when he invented and began selling The Rockman, a headphone amp the size of "a peanut butter sandwich." In a sense, the Rockman was to guitar amplifiers what the

Walkman was to stereos. It revolutionized the process of practicing electric guitar by allowing junior guitar heroes to practice silently while achieving a variety of processed sounds. In addition, it duplicated—in a small, solid-state transistor device—the amplified sound that Scholz achieved with his stacks of tube amplifiers in the band, Boston. Thanks to Scholz, you could practice at home without disturbing your neighbors and recreate the sound of huge guitar amplifiers in a recording studio.

Below is the patent abstract for the Bass Rockman, a sequel device Scholz created for bass guitarists.

Abstract:

An electronic audio signal processor circuit particularly suited for electrical instruments as an electric bass guitar for providing controlled distortion and tone alteration. The circuitry includes a compressor circuit at the input operated in conjunction with a detector which in accordance with the invention is an RMS detector. Also, at the input circuitry is a distortion switch which controls the type of distortion that is generated. This distortion switch is used in conjunction with a distortion amplifier, the output of which couples to a resistive sensing network. The network feeds the audio signals to a low EQ circuit, a mid EQ circuit and a high EQ circuit. Associated with the high EQ circuit is a clipper switch and at the output of the EQ circuitry is an EQ switch for providing preferred predetermined frequency response wave forms. A high frequency compressor and associated switch is also associated with the EQ switch. The output circuitry includes a chorus circuit and associated chorus control switch. Appropriate mixing is provided at the output.

3. Music Annotation System for Performance and Composition of Musical Scores: U.S. Pat. 6,483,019

Illustration 2-5

In 2001, when the members of the San Diego Symphony performed *The Nutcracker,* they achieved particular distinction for something they didn't do—namely, take their hands from their instruments to turn the pages of sheet music. Instead, the sheet music was stored digitally and displayed on a series of LCD music stands. This system, known as *MusicPad Pro,* was invented by Michael Hamilton (U.S. Pat 6,483,019) and sold by Freehand Systems, a California company. When it was time to turn the page, each musician pressed a wireless foot pedal to change the display. The system also enables a user to scan sheet music for use on the *MusicPad Pro,* annotate the music on screen, zoom in and out, and look ahead in the score, if necessary. Symphony conductor John Stubbs told a local TV reporter, "Musicians have been dreaming about this for years."

Below are the abstract and claim for the patent for this novel update on the music stand (see Illustrations 2-5 and 2-6).

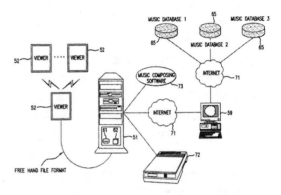

Illustration 2-6

Abstract:

A system for displaying music. An Internet server stores the music. A computer accesses the Internet server and downloads a particular musical composition. The computer stores the particular musical composition in a computer memory. A plurality of viewers is coupled to the computer. The computer retrieves, from the computer memory, the particular musical composition, and sends the particular musical composition to the plurality of viewers. The plurality of viewers displays the particular musical composition retrieved from the computer memory. The computer controls display of the particular musical composition on the plural-

ity of viewers. Each viewer has a stylus. Each stylus is used for annotating the particular musical composition with annotations.

I claim:

1. A system for displaying music, comprising:

an Internet server for storing the music;

a computer, having a computer memory, for accessing the Internet server and for downloading a particular musical composition, having a plurality of groups of music, with each group having a variation in the particular musical composition corresponding to a particular musical instrument;

said computer for translating the particular musical composition to an FHS file format, including a header chuck, a page chuck, a text chuck, and an end chuck;

said computer for storing, using the FHS file format, the particular musical composition in said computer memory, said computer for retrieving, from said computer memory, the particular musical composition stored in said computer memory;

a plurality of groups of viewers, coupled to said computer, with each group of viewers having at least one viewer, with the plurality of groups of viewers corresponding to the plurality of groups of music, respectively, with the plurality of groups of viewers for displaying, using the FHS file format, the plurality of groups of music of the particular musical composition retrieved from said computer memory, with said computer for controlling display of the particular musical composition on each of the plurality of groups of viewers;

a plurality of styluses, with a stylus located at each viewer within each group of the plurality of groups of viewers, respectively, with each stylus for annotating, at a respective display, the respective particular musical composition with annotations, thereby the plurality of styluses generating a plurality of annotations corresponding to the plurality of groups of viewers, respectively; and

said computer for storing the plurality of annotations as a combined-annotated file or as a plurality of viewer-annotated files, for later display with the particular musical composition, and for uploading the combined-annotated file or the plurality of viewer-annotated files to the Internet server.

F. Architecture

Of all the forms of artistic expression, architecture seems most directly tied to science. As the great Swiss-French architect Le Corbusier wrote, "Behind the wall, the Gods play with numbers, of which the universe is made up." Much of Le Corbusier's architectural theory was based upon the harmony of proportional measurement, derived from the Golden Section (also known as "divine proportion"), the Golden Rectangle, and the Fibonacci Sequence.

The Golden Section is a geometric proportion in which a line is divided so that the ratio of the length of the longer line segment

(A) to the length of the entire line (C) is equal to the ratio of the length of the shorter line segment (B) to the length of the longer line segment (A).

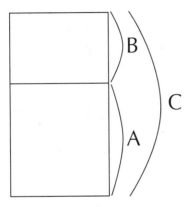

Illustration 2-7

This proportion can be found in the Greek architecture of the Parthenon, the Renaissance architecture of Leon Battista Alberti's Santa Maria Novella church, in Florence, and in the design of the pyramids in Egypt. The Golden Section also figures into painting (da Vinci's *The Last Supper*), music, and narrative storytelling—many writers believe that the climax of a work should occur at the Golden Section—approximately two-thirds of the way through the work. The use of the Golden Section demonstrates that architecture, like so many creative languages, relies on the precision (and mystery) of science.

Below we discuss three mundane architectural innovations that received utility patents: a layout for a health spa, a method for curving drywall, and a device that enables escape from high-rise fires.

1. Health Spa for Exercise, Recreational and Social Activities: U.S. Pat. 4,650,179

Frank Bond's 1987 patent, "Health spa for exercise, recreational and social activities," describes the layout of a health spa that, according to Bond, does more than cater to the physical needs of the patrons. Casting a critical eye towards other health club designs, Bond states in his application, "While the club members get a good workout, they do not necessarily have fun, nor is the somewhat sterile atmosphere conducive to developing important social contacts."

Bond's invention seeks to rectify these problems. When reviewing his claims, below, note that the structural relationships are described very broadly, as the inventor tries to claim a large family of such layouts.

I claim

1. *A health spa for exercise, reaction and social activities, the spa being housed within an enclosed building and comprising first, second and third portions, the first portion including a track disposed on a given level and having respective end portions, exercise equipment within the track, the*
    third portion including a lounge area substantially adjacent to one end portion of the track,
  the lounge area being spaced from the track by a wall and being elevated above the level of the track, the lounge area including a bar and tables for rest and socialization, the second portion includ-

ing a plurality of substantially enclosed courts disposed laterally of the lounge area, wherein the lounge area is between the track and the courts, the courts being substantially on the same level as the track, and the second portion including a pool disposed on a lower level than the courts.

2. *The health spa of claim 1, wherein the pool is directly below the courts, and wherein the lounge area has a portion provided with a glass wall overlooking the pool, whereby activities in the pool may be viewed from the lounge area.*

Illustration 2-8

2. Prefabricated Curved-Profile Architectural Element and Method for Prefabricating This Element: U.S. Pat. 6,446,399

One of the key innovations for construction has been the use of prefabricated components. The following patent demonstrates how to prefabricate curved drywall pieces.

To apply drywall to a curved space (see, for example, Illustration 2-8), the builder used to have to either wet the drywall and bend it into position (a difficult and labor intensive process that only works with large sheets of drywall) or have a specially made curved gypsum created for the space. Both methods discouraged the use of drywall in curved spaces. To simplify this task, in 2002, Yves Lecours of Quebec devised a process for prefabricating curved pieces of drywall. A summary of his system is provided in the abstract to his patent, U.S. Pat. 6,446,399

Abstract:

A prefabricated architectural element has a curved profile and has at least one curved brace member. A bendable panel is applied to the curved brace member, bent on this brace member to form the panel with the curved profile, and fastened to the curved brace member. Finally, the prefabricated architectural element comprises a uniform, smooth and regular surface finish on an outer face of the panel opposite to the curved brace member. A method of prefabricating this curved-profile architectural element comprises providing at least one curved brace member, providing a bendable panel, and applying the panel to the brace member. Application of the panel to the brace member comprises forming the panel with the curved profile by bending this panel on the brace member, and fastening the panel to the brace member. To complete the method, an outer face of the panel, opposite to the brace member, is finished in a uniform, smooth and regular surface. Preferably, the panel is a generally rigid panel in which laterally adjacent and parallel grooves are cut. Also, the outer face of the panel is finished by applying tape and drywall compound. Advantageously, the panel is applied to a plurality of curved brace members appropriately spaced apart from each other.

The patent includes the following first claim:

What is claimed is:

1. A prefabricated architectural element presenting a curved profile, comprising:
   at least one curved brace member;
   a bendable panel:
   applied to said at least one curved brace member;
   bent on said at least one curved brace member to form the panel with the curved profile; and
   fastened to said at least one curved brace member; and
   a uniform surface finish on an outer face of the panel opposite to said at least one brace member;
   wherein the bendable panel is a scored gypsum drywall panel.

3. Skid-Out High-Rise Fire Escape Device: U.S. Pat. No. 4,709,782

When designing buildings, architects must consider both conventional and emergency means of escape. Because it is sometimes difficult to escape from a fire in a tall building —stairways may be full of smoke or fire

trucks unable to reach to the height of the fire—architects have long wished for a system to transport people out of high-rise fires. Traditionally fire escapes were used, but they pose a few problems. They are expensive to install, require a great deal of maintenance, and can be used by intruders to gain access to the building. And they can be very unsightly, destroying the graceful lines of the building that the architect worked so hard to create.

Other solutions have been proposed—a hollow rail-track escape mechanism (U.S. Pat. 4,121,689), a carriage with guide rollers that engage a gear track assembly (U.S. Pat. 4,406,349), and a personnel lowering device adapted to be clamped to a vertically mounted I-beam (U.S. Pat. 4,485,891). Henry Lipinski designed and patented an escape system notable for its minimal effect on the architectural appearance of the building. Reminiscent of *Spiderman*, it uses a vertical skid trailer attached to the side of the building (see Illustration 2-8). Below are the abstract and first claim for Mr. Lipinski's escape device.

Abstract:

A high-rise fire escape device gravity operated and particularly adaptable for use in high-rise building and modern skyscraper structures as an escape apparatus from any floor of a building for use in the rescue of an occupant who may be trapped and prevented from using the conventional stairways or elevator due to a natural or man-made disaster such as fire, electrical or power failure, building collapse or personal injury of the occupants, etc. The apparatus or device comprises the combination of a vertical skid track member attached to the wall of a building with a skid which is inserted into a guide channel located in the track. The skid track is designed to be attached to either a new or existing building with access to the skid track being available at the outside of the building at predetermined locations, such as, building corners or a plurality of locations intermediate to the corners between the building windows so as not to impede the architecture design of the building. The skid track has a back and guide portion with a plurality of spring loaded or hinged skid track doors which allows the insertion of a skid to which the occupant of a building may be attached. The skid is so designed to allow its movement down the vertical skid track with the occupant attached, with its rate of descent being controlled by a plurality of descent retarders suitably disposed along the skid track's entire length. The descent retarder is disposed within the back section of the skid track and partially protrudes into the guide channel of said track. As the skid moves down the guide channel of the skid track it comes into fractional contact with the biased plane frictional surface of the plurality of protruding descent retarders disposed along its vertical axis causing the descent retarder to be displaced in a horizontal direction perpendicular to direction of the skid movement. The movement of the descent retarders in a horizontal direction is resisted by means just as a plurality of springs interposed between the rear of the descent retarders and the inside the back portion of the skid track. While the majority of the descent retarders are spaced uniformly along the entire length of the vertical skid track, there are some

that are placed in a closer or cluster configuration near the end of the vertical skid track to more greatly impede the rate of descent or velocity of the occupant user so as to prevent forceful contact with the ground. During an emergency, a building occupant may put on a harness of any standard construction and attach it to the skid which can easily be inserted into the guide portion of the vertical skid track through any of the plurality of track doors disposed along said skid track.

I claim:

1. An emergency gravity operated fire escape apparatus particularly useful for egressing from high-rise type structures, which in combination, comprises:

a skid track vertically disposed and in a spaced relationship to a wall of a structure having a ground end, said skid track having a front side and a back side with a partition interposed between the front and the back side forming a guide channel and a back section having an inside wall, a longitudinal aperture disposed the length of the front side of said skid track and a plurality of doors disposed along said skid track's front side;

a plurality of descent retarders uniformly disposed within the back section of said skid track and partially protruding into the guide channel of said track through a rectangular aperture disposed within the partition, said descent retarder having a plane frictional surface and rear portion;

means for controlling said descent retarders' horizontal displacement, said means for controlling being disposed within the back section of said skid track and placed between the rear of said descent retarder and the inside of the back side of said skid track; and

a skid disposed within the guide channel of said skid track, said skid having a back and bevel front portions with a handle affixed to the back and a loop affixed near the bevel front portion; whereby a harness may be attached to the loop of said skid, allowing the user to safely and slowly descend to the ground during an emergency exit from a high-rise structure.

G. Sculpture

The term "sculpture" conjures up Auguste Rodin's mesmerizing *The Thinker* or Henry Moore's *Draped Reclining Figure*. But sculpture is not limited to huge pieces crafted in bronze or stone. It is a conceptual art in which figures or designs are shaped in the round or in relief requiring an awareness of geometry, symmetry, rotation, and reflection.

Though works of sculpture have traditionally been protected under copyright and design patent law, the techniques of creating sculpture, particularly the methods of shaping and displaying unorthodox materials—for example, kinetic works with moving parts, embedded electronics, and substances such as ice, salt, and sand—may be protected under utility patent law. Below we describe two innovations—a method of sculpting with water and a method of sculpting with light—that received patents.

1. Simulated Wave Water Sculpture: U.S. Pat. 5,899,634

The Bible tells us that Moses parted the Red Sea with the help of God, but Thomas Lochtefeld managed to create a similar man-made water effect without divine intervention. In 1999, he patented his innovation "Simulated wave water sculpture" (see Illustration 2-9) which propels water in such a way as to allow an observer to walk within a tunnel of cascading liquid.

His patent includes the following abstract and claim:

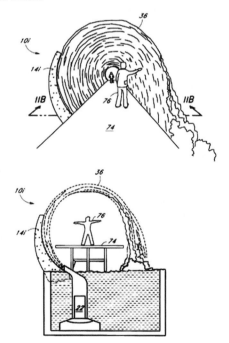

Illustration 2-9

Abstract:

A water sculpture is provided having an upwardly inclined flow surface. A flowing body of water is caused to flow upon the flow surface simulating various desired wave shapes. A variety of aesthetic wave shapes can be created, such as an unbroken wave face, a white water bore, a spilling breaking wave, or a tunnel wave. In one embodiment a walk-through water sculpture is provided such as for an entrance way of a building or the like.

What is claimed is:

1. A water sculpture comprising:

> *a flow surface adjacent a platform or walkway with at least a portion thereof having a generally inclined slope;*
>
> *at least one source of water for providing a sheet flow of water*
>
> *onto said flow surface such that said sheet flow of water flows*
>
> *upwardly onto said inclined slope and substantially conforms to said flow surface; and*
>
> *said flow surface having a shape adapted to simulate a desired wave form wherein at least a portion of said flow of water assumes an airborne trajectory over said walkway to form a tunnellike passageway.*

As with many other examples throughout this chapter, the breadth of Lochtefeld's claim illustrates the power of utility patent versus copyright. The patent permits the inventor to claim rights over a large class of works using the technique, not merely a particular water sculpture.

2. Lighted Sculpture With Translucent Colored Panels: U.S. Pat. 5,955,156

Terry Hermanson of New York City patented a method of sculpting with light in his 1999 patent (see Illustration 2-10) "Lighted sculpture with translucent, colored panels." Mr. Hermanson's rights, defined by the claims (below), give him a monopoly over use of his method of securing translucent panels to a frame to depict the outline of a figure. If Mr. Hermanson had instead gotten a design patent, his rights would have been limited to the specific imagery depicted in the patent drawings—that is, the reindeer shown in

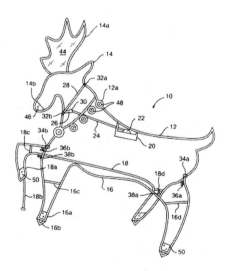

Illustration 2-10

Illustration 2-10. (For more on design patents, see Chapters 3 and 8.) The utility patent included the following abstract and claim:

Abstract:
A lighted display device includes a sculpted frame formed of thin wire or tubing. The frame outlines a character or an object and has one or more closed portions defined by the wire or tubing enclosing an area or partially enclosing an area. The display further includes a string of lights disposed along selected portions of the frame, and at least one translucent panel disposed in the closed portions or partially-closed portions of the frame.

I claim:
1. A lighted display device comprising:
   a sculpted frame outlining a character or an object;
   a series of lights disposed along said frame; and
   a translucent panel secured to said frame, at least a portion of the perimeter of said panel being outlined by at least a portion of said series of lights.

H. Film

Science has always been instrumental in film-making—after all, the Oscars are awarded by the Academy of Arts and Sciences. Over the years, Hollywood has handed out hundreds of Academy Awards for technical achievement and scientific/engineering innovations. Oscar winners have included inventors of script software, computerized methods of subtitling, fire protection barriers for stunt workers, cranes, tripods, dollies, aerial cameras, machines that produce snow, ice, and wind, reverberation systems, infrared film, Walt Disney's multiplane camera (which allowed for the illusion of depth and perspective in cartoons), flameproof foliage, high-speed film, and a macro zoom lens.

Below we discuss three innovations intended to assist filmmakers: a system related to syncing sound and film image, a method for annotating scripts, and a system for broadcasting the film's soundtrack in a movie theater.

1. System for Recording a Time Code Signal on Motion Picture Film: U.S. Pat. 4,504,130

One need only look at the history of clapperboards—slates that are held before each filmed sequence to provide a record of the take—to see Hollywood's technological evolution.

Originally, these devices were simple chalkboards with a movable black and white striped clap stick. The name of the film, the director, camera, date, number of the scene, and the version or "take" number were all written on the board. Before the director shouted "Action," the cameras photographed the clap board as an assistant snapped its movable upper stick. The writing on the clap board served as an indexing device that enabled a director to later find a favorite take.

The clap stick—the portion that snapped down atop the board—also served an important function. Because the soundtrack was recorded separately from the film, the sound of the clap was necessary to ensure that the soundtrack and film were synchronized. Audiences are pretty quick to notice when the dialogue appears to lead or follow the movement of the actor's lips. To ensure synchronicity in the editing room, the sharp, separately recorded sound of the "clap" was matched up to the visual image of the clapper snapping closed.

At the end of the 20th century, a digital video technique known as "time code" was developed, which enabled a far more precise means of synchronizing soundtracks. The time code signal could be recorded directly on the video tape and the audio tape for perfect synchronization.

The problem was that time code could not be encoded on motion pictures because motion picture cameras don't transport film at a continuous rate. (Because it's a mechanical device, the film moves intermittently.) In 1985, inventors Steven Bell and Ivan Kruglak obtained a patent for recording continuous time code on film. (A related time code patent was also granted to H.M. Denecke, U.S. Pat. 4,646,167.)

The ability to record time code altered the way that the clap board operated. Nowadays, thanks to Kruglak and Denecke, these boards are referred to as time code slates, TC slates, or sync slates, because they include a blinking LED display with time code—a reference to the exact frame spot within the recorded film. These devices can sync with the digital time code on the film, enabling even more incredibly precise marking, editing, and synchronizing. In 1998, Kruglak and Denecke each received individual Technical Achieve-

ment Academy Awards for their contributions to the development of time code slates.

Below is the abstract and first claim from the Bell and Kruglak patents.

Abstract:

An apparatus and related method for recording a continuous digital time code on motion picture film as it is advanced intermittently by a motion picture camera. The apparatus controllably adjusts the time durations of the successive bits of the signal it records, to compensate for the variable velocity profile of the intermittently advancing film. As a result, the apparatus records the time code signal as a continuous signal with a uniform time base, even though the film is being moved in an intermittent and nonuniform fashion.

We claim:

1. *Apparatus for recording a time code signal on film while it is being intermittently advanced by a motion picture camera, each intermittent film advancement following a variable velocity profile, the apparatus comprising:*

   transducer means disposed adjacent the film;

   signal generating means for coupling a time code signal to the transducer means, to record the signal on the film as the motion picture camera advances the film past the transducer means; and

   timing means for producing a timing signal indicative of the instantaneous velocity of the film relative to the transducer means, as the film is advanced intermittently past the transducer means;

> *wherein the signal generating means*
> *includes time base adjustment means,*
> *responsive to the timing signal, for*
> *adjusting the time base of the time code*
> *signal coupled to the transducer means,*
> *to compensate for the variable velocity*
> *profile of the film such that the time code*
> *signal is recorded on the film with a*
> *substantially constant time base.*

2. Method and Apparatus for Annotating a Document: U.S. Pat. Application 20020129057

It's neither crass nor cynical to say that Hollywood films are engineered products. For example, regardless of their genre—Westerns, war movies, musicals, romantic comedies—films are based upon a handful of plot formulas. These formulas—the most famous of which is "boy meets girl, boy loses girl, boy gets girl" (think of *Tootsie, Sleepless in Seattle,* or *Pretty Woman*)—help to create predictable products. Special effects, use of popular music, audience analysis, marketing research, familiar performers, and the ubiquitous happy ending also contribute to a mass-marketed product aimed at generating maximum revenue (hopefully within a very short period of time). All of this engineering is—like the creation of a new car or soft drink—a collaborative process.

An example of coerced collaboration can be seen in the film, *The Big Picture,* in which a young director's introspective plot for a small film set at a winter lodge is quickly modified by studio tinkering into a beach blanket ménage a trois. This satire reflects the fact that to achieve success, the typical film script

is commonly the subject (or victim) of mass collaboration.

Director/Screenwriter Paul Schrader (who wrote *Taxi Driver*) stated that screenwriting is not really an art form "because screenplays are not works of art. They are invitations to others to collaborate on a work of art." It makes sense, therefore, that the tools used to collaborate upon and create these scripts are the subject of patents.

As this book went to press, director Steven Spielberg was awaiting response to his application for a patent for a method of recording audio annotations to a script. (U.S. Patent applications can be viewed at the USPTO website (www.uspto.gov/patft) starting 18 months after filing.)

Spielberg's application seeks to claim the following:)

1. An apparatus for annotating a document comprising:
> *a processor;*
> *memory coupled to said processor, said*
> *memory comprising at least one text*
> *document;*
a document processing engine configured to
> *obtain said at least one text document from*
> *said memory and convert at least a portion*
> *of said at least one text document to at least*
> *one audio file;*
an audio output device configured to play
> *said at least one audio file to a first user;*
an audio input device configured to obtain at
> *least one verbalized comment from said*
> *user about said at least one audio file*
> *wherein said at least one verbalized com-*
> *ment is stored as an audio comment file;*

an annotator, said annotator configured to associate said audio comment file with a location in said text document that corresponds to said audio file playing when said first user provided said at least one comment.

By the way, as of publication of this book, Mr. Spielberg has another patent application pending (U.S. Patent Application 20030075070) for a "Switcher track and sled."

3. THX Surround Sound: U.S. Pat. 4,569,076

Film critic Stanley Rosen wrote, "A case can be made that *Star Wars* ruined the movies, both for causing the demise of the great 1970s-era, realism-rooted dramas and for ushering in the new generation of manipulative, formulaic effects-driven blockbusters .... The post-*Star Wars* era has been marked by big-budget films studiously trying not to surprise us. As much as possible, they try to be a sequel or a remake—or at least modeled on a bigger hit."

After the release of George Lucas's *Star Wars* (and to some extent, Steven Spielberg's *Jaws* and *E.T.*), films began to be seen as events, infused with an amusement park sensibility. Narrative, the glue for the first 50 years of filmmaking, was now just a thinly veiled means of connecting dazzling and eye-popping effects. Although filmmaking originated as a silent visual experience (and many purists believe the art form died with the advent of sound), George Lucas recog-

nized that the need to over-stimulate film audiences required more than the dazzling visuals provided by his company, Industrial Light and Magic. So in the early 1980s, his LucasFilms company created and patented THX Surround Sound, a method for dispersing sound in a motion picture theater so that aural effects seem to come from all sides. The audio system's tagline, "Let's see it in THX," demonstrates that the patents for film apply not only to what we see, but to what we hear as well. The abstract and one of its claims are included below.

Abstract:

A motion picture loudspeaker system is described in which the loudspeaker elements are integral with an acoustical boundary wall such that the characteristics of the vented box woofers are optimized. In order to overcome high reflection problems as sound from the tweeters is reflected by the motion picture screen and the acoustical boundary wall, frequency dependent acoustical absorptive material is attached to the wall to inhibit high frequency reflections with minimal effect on the bass optimization. The system includes the use of a steep slope crossover network having a crossover frequency such that there is a first order match of the woofer and tweeter dispersion at the crossover.

I claim:

1. A loudspeaker and motion picture screen system for use in a theater, the system comprising

*a motion picture screen which is substantially
transmissive to low frequency sound
energy and which becomes increasingly
reflective as the frequency of the sound
energy rises in the high frequency region,*

*acoustical boundary means substantially
parallel to, spaced from, and at least
partially coextensive with said screen,
said acoustical boundary means having
the acoustic characteristics of reflecting
low frequency and high frequency
sound energy,*

*loudspeaker means adjacent said acoustical
boundary means, said loudspeaker
means including at least low frequency
and high frequency loudspeaker elements
radiating sound energy towards said
screen, the screen facing portion of the
low frequency loudspeaker element or
elements substantially flush with said
acoustical boundary means, and*

*sound absorptive means adjacent said
acoustical boundary means in the vicinity
of said high frequency loudspeaker element or elements, said absorptive means
having acoustic characteristics such that
high frequency sound energy is substantially absorbed, whereby the reradiation
of reflected high frequency sound energy
from said screen is reduced.*

I. Fashion

In the fall of 1991, two hikers in the Italian
Alps encountered a dead body buried in the
ice. They alerted authorities, who retrieved
the body initially assuming it was the remains
of a hiker—one of the many who were peri-
odically lost in the area. To the surprise of all,
the dead man, named Otzi, had lived 5,300
years ago, during the Neolithic or New Stone
Age. This body was much older than the
many well-preserved mummies of Egyptian
royalty. Fortunately for science, Otzi aged
well—as did many artifacts found with Otzi,
including his clothing.

Apparently, Otzi had been warmly dressed
in leggings, loincloth, and a jacket made of
deer and goat hides, as well as a cape made
of grass and bast (the long tough fibers of the
linden tree). His cap was made of brown
bearskin, and his shoes were stitched from
hide and insulated with grass. A belted pouch
contained materials for starting a fire. In short,
the well-dressed man of 3300 BCE, was built
for survival; his fashion was purely functional.

If Otzi were alive today, he might stay warm
in his cave with an Old Navy polar fleece
track suit, and he might find Nike's Air Jordans
perfect for fleeing attacking mountain lions.
But today's $40-billion-a-year apparel industry
isn't built upon supplying survival duds—it's
intended to efficiently and aesthetically fill the
closets of the billions of consumers inhabiting
the planet. To maintain this efficiency, the
processes and equipment used in textile
manufacturing have long been a rich subject
of innovation—the Luddites, after all, were
fighting against new inventions in textile
production. Below we describe two patents
that apply to the fashion industry: a detachable
body stocking, and a system to help people
shop for clothing.

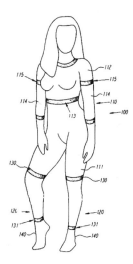

Illustration 2-11

1. Detachable Multisectional Body Stocking Hosiery: U.S. Pat. 5,729,836

Hosiery and underwear have been staples of women's fashion for several centuries. However, the idea of combining stockings and underpants did not occur until the late 1950s, when Allen Gant, Sr., invented pantyhose. Glen Raven Mills introduced the product in 1959, and it became an immediate smash that evolved during the 1960s. (An opaque nylon top was added and a seamless version was available for miniskirters.)

The concept of combining (or separating) several garments is still alive today, as evidenced by a patent issued in 1998 for "Detachable multisectional body stocking hosiery" (see Illustration 2-11). Below is the patent abstract and claim:

Abstract:

Multisectional body stocking having a plurality of various sections is connected by elastic attachment materials on each section in an overlapping manner. The multiple detachable hosiery sections allow the user to mix or match hosiery sections, or change the number of hosiery sections, to accommodate fashion desires, changes in clothing or a run in a particular hosiery section. The result is a versatile multisectional body stocking hosiery system which allows a user to use some of the various sections in many different combinations.

I claim:

1. A multisectional body stocking made of hosiery material, comprising;

a pair of leg portions made of hosiery material; and

a body portion made of hosiery material detachably connected to said pair of leg portions by a non-protruding elastic means, said body portion extending from said pair of leg portions to a portion of a body of a person wearing the body portion which is above the hips and proximate to the waist.

2. System and Method for Fashion Shopping: U.S. Pat. 5,930,769

Have you ever forgotten your size when making a clothing purchase? Do you wish you could keep your measurements on hand when buying clothing in person or online? Inventor Andrea Rose feels your pain. She invented a business method for shopping that minimizes purchasing problems.

How does Ms. Rose's system work? The customer, with the aid of a salesperson, provides information (body measurements and a digital photograph of the customer's face) and the system determines a "body type." Based on this, available garments are recommended that best compliment the customer's size and shape.

In short, no more dragging hundreds of garments back to the fitting room! To get another view of this invention and to see how some methods are visualized, see Illustrations 2-12, 2-13, and 2-14.

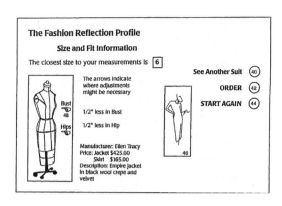

Illustration 2-13

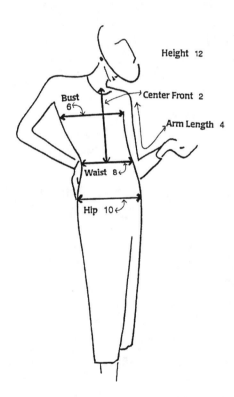

Illustration 2-12

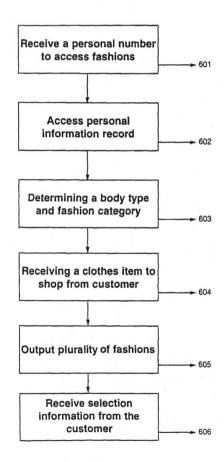

Illustration 2-14

The abstract and claim are below.

Abstract:

The present invention provides a method of manual fashion shopping and method for electronic fashion shopping by a customer using a programmed computer, CD-ROM, television, Internet or other electronic medium such as video. The method comprises receiving personal information from the customer; selecting a body type and fashion category based on the personal information; selecting fashions from a plurality of clothes items based on the body type and fashion category; outputting a plurality of fashion data based on the selected fashions; and receiving selection information from the customer.

What is claimed is:

1. *A method of fashion shopping by a customer comprising the steps of:*

   receiving personal information from the customer;

   selecting a body type and fashion category based on the personal information;

   selecting fashions from a plurality of clothes items based on the body type and fashion category;

   outputting a plurality of fashion data based on the selected fashions;

   receiving selection information from the customer; and

   processing order information to place an order for the selected fashions.

J. Photography

Perhaps because he had been trained as an engineer, Alfred Stieglitz was at ease with the mechanics of photography and was comfortable harnessing that technology for art. As a result, he, more than any other modern photographer, established photography as an art form. He wrote, "If only people would broaden their concepts to include concern about the brotherhood of man and the machine, the world would be a great deal better."

That brotherhood between man and machine is clearly evident in photography. Digital cameras have eliminated the landmark breakthrough that defined photography—photosensitive emulsion film. Software such as Adobe *Photoshop* have to some extent-eliminated darkrooms (and have become verbs in the world, as in "That photo needs to be 'shopped'"). Below are two photographic patents: a method for eliminating the photographic effect known as "red eye," and a system for digitally indexing photographs.

1. Covering an Area in Printed Photograph: U.S. Pat. 6,027,263

Sometimes, an innovation leads to an unexpected problem. The use of flash technology, for example, enabled photos to be taken in low natural light. On the other hand, it led to a phenomenon known as red eye, caused when the flash reflects off the red retina of an eyeball. The effect can be eliminated by pointing the flash elsewhere—that is, anywhere but into the subject's eyes. But often, especially with inexpensive cameras, that's not possible. The effect can easily be removed from digital photos by using photo manipulation software such as Adobe *Photoshop.*

A simple, innovative way to eliminate red eye from printed photographs is to press a "cover up" on the photography, a substance that sticks to the photo and is closer to the white color of the eye, as described in the invention below (U.S. Pat. 6,027,263), titled "Covering an area in printed photograph."

Abstract:

A sheet, having material deposited thereon, is placed over a printed photograph and the material is then transferred onto the printed photograph to cover a selected area in the printed photograph. The sheet has rub-on material deposited thereon, where the rub-on material is shaped and sized on the sheet for covering an image of a pupil of a person such a red-eye affected image of a pupil.

What is claimed is:

1. *A sheet having a transparent rub-on material of a selected color deposited thereon for transferring the material onto a printed photograph to cover an image of a pupil in an image of an eye having red-eye effect, wherein the selected color is selected to neutralize said red-eye effect when the material covers the image of the pupil.*

2. *The sheet of claim 1 wherein the material is shaped as substantially a plurality of circles.*

3. *The sheet of claim 1 wherein the selected color is cyan.*

2. System and Method for Selecting Photographic Images Using Index Prints: U.S. Pat. 6,549,306

In 1873, the author Mark Twain (Samuel Clemens) was awarded a patent for a self-adhesive scrapbook (U.S. Pat. 140,245). More than a century later, we still use scrapbooks —but unlike Twain's innovation, many of them are not bound, do not use paper or adhesive, and exist solely in the digital domain. The patent below (U.S. Pat. 6,549,306), describes a popular online process—a method of creating an index (or scrapbook) of photographs and then selecting prints from that collection. Almost every Internet service provider (such as Yahoo! or AOL) offers such services. (See Illustration 2-15 for a diagram of the process.) Here are the abstract and one claim from the patent, which has been assigned to the Eastman Kodak Company.

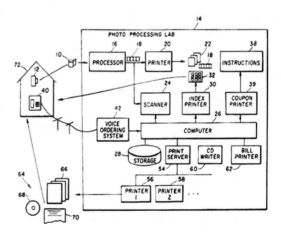

Illustration 2-15

Abstract:

A method for remotely selecting and ordering photographic prints, includes the steps of: sending a photographic film bearing a plurality of latent images to a photofinisher; developing the photographic film to produce visible images and scanning the visible images to create a digital image file at the photo finisher; producing an index print having a plurality of images from the photographic film along with an index number associated with each image and an order number; sending the index print to a customer; selecting images for which prints are desired from the index print; ordering photographic prints via telephone from the customer's home to the photofinisher, specifying the order number and the index numbers associated with the images for which prints are desired; and making photographic prints of the selected images at the photofinisher and sending the photographic prints to the customer.

What is claimed is:

1. A method for remotely selecting photographic prints by a customer with respect to a plurality of digital images stored by a digital image center; comprising the steps of:

a) storing a plurality of digital images at the digital image center;

b) producing an index having a visual representation of each of the plurality of stored digital images;

c) providing the index to the customer at a remote location from the digital image center;

d) facilitating electronically ordering of a photographic print over a communication network by said customer using said index at said remote location;

e) producing said photographic print using one of said stored digital images in response to said ordering; and

f) delivering said photographic print to said customer.

K. Sex/Pornography

Adult entertainment—as the porn business prefers to be known—is a $56-billion-a-year global industry. According to one researcher, adult e-commerce sites account for at least $2 billion annually—the biggest source of revenue on the Web. The industry is also the source of a lot of inventions that eventually are mainstreamed—including Web commerce innovations such as banner advertising, referral fees for click-throughs, partnership programs, customer billing methods, and some encryption technology, all originally developed for use on adult sites. A study in 2003 reported that the majority of files swapped by peer-to-peer systems on the Internet dealt with sexual multimedia—far exceeding bootlegged music.

Sex, invention, and patents have been intertwined since 1846, when the first patent in the United States for a sexual aid (U.S. Pat. 4,729) was awarded to Dr. John Beers, for a gold wire and oiled silk vaginal diaphragm. Less brutal to women than many sexual aid inventions in the decades to follow, Beers' intention was to provide a mechanical device that prevented conception, could be controlled by the woman, did not detract from the act of sex, and could be profitably marketed. (For an excellent history of patented sex devices, read *American Sex Machines: The Hidden History of Sex at the U.S. Patent Office,* by Hoag Levins (Adams Media).) Below, we provide two patents that illustrate how art and entertainment relate to sexual inventions; a two-seat lovemaking device and a musical condom.

1. Couple's Intimacy Reciprocating and Pivoting Two Seat Assembly: U.S. Pat. 5,385,154

Below is the first claim for a patent aptly titled "Couple's intimacy reciprocating and pivoting two seat assembly" (see Illustration 2-16), issued in 1995 for a sex-furniture device. Despite the obtuse language used in the claims, the purpose of the furniture is obvious. (Don't look for this in your next Pottery Barn catalog.)

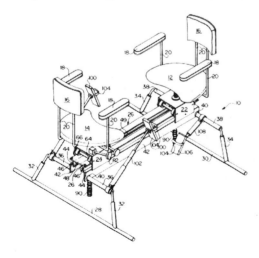

Illustration 2-16

The first claim reads:

1. *An intimacy chair assembly to assist a human male and female couple to engage in sexual intercourse with reduced effect of gravity or the reduced expenditure of substantial energy comprising:*

   a seat for each of said female and male of said couple operatively associated with said assembly,

   said male and female seats positioned to substantially face each other,

   means positioned on said assembly for reciprocating movement of each seat independently of the other seat and selectively continually toward and away from the other seat in a substantially longitudinal direction,

   means positioned on said assembly and connected to each of said seats for independently and selectively continually pivoting each seat about a horizontal axis relative to the other seat,

   whereby said couple seated upon said seats may control their engagement in sexual intercourse while substantially supported by the seats thereby reducing the amount of energy required or the body control necessary.

2. Force-Sensitive, Sound-Playing Condom: U.S Pat. 5,163,447

Many people have seen the connection between music and romance, but Paul Lyon's musical condom combines them in a truly new and nonobvious way. After all, how

United States Patent [19]

Lyons

[11] Patent Number:	**5,163,447**
[45] Date of Patent:	Nov. 17, 1992

US005163447A

[54] **FORCE-SENSITIVE, SOUND-PLAYING CONDOM**

[76] Inventor: **Paul Lyons,** 295 Elm St., Southbridge. Mass. 01550-3009

[21] Appl. No.: **728,607**

[22] Filed: **Jul. 11, 1991**

[51] Int. Cl.⁵ **A61F 6/04**
[52] U.S. Cl. **128/844;** 128/883; 446/220
[58] **Field of Search** 128/842, 844, 885, 886, 128/883, 884; 604/347–353; 446/220–226, 404

[56] **References Cited**

U.S. PATENT DOCUMENTS

| 494,436 | 3/1893 | Orth | .... | 128/883 |
| 745,264 | 11/1903 | Todd | .... | 128/886 X |

FOREIGN PATENT DOCUMENTS

| 680088 | 10/1952 | United Kingdom | .... | 128/886 |
| 2036560 | 7/1980 | United Kingdom | | |

OTHER PUBLICATIONS

Frederick's of Hollywood, catalog, vol. 70, Issue 356, Version 0600, ©1990, p. 68: "Wedding Surprise"

Primary Examiner—Robert A. Hafer
Assistant Examiner—David J. Kenealy
Attorney, Agent, or Firm—David Pressman

[57] **ABSTRACT**

A force-sensitive sound-playing condom comprising: a condom body (10) having a distal end and a proximal end, and a miniature force-sensitive sound-playing unit (14) attached to the condom at its proximal end. The proximal end of the condom is made in the form of a semirigid rim (12) having a lower part with an opening (16) coinciding with the cavity of the condom, and an upper part extending radially upwardly from the body of the condom and supporting the sound-playing unit (14). The latter contains a chip-controlled piezoelectric sound transducer which plays a melody or voiced message when during intercouse the contacts (28 and 30) of the sound-playing unit (14) are closed and the transducer is activated.

19 Claims, 1 Drawing Sheet

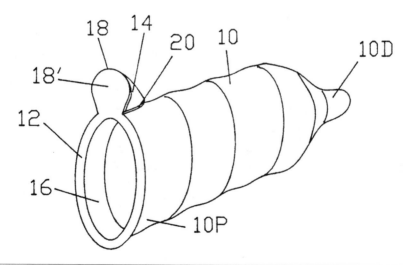

Illustration 2-17

many inventors cite a Frederick's of Hollywood catalogue as prior art?

As the patent describes, "The music or voice message may be played once (e.g., an overture or melody may be played for about 20 seconds), or it may be repeated continuously for several minutes to coincide with the duration of coitus. A voiced message may be a warning about safe sex, or a compliment to the couple for using a condom. Suitable melodies (if music is played) may be The 1812 Overture, 'The Ode to Joy' from Beethoven's Ninth Symphony, the song, 'Happy Birthday to You,' 'The Anniversary Waltz,' or any popular love song." (See Illustration 2-17.)

Below are the abstract and claim from the patent.

Abstract:

A force-sensitive sound-playing condom comprising: a condom body (10) having a distal end and a proximal end, and a miniature force-sensitive sound-playing unit (14) attached to the condom at its proximal end. The proximal end of the condom is made in the form of a semirigid rim (12) having a lower part with an opening (16) coinciding with the cavity of the condom, and an upper part extending radially upwardly from the body of the condom and supporting the sound-playing unit (14). The latter contains a chip-controlled piezoelectric sound transducer which plays a melody or voiced message when during intercourse the contacts (28 and 30) of the sound-playing unit (14) are closed and the transducer is activated.

What I claim is:

1. A force-sensitive sound-playing condom, comprising:

a condom body, and

force-sensitive sound-playing means for emitting a predetermined sound, said force-sensitive sound-playing means being attached to said condom body,

said condom being donnable upon an erect penis without activating said force-sensitive sound-playing means,

said force-sensitive sound-playing means being designed to emit said predetermined sound in response to a predetermined external force created during the act of sexual intercourse.

L. Books/Publishing

In *Technopoly*, author Neil Postman notes that 50 years after the printing press was invented, more than eight million books had been printed, making available a wide range of information on such topics as botany, religion, politics, and medicine, that had previously been inaccessible to readers. This, in turn, led to innovations in the form of books—for example, pagination with Arabic numerals, indexing, annotation, cross-referencing, paragraphs, title pages, and running heads. "By the end of the sixteenth century," writes Postman, "the machine-made book had a typographic form and look comparable to books of today."

Even though the general form of the book materialized four centuries ago, innovators still continue to play with the format, structure, and method of dispensing bound, printed information. The patents described below— one for a do-it-yourself storytelling process and the other for book-marking audio books— demonstrate two publishing innovations.

1. Do-it-Yourself Storytelling Book: U.S. Pat. 6,210,172

In his 1966 book, *Hopscotch,* the Argentine novelist Julio Cortázar created an innovation that predates the hyperlink. Cortázar's book had 155 chapters. Chapters one to 56 were intended to be read sequentially in the normal fashion. However, at the end of each of these chapters is the number of an alternative chapter the reader can select. For example, Chapter 2 ends with a link to Chapter 116, which itself has a link to Chapter 3, thereby giving the reader the choice of reading Chapter 116 or not. Cortázar's book was cited a few years later as an inspiration by computer programmers creating the first computer-based hypertext systems.

As Cortázar demonstrated, it's always possible to come up with a new way to tell a story. One patented innovation issued in 2001 and described below (U.S. Pat. 6,210,172) provides for a "Do-it-yourself storytelling book." Here are the abstract and claim:

Abstract:
A storytelling book with clear loose-leaf page holders is provided so that a person, such as a child, can illustrate and narrate with text a story of his or her own invention on a series of insertion pages and then present that story to an audience. A selected number of pages comprising the insertion pages created by the storyteller, and corresponding insertion pages, are arranged in book-like fashion and bound together so that the book may be disposed either with the pages flat on a support or in easel-like disposition. A first side of one of the pages is disposed in proximity to a second side of an adjacent page when the book-like arrangement is in a closed condition. The pages are disposed so that the person listening to the story sees the first sides and their respective illustrations or pictures while the storyteller or reader sees the second page sides and their corresponding text.

What is claimed is:
1. The method of creating and preparing a story to be read to a person or persons forming an audience comprising:

 a) providing a storytelling flip-over picture book;

 b) providing said book with a plurality of page holders;

 c) providing binder means for binding the plurality of page holders in an easel-like arrangement;

 d) providing at least two original insertion pages which have a space for pictures illustrating a story;

 e) creating pictures on said two original insertion pages;

 f) providing at least two corresponding insertion pages;

 g) generating on said two corresponding insertion pages corresponding to the pictures on said original insertion pages;

b) *creating book pages by holding said original insertion pages and said corresponding insertion pages using said page holders such that said original and corresponding insertion pages are arranged in diametric contraposition.*

2. Method and Apparatus for Audibly Indicating When a Predetermined Location Has Been Encountered in Stored Data: U.S. Pat. 5,872,712

Audiobooks are the fastest growing segment of the book industry, with over 60 million sold annually. To some extent, publishers can thank traffic gridlock for this phenomenon, because most listening—55%—takes place in vehicles (37% of audiobook buyers listen at home, 3.5% while exercising or jogging, and 3.5% while at work); 40% of all audiobook sales are motivational, inspirational, and self-help recordings. Approximately 58 million people in the United States and Canada have listened to audiobooks. According to one source, the over-40 crowd is turning to audio books as "an alternative to hunting for their reading glasses."

Audiobooks are traditionally sold in cassette or compact disc form, but Audible.com, an Internet company, realized that a lot of listeners would love to listen without all the multiple tapes or compact discs. The company pioneered a method of providing compressed downloadable audio. Using this technology, an unabridged version of *Moby Dick* can be loaded onto a cigarette-pack-sized MP3 player. Audible acquired several patents related to its technology, but one of the most important is a method of book-marking digital data. This permits a listener to stop listening, then later return to the same spot in the audio book. Below are the abstract and first claim for this post-Gutenberg publishing breakthrough.

Abstract:

A method and apparatus for audibly indicating when a predetermined location has been encountered in stored data is disclosed. A predetermined location is first identified. An audible indicator associated with the predetermined location is then generated when the predetermined location is encountered. The predetermined location can be an electronic bookmark, a section boundary or a program boundary. The invention includes a method and apparatus for audibly setting an electronic bookmark in stored data by selecting a location within the stored data, associating an electronic bookmark with the location, and generating an audible message for the electronic bookmark.

We claim:

1. *A method for audibly indicating when a predetermined location has been encountered in stored data, said method comprising the steps of:*

    identifying said predetermined location; and

    generating an audible indicator associated with said predetermined location when said predetermined location is encountered.

M. Crafts

Of all of the fields we examine in this chapter, crafts art—such as jewelry, leather work, glassblowing, and pottery—has the greatest collection of prior art, including centuries of techniques and artifacts. You'd think that in a field with this much prior art, it would be difficult to come up with something patentable. Not true.

Consider the craft of batik, a 2,000-year-old method of dyeing designs in cloth by first coating the cloth with removable wax over the parts not to be dyed. Batik got its name ("to dot") from artists in Java, where the art reached its golden age and where Dutch artisans introduced the tool known as the Cap (or Chop), a metal block used to stamp a pattern with a block of wax. Thereafter, batik art was classified as either Batik tulis (hand-drawn) or Batik cap.

Despite its ancient origins, there have been consistent innovations in batik. The USPTO has its developed own classifications for batik innovations—Class 8, Subclass 447, wax processes for production of patterns by preventing coloration in local areas. (We talk more about patent classifications in Chapter 5 and Appendix B). Below are two examples of patents form this subclass.

1. Method of Producing a Mosaic Expression on Fabric: U.S. Pat. 4,675,023

In June 1987, Barbara Hyink received a patent (U.S. Pat. 4,675,023) for a "Method of producing a mosaic expression on fabric"

(see Illustration 2-18). What the inventor claims is novel and nonobvious, according to her patent, is the ability to use batik to create a random mosaic appearance simulating stained glass. The patent abstract states:

Once the fabric and its basic color is [sic] *selected, a coating of melted wax is applied to one surface thereof. After the wax is dry, the fabric is crackled so as to form random and skewed cracks. Dye is then applied which penetrates the cracks and is absorbed by the fabric, whereby random skewed lines are left in the fabric after the wax is removed. The random skewed lines define a multiplicity of contiguous areas to be selectively painted so as to render a mosaic-like work of art.*

In other words, after the wax is poured on the fabric, the artist breaks it up and then pours ink through the cracks. The artist then pulls the wax off, and paints in between the

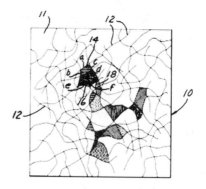

Illustration 2-18

lines to create the appearance of mosaic stained glass.

What's remarkable about this batik patent is that it does not grant rights over any *specific* design. Instead, it effectively gives her control over *all* designs that are randomly created using her patented process. In other words, if she sees a batik print for sale at a store and that print was made using her method, she can sue just about everyone who played a role in getting that print to market, from the artist to the shopkeeper.

2. Method of Producing a Batik Type Image on Cloth: U.S. Pat. 5,400,257

In 1995, Michael Krinsky and Michal McGloin received a batik patent (U.S. Pat. 5,400,257) for a "Method of producing a batik type image on cloth." Like Hyink, their patent is far broader than the form of protection granted by copyright—they can stop anyone who uses their process. But unlike Hyink's creation, Krinsky and McGloin's innovation does away with the "handmade" aspect of the craft. These two have gotten rid of all that messy wax—by using color film separations, high-tech inking processes, and computer graphics, this innovation simulates the look of batik. In Illustration 2-19, you see the patented process that is claimed by Krinsky and McGloin. Below is a summary of their invention.

A method for producing a Batik-type image on cloth. Artwork is generated manually or via a computer graphic art program, which contains an outline of a Batik-type image to be produced on cloth. The outline simulates

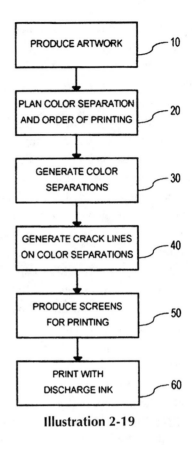

Illustration 2-19

wax drip lines. Coloration is then added to selected areas, and the artwork is color separated into individual images. Simulated wax crack lines are then added to the color separations. Screens for each individual color are produced, and the cloth is printed using a discharge type ink. The result is an image very similar to Batik style dyeing.

N. Live Performance

Today, audiences for live theater are wowed by the magic of mechanical props and fireworks—for example, the use of a full-size helicopter in the musical, *Miss Saigon*. But the gadgetry and science of live theater dates back centuries. The 17th century artist and architect Gian Lorenzo Bernini—designer of the piazza and colonnade of St Peter's in the Vatican—understood the magic of theater. He was an innovative designer of stage settings and gadgetry. His mastery of fireworks enabled him to thrill audiences with bursts of light, motorized angels and devils, and elaborate sets, which led the way to a modern concept of stage production. Elaborate stage sets and mechanical props were also popular in European ballet performances. King Louis XIV so loved these theatrical events that he often participated—he acquired his nickname "the Sun King" from an elaborate sun-styled headdress he wore in a performance.

In modern times, innovation continues in live performances, as demonstrated by the exciting and elaborate performance devices used by the Blue Man Group and Cirque du Soleil. And, as the following patents—for a movable seating system and an improved fog machine—demonstrate, there is still plenty of room for innovation.

1. Amusement Attraction: U.S. Pat. 6,428,419

There is a great convenience to viewing theater and movies on television and over the Internet. But such viewing is always a pale comparison to the live performance, especially in venues designed with the audience in mind. The following patent improves on movable seating systems at live venues. Note, that this patented system can also be used in an amusement park, which demonstrates one of the advantages of a utility patent over a design patent—you can claim multiple uses of a new invention in one utility patent application. Below are the patent abstract and claim:

Abstract:
An amusement ride or theater attraction has a moveable floor for guest loading and unloading. A screen displays images. A motion base moves guests in at least one degree of freedom. The moveable floor that has a cutout for the motion base. The moveable floor is positioned to a raised position during guest loading and unloading. The moveable floor is lowered to a lowered position during ride operation, with the motion base passing through the cutout. Loading and unloading of passengers is simplified, without limiting motion base movement during operation of the ride.

What is claimed is:
1. An amusement attraction comprising:
a screen for displaying images;
*   at least one motion base supporting a*
*   passenger platform; and*
*   a moveable floor including a cutout*
*   aligned with the motion base,*
*   so that the moveable floor can move from*
*   an up position for guest loading and*
*   unloading, to a down position, during*
*   operation of the ride.*

With the following narrowing dependent claims:

2. An amusement ride according to claim 1, the motion base further comprising a ride vehicle mounted on the motion base.

3. *An amusement ride according to claim 1, wherein said moveable floor includes a plurality of tiered levels.*

4. *An amusement ride according to claim 3, further including at least one set of stairs leading from a lower tier level to a higher tier level on the moveable floor.*

2. Fog Producing Apparatus: U.S. Pat. 4,911,866

According to legend, the University of Montana theater is haunted by a solitary ghost who can sometimes be seen sitting in the theater during late-night rehearsals. One night during a production of *Macbeth*, the actresses playing the three witches heard screaming offstage. (No one else heard anything). After that, a stage collapsed and then, most mysterious of all … a fog machine wouldn't turn off. The device eventually flooded the theatre with a misty haze.

No doubt the Montana theater ghost was as fascinated by the fog machine as are attendees at heavy metal concerts, ice capades, and other theatrical events. The artificial fog machine is one of the most popular theatrical effects used in the entertainment industry.

Fog machines have evolved, particularly in regard to the fuel used to generate the fog. Many modern machines devour bottles of fog juice, composed of hazardous organic polyoils. The patent described below, owned by the Walt Disney Company, describes a fog machine innovation that uses water.

The abstract and first claim are provided below.

Abstract:

A fog producing apparatus for suspending fine particles of water in air in an economical and reliable manner. Ultrasonic transducers potted in an electrically insulative and liquidproof material are placed in a container in which a predetermined water level is maintained by a float and valve device. Alternatively, the potted transducers are suspended below floats floating on the surface of the water whereby the critical water depth over the transducers is automatically maintained. In addition compressed air is conducted through the emanating fog plumes to provide a more homogeneous and dispersed fog effect. A copious amount of fog can thereby be efficiently and reliably produced to create theatrical or visual effects.

What is claimed is:

1. *An apparatus for producing fog, comprising an ultrasonic transducer module, said module including a transducer disc and circuitry means for oscillating said disc in the MHz frequency range, potted in an electrically insulative and waterproof potting material whereby only said disc remains exposed so that the entire module is submersible and functional within a body of water.*

O. Novelty Devices

Sheryl Crow will always be remembered for singing, "All I want to do is have some fun until the sun comes up over Santa Monica Boulevard." While the arts are "refined" fun, and sports "organized" fun, some fun is just fun fun. As we will see below, new machines and devices for fun are always needed.

Novelty, for patent purposes, means "new." But the term has a different meaning for consumers—wacky! A hat that holds two beer cans, chewing gum that turns the user's teeth black, or a wearable arrow that makes it seem as if the user has been shot through the head, are examples of some nutty novelty items. The two items described below—a wig flipping device and a machine that will kick you in the butt—may not have achieved as much sales as the preceding innovations. However, they are intended to entertain. And who are we to wonder, in a world that sells body glitter, pet rocks, and heart-shaped handcuffs, why anyone would buy them?

1. Wig Flipping Device: U.S. Pat. 5,372,549

Wigs have often been the subject of humor and entertainment—from the snatching of a toupee by the Marx Brothers to the hiding of a frog under a toupee in the 1945 comedy *The Poet and the Peasant*. In the 1950s, the phrase "flip your wig" was used as a synonym for hysterical behavior. The term "wig out" connoted similar behavior. Today, a consumer can choose from an endless collection of wacky wigs such as tinsel wigs, bald head wigs, neon wigs, and the well-liked rainbow clown wig. Capitalizing on the wacky wig factor, the device described in U.S. Pat. 5,372,549 truly enables one to flip one's wig. (See Illustration 2-20.)

Abstract:

A wig flipping device comprising a cap which is connected to a spring-loaded wig is disclosed. A releasable retention mechanism holds the wig to the cap and when a trigger mechanism is activated, the retention mechanism releases causing the spring to uncoil and raise the wig above the cap.

I claim:

1. *A wig flipping device comprising;*
    a cap adapted to be worn on a user's head;
    a wig;
    a spring having a first end connected to said cap and a second end connected to said wig, said spring having a compressed state and a released state; means to hold said spring in its compressed state, said means capable of releasing said spring to assume its released state, wherein when said spring is in said compressed state, said wig covers at least a portion of said user's head simulating the user's

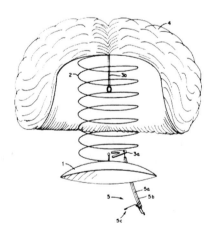

Illustration 2-20

real hair and when said spring is in said released state said wig springs away from said user's head in a surprising manner.

2. User-Operated Amusement Apparatus for Kicking the User's Buttocks: U.S. Pat. 6,293,874

Of course, one person's idea of fun may be another's idea of masochism. That's certainly the case with the ass-kicking amusement device patented in 2000 by Joe Armstrong. In case the vivid description proved in the abstract doesn't give you the full picture, see Illustration 2-21.

Abstract:
An amusement apparatus including a user-operated and controlled apparatus for self-infliction of repetitive blows to the user's buttocks by a plurality of elongated arms bearing flexible extensions that rotate under the user's control. The apparatus includes a platform foldable at a midsection, having first post and second upstanding posts detachably mounted thereon. The first post is provided with a crank positioned at a height thereon which requires the user to bend forward toward the first post while grasping the crank with both hands, to prominently present his buttocks toward the second post. The second post is provided with a plurality of rotating arms detachably mounted thereon, with a central axis of the rotating arms positioned at a height generally level with the user's buttocks. The elongated arms are propelled by the user's movement of the crank, which is opera-
tively connected by a drive train to the central axis of the rotating arms. As the user rotates the crank, the user's buttocks are paddled by flexible shoes located on each outboard end of the elongated arms to provide amusement to the user and viewers of the paddling. The amusement apparatus is foldable into a self-contained package for storage or shipping.

Unlike some of the holders of other patents cited in this chapter, the inventor of this spanking device had done considerable prior art research, described below:

Description of the Related Art:
Prior art devices include individual spanking devices that must be reloaded or reset after each individual spanking action. Typical prior art devices provide a paddle that can pivot once, upon being triggered, to spank a hand or buttocks of the user. In U.S. Pat. 920,837, issued to De Moulin, a device is disclosed for lifting and spanking of the user for secret society initiation ceremonies. The

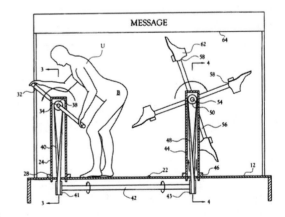

Illustration 2-21

device includes a trick lifting machine having a spring member, lever, and manual actuation for triggering the paddle release. The actuation by a user releases the spring member, pivoting the paddle, and striking a user straddled over the device. The spring and paddle are reset after each actuation.

This and other known devices of the type, disclose spring activated, individual paddle actions that must be reset after each contact with the user, with associated repositioning of the user in a posture to accept the next individual paddle action.

Therefore, it is an object of the present invention to provide an amusement apparatus which is user-operated and controlled, and is designed to inflict repetitive blows on the user without resetting of the apparatus and/or repositioning of the user between blows.

It is another object of the present invention to provide an amusement apparatus having a user controlled crank regulating the frequency and force of the blows inflicted upon the user's buttocks.

It is another object of the present invention to provide an amusement apparatus for self-inflicting repetitive blows to a user and which is foldable into a self-containing package for storage or shipping.

P. Toys

All toys are, to some extent, a reduction of adult behavior to child's play. For example, three of the bestselling toy inventions were architecturally inspired. A.C. Gilbert came up with the idea for the Erector Set while watch-ing the construction of a power line tower. Lincoln Logs were based on the log-shaped pieces joined together to construct the foun-dation of Frank Lloyd Wright's Imperial Hotel in Japan. (The observer/inventor was Frank's son, John Lloyd Wright.) And LEGOs were created by Ole Kirk Christiansen, a master carpenter and joiner who probably had no idea that children around the world would eventually spend five billion hours every year playing with his LEGO bricks (327 billion LEGO elements have been molded since 1949).

Below we look at four toy patents, all based on adult behavior—a unique squirt gun, a crushable car toy (based on Monster Truck exhibitions), a talking stick horse, and a child's video camera.

1. Squirt Gun (Super Soaker): U.S. Pat. 4,591,071

Most toys are built upon other toy concepts. Remote controlled vehicles, for example, are based on simple toy cars, which in turn are derived from rolling toy vehicles such as trains and carriages, popular in the 19th cen-tury. Lonnie Johnson, an ex-NASA engineer, improved upon a staple of every child's toy weapons arsenal—the squirt gun—when he created one of the most popular toys of the 1990s, the Super Soaker. Below are the abstract and one of the claims.

Abstract:
A toy squirt gun which shoots a continuous high velocity stream of water. The squirt gun is configured as a structure facilitating partial filling with water leaving a void for compressed

air. The squirt gun includes a nozzle for ejecting water at high velocity, a pressurization pump for compressing air into the gun to pressurize water contained therein, and a trigger actuated flow control valve for shooting the gun by controlling flow of pressurized water through the nozzle. A battery-powered oscillator circuit and a water flow powered sound generator produce futuristic space ray gun sound effects when the gun is shooting.

What is claimed is:

1. A toy squirt gun for shooting a continuous stream of water, comprising:

   (a) a structure means for containing water and air under high internal pressure, said structure means being configured to facilitate partially filling with water leaving an internal volume for compressed air, a water fill port means, a pressurization pump means, a trigger means, a flow control valve means, a battery-powered oscillator circuit means, a flow actuated sound generator means and a nozzle means;

   (b) said fill port means being attached to said structure means and including a removable cap corresponding to an aperture in said structure means, whereby said fill port means provides access for partially filling said squirt gun with water, the cap being resealable so as to not permit leakage when said squirt gun is operating under high internal pressure;

   (c) said pressurization pump means being operably coupled to said structure means, providing hand-held support for said squirt gun and operating to compress

air into said structure means, said pressurization pump means including a movable member means for facilitating manual actuation thereof;

   (d) said nozzle means being coupled to said structure means, said flow control valve means being fluidly coupled via a passageway within said structure means to said nozzle means, said control valve controlling flow of pressurized water to said nozzle means; to shoot said squirt gun said trigger means being manually actuated to open said control valve means and thereby permit pressurized water flow through said nozzle means, said water flow exiting said nozzle means and thereby said squirt gun at high velocity;

   (e) said flow actuated sound generator means including a rotatable impeller means mounted integral and within said structure means and interposed between said control valve means and nozzle means and adapted to rotate when flowing water moves from said control valve means to said nozzle means, and also including vibration means mounted externally on said structure means and operably coupled to said impeller means for activation upon rotation of said impeller means; wherein said vibration means comprises a horn cylinder means, a horn piston means, a first reed vibrator means and a second reed vibrator means, said first and second reed vibrator means being attached to said cylinder means, said piston means being positioned inside said cylinder means, rotation of said impeller means causing said horn piston means to cycle back and forth inside said horn cylinder means and thereby alternatingly force air through said first and second vibrator means causing said first and second vibrator means to vibrate and produce pulsating sounds; and

(f) said battery operated oscillator circuit means being attached to said structure means and including a switch means for controlling on and off states of said circuit means, said switch means being coupled to said trigger means to simultaneously switch said circuit means to an on state when said trigger means is actuated to shoot said squirt gun, said circuit means operating to produce pulsating sounds when switched to an on state.

2. Crushable Toy Car Apparatus ("Monster Truck Crusher"): U.S. Pat. 5,131,880

Bob Chandler had a novel idea in the 1970s—why not put 66-inch tires on a four-wheel-drive truck? In 1981, he had another idea—why not use that truck with big tires to crush a car? Nine months later, a promoter booked Chandler to crush a car with his truck at a tractor pull, and that event spawned a distinctly American phenomenon known as the Monster Truck Rally, which attracts 15 to 20 million Americans every year.

In order to capitalize on this national obsession, Mark and Charles Nesbit invented a crushable toy car apparatus (see Illustration 2-22) that enables users to simulate the monster truck experience in their very own living rooms. Below are the abstract and the first claim for the invention.

Abstract:
A crushable car body (20) having a pressurized deformable bladder (50) associated with the upper car body portion (30) such that when downward pressure was exerted on the roof (31) of the car body (20) the car body (20) would be deformed to simulate a crushed car; and, wherein the reintroduction of positive pressure into the deformable bladder will return the car body (20) to its original configuration.

We claim:

1. *An inflatable recrushable toy car apparatus for use with an inflation means and a crushing vehicle in combination with a ramp arrangement; wherein, the toy car apparatus comprises:*

   a car body having a roof, hood, trunk, wheels and chassis and further including an upper body portion deformable from a normal body portion configuration to

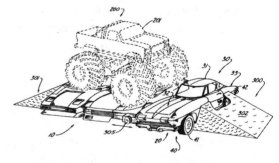

Illustration 2-22

a crushed body portion configuration and vice versa; and, a lower body portion: and,

an inflatable bladder operatively associated with said inflation means and at least the upper body portion of said car body; wherein, the bladder is provided with: a valved inlet port for admitting air from said inflation means at an above atmospheric inflation pressure to restore the upper body portion of the car body to a normal body portion configuration; and, an overpressure responsive valved outlet port responsive to an increase in the pressure of the above atmospheric pressure air within the bladder for allowing the air within the bladder to escape to produce the crushed body portion configuration, in response to an external force being transmitted to the upper body portion by said crushing vehicle to produce the opening of said overpressure responsive valved outlet port.

3. The Talking Stick Horse: U.S. Pat. 6,524,156

In D.H. Lawrence's short story, "The Rocking Horse Winner," a young boy develops an obsession with a toy rocking horse. Only when riding the toy horse can the child hear the name of winning race horses. With the help of a handyman, he uses this information to bet, giving his winnings to his greedy mother.

Our cultural fascination with talking animals —for example, Mr. Ed.—is evident in the following interactive children's toy, "Talking

stick horse." Below is the abstract and a narrowly drafted first claim.

Abstract:

An interactive ride-on toy, having a stuffed toy horse's head which includes ears, a movable mouth and is connected to a stick. One or more buttons, each with an icon depicting an image, is positioned on one or both ears of the horse's head. An electronically programmed chip responds to activation of the button to operate a speaker and a mechanism for moving the horse's mouth, the speaker playing sounds relating to the image depicted on each button.

What is claimed is:

1. An interactive ride-on toy, comprising:

a toy animal's head, having a movable mouth;

> *a riding member connected to said head;*

> *at least one button on said head;*

> *an electronically programmed chip for responding to activation of the button; and*

a speaker and a mechanism for moving said mouth located within the head, wherein the chip is programmed to operate both the speaker and the mechanism in response to activation of the button.

4. Fisher-Price PXL 2000 Camera: U.S. Pat. 5,010,419

When Fisher-Price unveiled its PXL 2000 Camera in 1987, it had high hopes. The battery-operated video camera was simple to use, could be plugged directly into a television for playback, and—in a radical departure from existing video technology—did not require expensive and large video cassettes (see Illustration 2-23). The video and audio could both be recorded on a standard audio cassette tape.

Alas, the camera was a flop, primarily because Fisher-Price misjudged the market. Kids wanted color, not black and white, and certainly not the slow-moving, dark and grainy pixilated black and white imagery produced by the PXL 2000.

But, then something unusual happened. The toy that children shunned became a popular tool for video artists, fascinated by its unique (and some say, disturbing) visual qualities. These video artists nicknamed the phenomenon Pixelvision, and soon the distinctive imagery even began appearing in major motion pictures—for example, Michael Almareyda's 1994 horror film, *Nadja*, in

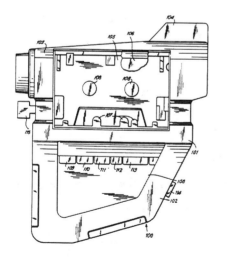

Illustration 2-23

which Pixelvision imagery is used to provide the vampire's point of view. Recently, a DVD, *The Art of Pixelvision*, was released which included many award-winning Pixelvision shorts. The camera—which often breaks down and for which no replacement parts are available—is no longer sold, though used versions fetch approximately $400 when they appear on Ebay. Reportedly, a Japanese version of the camera entitled Sanpix has recently been released.

Below are the abstract and first claim from the PXL-2000 patent.

Abstract:

The invention is generally directed to a video apparatus for storing video images on a recording medium and replaying the stored images on a display. A camera mechanism converts light images into electrical video signals. A processor circuitry coupled to the camera mechanism includes means for converting the electronic video signals into a low bandwidth frequency modulated storage signal with the bandwidth substantially lower than in a standard television video signal. A recording mechanism coupled to the processing means stores the low bandwidth frequency modulated storage signal on an audio cassette, which has a standard speed allowing storage of an audio bandwidth signal. The recording mechanism includes a drive mechanism for driving the audio cassette at higher than normal speed to increase the bandwidth storage capacity of the audio cassette. A recording head mechanism stores the low bandwidth frequency modulated storage signal on the audio cassette. The video apparatus also includes a switch mechanism for switching the video apparatus from a record mode where video images are stored on an audio cassette to a playback mode where the stored images are read off the audio cassette and displayed on the video display. In playback mode, the low bandwidth video signal is converted to a higher frequency standard television bandwidth video signal for display. The rate conversion from a low bandwidth video signal to a standard television video signal is performed by a "ping-pong" digital memory system. The video apparatus also adjusts the sensitivity of the camera mechanism by adjusting the exposure time of the camera mechanism based on the incident light.

We claim:

1. A video apparatus for storing video images on a recording medium comprising:

camera means for converting light images into electrical video signals;

processing means coupled to the camera means including means for converting the electronic video signal into a low bandwidth frequency modulated analog storage signal with a bandwidth substantially lower than a standard television video signal; and recording means coupled to the processing means for storing the low bandwidth frequency modulated analog storage signal on an audio cassette having a standard speed allowing storage of an audio bandwidth signal, the recording means including drive means for driving the audio cassette at higher than normal speed to increase the bandwidth storage capacity of the

audio cassette and recording head means for storing the low bandwidth frequency modulated analog storage signal on the audio cassette.

Q. Decorative/Gift Arts

Hallmark Cards was founded in the 19th century by Joyce Clyde Hall, who sold postcards from his rented room at the YMCA. He later expanded to greeting cards, and eventually created the gift-wrap industry when he ran out of tissue paper to wrap gifts and began selling French envelope linings for that purpose. His company, Hallmark Cards, Inc., pioneered a new industry in America, specializing in cards, wrapping paper, and small gifts, all of which communicated friendly messages while exploiting social conventions (Mother's Day, weddings, and so on). Today the company founded by Hall generates over $4 billion in annual revenues. Below we examine two patents for innovations in the decorative/gift market—a method for transferring holographs to wrapping paper and a scented postcard.

1. Holographically Transferable Images: U.S. Pat. 5,939,177

Holographs are popular for security purposes—for example, the Microsoft holograph signifying authenticity—because they are so difficult to duplicate. But holographs are also popular for their amusement and decorative value.

U.S. Pat. 5,939,177 is for a method of producing "holographically enhanced" paper

The Decorative Bow: Worthy of a Patent?

Hallmark Cards, Inc. was recently issued a patent for an invention that appears to have been created much earlier. Filed in 2000 and issued in May 2001, their U.S. Pat. 6,237,819, titled "Decorative bow," has the following first claim:

1. A decorative bow comprising:

a plurality of ribbon-like strands, each of the strands having a zigzag shape with a plurality of folds in regularly alternating directions distributed along a length of said each strand;

a base member to which the plurality of strands are secured.

In its patent for the decorative bow, Hallmark Cards claims:

"[C]onsumers who are tired of the conventional look of decorative bows are often attracted to decorative bows that have more unique structures and interesting appearances. Thus, there is a need for a decorative bow that has a structure that is visually appealing and highly distinctive from the conventional flower-like decorative bows."

Hallmark claims that its decorative bow "has an attractive appearance very distinct from that of conventional flower-like bows," yet the accompanying patent drawings (see Illustrations 2-24 and 2-25) appear to show a fairly ordinary decorative device. Is this truly novel? Is the USPTO correct when it endorses this as being a nonobvious invention? Should Hallmark

have the right to stop others from making, using and selling this bow? Again, the power and strength of an art and entertainment patent depends upon the depth of prior art research that accompanies the application and examination. When the time comes to go after infringers, Hallmark may find that others will challenge the patent.

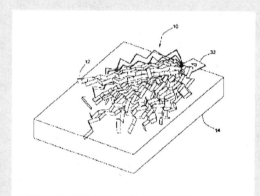

Illustration 2-24

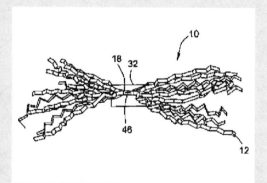

Illustration 2-25

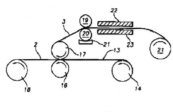

Illustration 2-26

(see Illustration 2-26) by "laminating a metallized holographic image on a polymeric substrate to paper wrapping element under temperatures and pressure requisite to obtaining such lamination." Thanks to this invention, you may someday find holographs produced on wrapping paper. Below are the abstract and first claim for this invention.

Abstract:

A holographic image that has been transferred from a conventional polymeric support to a wrapping paper element is described in this invention. A host of images may be envisioned and since this image, on a wrapping paper element, may then be wound up in a roll, it can be used as a wrapping element for a host of applications such as in wrapping of gifts and in papers used for advertising and the like. This element and process permits the wide spread use of such holographic images, such use not being available until now.

I claim:

1. *A wrapping paper element having a metallized holographic image adhered thereon, said metallized holographic image having been transferred to said wrapping paper element from a second support, said second support comprising in order:*

   a. *a polymeric support having a holographic image therein;*

   b. *a metal applied over said holographic image to enhance said holographic image by metallization thereof, said metal forming the metallized holographic image; and,*

   c. *an adhesive layer coated on said metallized holographic image on said polymeric support and subsequently dried, wherein said metallized holographic image is transferred to said wrapping paper element by laminating said dried adhesive layer of said second support to said wrapping paper element at a temperature between 0.degree. C. and 250.degree. C. and a pressure between 0.15 and 1,000 pounds per square inch and then delaminating the polymeric support having a holographic image therein from the metallized holographic image to substantially transfer all of said metallized holographic image to said wrapping paper element leaving said polymeric support having said holographic image remaining therein capable of being re-metallized for reuse.*

2. Scented Postcard:
U.S. Pat. 5,148,983

It used to be that a love letter might be doused with a hint of perfume. For some, that's apparently not enough. In 1992, Ralph Muniz patented the scented postcard (see Illustration 2-27). For example, a tourist in Florida can now send a postcard that smells like an orange or grapefruit.

Below are the claims for this invention.

1. *A souvenir device comprising:*

   a pair of members joined together to define an internal storage cavity between their opposing surfaces;

   graphic indicia carried on at least one exterior face of said joined pair of members;

   a pad carried in said internal storage cavity holding a quantity of a scented substance;

   means internally communicating said scented substance exteriorly of said joined pair of members;

   said communicating means comprises a plurality of open-ended passageways extending between said internal storage cavity and edge marginal regions of said joined pair of members; and

   said plurality of passageways are defined between opposing surfaces of said members and opposing surfaces of a plurality of raised portions carried on a selected one of said members.

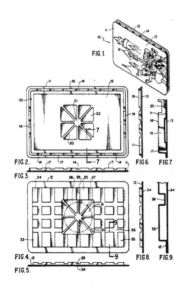

Illustration 2-27

R. Advertising

There are over 6,000 ad agencies in the United States, and the top three—Omnicom Group, Interpublic Group, and Grey Global—generate over $14 billion annually in revenues. Not bad, considering that ad agencies didn't even exist until the middle of the 19th century. Worldwide, over $350 billion is spent annually on advertising in newspapers, television, direct mail, radio, magazines, the Internet, and outdoor signs. According to one report, we are so inundated with advertising in this country that you may encounter from 500 to 1,000 advertisements in a single day.

This sheer mass of advertising makes it hard for advertisers to distinguish their message. For example, a pizza chain in Oregon, Pizza Schmizza, tried to get its advertising message out by having homeless people wear sandwich signs such as "Pizza Schmizza paid me to hold this sign instead of asking for money" (In return for a 40-minute shift, the company gave the homeless workers a few dollars and fed them pizza and soda.)

Not surprisingly, innovation is essential in advertising—and that innovation is increasingly being patented. Below are examples of three advertising patents, including an advertising method for the Internet, a mechanical advertising device, and a printed advertising device.

1. Internet-Based Advertising Scheme Employing Scavenger Hunt Metaphor: U.S. Pat. 6,102,406

Do you wish there was more advertising on the Internet? Do you want advertisers to have additional ways to get personal information from you? Would you like it if you could get both of these wishes to come true and also participate in a quiz or test in which you were forced to visit advertisers' websites? If so, then you'll be glad to learn about U.S. Pat. 6,102,406 (issued in 2000), titled "Internet-based advertising scheme employing scavenger hunt metaphor."

Because fewer than 2% of Internet surfers ever click through on banner ads, advertisers are always seeking new ways of getting the gullible to follow marketing links—and hopefully give up valuable personal and consumer information in the process, which the advertiser can database and use for further advertising purposes. The following abstract and claims describe a process of getting Web surfers to follow advertising links in the hopes of winning a contest. A flow chart demonstrating the process is shown in Illustrations 2-28 and 2-29.

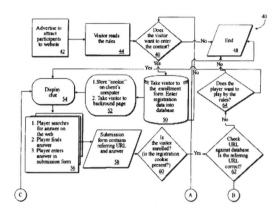

Illustration 2-28

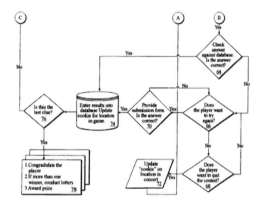

Illustration 2-29

Abstract:

An Internet-based service configured to operate a scavenger hunt in which participants are required to answer questions using information obtained from one or more Web sites visited in response to hints suggesting where such information may be located. Each preceding question must be successfully answered before a next question is presented. Generally, a correct answer requires verification that a respondent visited the Web site at which the information required in the answer is located. This, in turn, may require that the respondent reached the Web site at which the information required in the answer is located through an authorized path including at least one predetermined Web address. Such verification may be achieved by using referring uniform resource locator (URL) information regarding the at least one Web address as a security key to allow access to a location at which the respondent may enter the answer. The security key provides access to a secure database used to store answers provided by the participants in the scavenger hunt. Unique security keys for each question used in the scavenger hunt may be required to obtain access to the secure database.

What is claimed is:

1. An Internet-based service configured to operate a scavenger hunt in which participants are required to answer questions using information obtained from one or more Web sites visited in response to hints suggesting where such information may be located, wherein each preceding question must be successfully answered before a next question is presented.

2. Advertisement System for an Airport Facility: U.S. Pat. 6,275,201

So much luggage to push and so little space to advertise. That was the dilemma faced by

two German inventors who believed that the advertising space at airports could be increased exponentially if every advertising board could contain multiple advertising messages, each triggered by a transponder on the cart carrying your luggage (see Illustration 2-30). In other words, as you approached an airport advertisement it could change repeatedly as you passed or be customized for you—for example, if you landed on a flight from Germany, the message might appear in German.

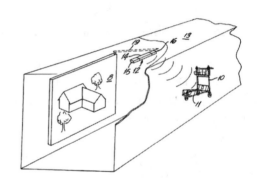

Illustration 2-30

The abstract and first claim for U.S. Pat. 6,275,201 (issued in 2001) are provided below.

Abstract:

An advertisement system for an airport facility having a plurality of gates connected by passageways and aisles and provided in departure and arrival buildings with restaurants and shops, with information carriers emitting written and picture messages and provided on information boards, and with a plurality of luggage pushcarts for transporting luggage of airport passengers inside the facility, the advertisement system including a plurality of advertisement panels each having a standard advertisement message and at least one different advertisement message stored in the advertisement panels, and elements which arbitrary [sic] change the messages so that one of the advertisement messages is displayed at a time.

What is claimed is:

1. An advertisement system for an airport facility having a plurality of gates connected by passageways and aisles and provided in departure and arrival buildings with restaurants and shops, with information carriers emitting written and picture messages and provided on information boards, and with a plurality of luggage pushcarts for transporting luggage of airport passengers inside the facility, the advertisement system comprising:

a plurality of advertisement panels each having a standard advertisement message and at least one different advertisement message stored in the advertisement panels; and

means for arbitrary [sic] changing the message so that one of the advertisement messages is displayed at a time,

wherein a controlled turn-on time, which is dependent on an arbitrary number and distribution of airport passengers, is associated with turn-on/off advertisement areas for advertisement panels available in the airport facility,

wherein a limited turn-on time is associated with each advertisement message, and wherein the message changing means comprises a plurality of sets of interrogatable transponders with the transponders of each set emitting particularly coded signals, which correspond to a particular message, and arranged on a group of luggage pushcarts of the plurality of luggage pushcarts available in the airport facility, whereby the particular message is displayed dependent on a frequency the luggage pushcarts of the group of luggage pushcarts passing a particular location.

3. Advertising Brochure and Method for Its Use: U.S. Pat. 6,276,724

If you're old enough, you might remember a time when you could open a magazine and the only thing inside it was … the magazine. Nowadays, publications are packed with advertising inserts of all shapes and sizes, including sniffable perfume inserts, insert cards, and elaborate advertising attachments that may include samples of toothpaste, software, or even sound chips.

But apparently, the state of insert advertising was not sufficient to Richard Zorn, who felt that printed inserts lacked the personal touch—as well as the impact—of beautifully printed brochures. And so Zorn's invention—"Advertising Brochure and Method for Its Use" (U.S. Pat. 6,276,724)—solves "the long-felt need for a high-quality, personalized magazine insert or attachment."

As you can see from Illustrations 2-31 and 2-32, the process includes creating a database with the customer's name and address, information that can later be "personalized" on the insert. So just in case you forget your name and where you live, the magazine insert may have a greeting such as, "Hello Jim Smith of 5327 Cabrillo Street, San Francisco." Below are the abstract, some views (Illustrations 2-33, 2-34, and 2-35) of how the invention can be used, and the first claim for the invention.

Abstract:

An advertising or promotional brochure is disclosed that is to be mailed in conjunction with a magazine or periodical. The brochure may include high-quality, glossy photographs, and be personalized with text and/or images that relate specifically to the magazine subscriber. In addition, the brochure may include coupons for sales discounts, bank promotional checks, and other promotions that may be redeemed by the magazine subscriber. The brochure may be embodied as a multi-page pamphlet and may have an appearance and cover similar to the magazine to which it is attached.

What is claimed is:

1. A brochure for attachment to a periodical comprising:

a cover sheet having a first cover page with a variable print area within which is indicia identifying a magazine subscriber name and subscriber address, wherein the first cover page further includes postage indicia, and the first cover page is exposed to view for mailing of the periodical,

said cover sheet further having a second cover page with a removable attachment to a cover of the periodical, and

at least one insert sheet attached to an inside page of the cover sheet, the insert sheet having a detachable coupon.

S. Gambling

Gambling, like pornography, has been one of the forces behind the Internet explosion: 36% of a group of Internet users recently surveyed said they had gambled online; 13% had gambled for real money. As of 2003, Internet gambling was estimated to be a $6 billion industry. But before online gambling really takes off, a few problems have to be solved: casinos need to be able to check where you're surfing from (to make sure that gambling is legal in your state); and casinos need to be able to verify your identity and, ideally, your age. Currently Internet technology does not permit online casinos to answer these questions with 100% certainty, but that isn't stopping everyone involved from pursuing technological solutions. For example, research is currently being undertaken to locate users using global positioning systems (GPS), which will soon be incorporated in many mobile phone devices. (The use of GPS will enable phone wagering from mobile phones.) Visa is also working on technology to track the geographic location of users down to the zipcode from which they are calling. Similar innovations in database and tracking technology may enable casinos to determine a user's identity and age with more certainty. In short, the urge to

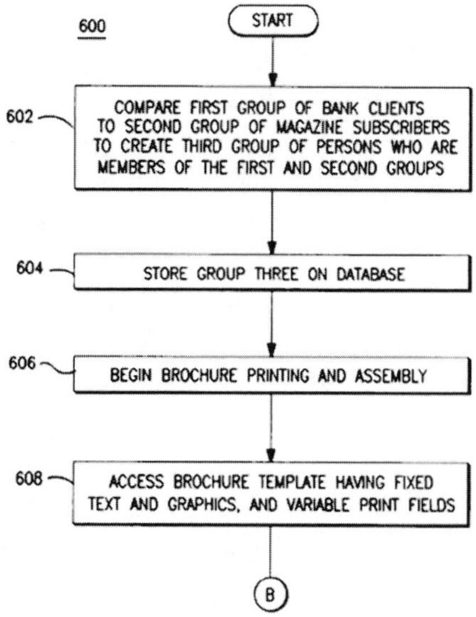

600
START
602 COMPARE FIRST GROUP OF BANK CLIENTS TO SECOND GROUP OF MAGAZINE SUBSCRIBERS TO CREATE THIRD GROUP OF PERSONS WHO ARE MEMBERS OF THE FIRST AND SECOND GROUPS
604 STORE GROUP THREE ON DATABASE
606 BEGIN BROCHURE PRINTING AND ASSEMBLY
608 ACCESS BROCHURE TEMPLATE HAVING FIXED TEXT AND GRAPHICS, AND VARIABLE PRINT FIELDS
B

Illustration 2-31

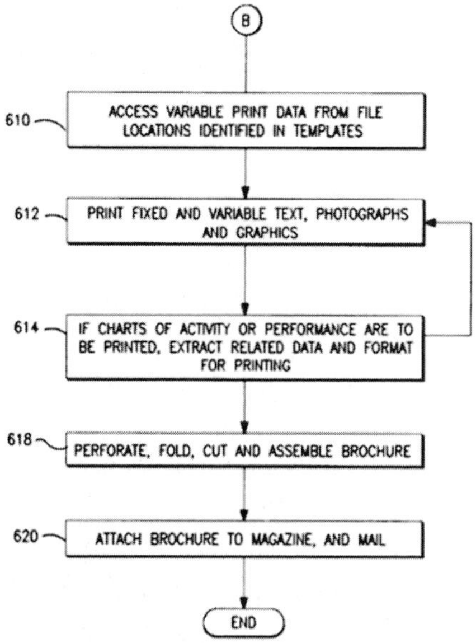

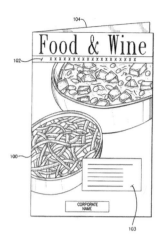

B
610 ACCESS VARIABLE PRINT DATA FROM FILE LOCATIONS IDENTIFIED IN TEMPLATES
612 PRINT FIXED AND VARIABLE TEXT, PHOTOGRAPHS AND GRAPHICS
614 IF CHARTS OF ACTIVITY OR PERFORMANCE ARE TO BE PRINTED, EXTRACT RELATED DATA AND FORMAT FOR PRINTING
618 PERFORATE, FOLD, CUT AND ASSEMBLE BROCHURE
620 ATTACH BROCHURE TO MAGAZINE, AND MAIL
END

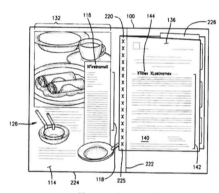

Illustration 2-32

104
Food & Wine
102
100
CORPORATE NAME
103

Illustration 2-33

132
116
220
100
144
136
226
XFirstnameX
XTitlex XLastnamex
126
140
222
142
114
224
118
225

Illustration 2-34

104
ADVERTISING LOGOS
112
100
113
"SUBSCRIBER NAME"
Inside this issue of "BROCHURE TITLE" we have included 8 money-saving checks at these locations
RETURN ADDRESS
PAID
110
108
SUBSCRIBER NAME ADDRESS
106

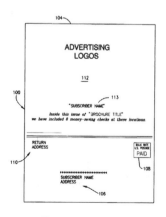

Illustration 2-35

gamble is leading to more and more innovative breakthroughs, many of which will surely filter down to other commercial uses.

Below, we look at two recently issued patents for more conventional gambling methods—a patent related to slot machines and another related to the use of gambling chips.

1. Free Long-Distance Calls on Slot Machines: U.S. Pat. 6,530,835

If any device epitomizes gambling technology, it's the slot machine. The first modern three-reel slot machine (first christened the "Liberty Bell") was created in 1895 by Charles Fey, a San Francisco electrician. Fey later invented a poker-based slot machine, the precursor of video poker. The machines were immediately popular, so much so that California soon outlawed them under antigambling laws. In order to outwit officials, Fey called his machines vending machines and programmed some of them to disperse chewing gum. From that was born the vending machine industry, in which coin-fed machines dispersed food. (The fruit and candy symbols found on modern slot machines are a reminder of the machine's evasive legal history.)

Initially casino owners placed slot machines in their lobbies to occupy the time of girlfriends and wives of heavy rollers. Soon, however, the machines accounted for over two-thirds of casino revenue.

Casino owners love gambling machines—slot machines, video poker, and video blackjack—because the casino retains a higher percentage of the amount gambled (the hold percentage or "vig") on these machines than on table games like roulette or craps. For that reason, the casinos want to keep the players at the machines for as long as possible.

Three inventors from Connecticut figured out a way to keep players hooked to the slot machines—connect them to free long-distance phone service ("Hi Honey, I lost $4,000"). As long as the player continues at the machine, the phone calls continue; once the last coin is spent, the line goes dead.

The abstract and first claim are shown below. For a simple flowchart depicting the invention, see Illustration 2-36.

Abstract:

A gaming machine that provides free long distance telephone calls, or audio entertainment, as a reward for the continued playing of the gaming machine. The player may continue the free long distance phone call, or continue receiving the audio entertainment, as long his play meets a predetermined level of usage criteria.

What is claimed is:

1. A method of providing telephone service, comprising:
   receiving currency deposited into a gaming machine;
   enabling a game play in response to the receipt of currency; and
   enabling a connection to the telephone service for a predetermined period of time in response to the game play.

US006530835B1

(12) **United States Patent**
Walker et al.

(10) **Patent No.:**   **US 6,530,835 B1**
(45) **Date of Patent:**   ***Mar. 11, 2003**

(54) **FREE LONG DISTANCE CALLS ON SLOT MACHINES**

(75) Inventors: **Jay S. Walker**, Ridgefield, CT (US);
James A. Jorasch, Stamford, CT (US);
Thomas M. Sparico, Riverside, CT (US)

(73) Assignee: **Walker Digital, LLC**, Stamford, CT (US)

(*) Notice: Subject to any disclaimer, the term of this patent is extended or adjusted under 35 U.S.C. 154(b) by 0 days.

This patent is subject to a terminal disclaimer.

(21) Appl. No.: **09/641,903**

(22) Filed: **Aug. 18, 2000**

Related U.S. Application Data

(63) Continuation of application No. 08/821,437, filed on Mar. 21, 1997, now Pat. No. 6,139,431.

(51) Int. Cl.[7] A63F 9/24; H04M 17/00
(52) U.S. Cl. 463/25; 463/20; 379/144.05; 379/93.13
(58) Field of Search .... 463/1, 12–13, 463/16, 20, 25–29, 40, 41, 42, 30, 36; 273/143 R, 292, 293; 379/90.01, 91.01, 93.13, 114.01, 114.03, 114.05, 114.11, 114.15–114.28, 115.02, 144.05, 143; 705/1, 14, 35, 41; 902/22, 23; 340/825, 825.33, 323 R, 870.01, 870.07, 870.16

(56) **References Cited**

U.S. PATENT DOCUMENTS

4,760,527 A   7/1988 Sidley 364/412

5,018,021 A	5/1991	Slater	358/349
5,179,517 A	1/1993	Sarbin et al.	364/410
5,259,613 A	11/1993	Marnell, II	273/138
5,276,312 A	1/1994	McCarthy	235/380
5,321,241 A	6/1994	Craine	235/380
5,429,361 A	7/1995	Raven et al.	273/138
5,456,648 A	10/1995	Edinburg et al.	482/4
5,655,961 A	8/1997	Acres et al.	463/27
5,755,621 A	5/1998	Marks et al.	463/42
5,770,533 A	6/1998	Franchi	463/42
5,909,486 A	* 6/1999	Walker	
6,113,495 A	* 9/2000	Walker	
6,139,431 A	* 10/2000	Walker	
6,229,879 B1	* 5/2001	Walker	
6,327,351 B1	* 12/2001	Walker	

OTHER PUBLICATIONS

"On the Light Side", The Associated Press, May 27, 1989, Domestic News Section.
Finnigan, David, "'Call Girls' Wow 'Em at Gaming Confab", Las Vegas Business Press, Oct. 7, 1991, vol. 8; No. 36; Sec 1; p. 1.
"Mirage Resorts, Incorporated Licenses Video Conferencing Technology From C–Phone Corporation; C–Phone Hardware and Software Drives State–of–the–Art Video Customer Service Network in Slot Machines at Treasure Island", PR Newswire, Jan. 15, 1997, Financial News Section.

* cited by examiner

Primary Examiner—Mark Sager
(74) *Attorney, Agent, or Firm*—Steven M. Santisi

(57)   **ABSTRACT**

A gaming machine that provides free long distance telephone calls, or audio entertainment, as a reward for the continued playing of the gaming machine. The player may continue the free long distance phone call, or continue receiving the audio entertainment, as long his play meets a predetermined level of usage criteria.

33 Claims, 9 Drawing Sheets

Illustration 2-36

2. System for Machine Reading and Processing Information From Gaming Chips: U.S. Pat. 6,514,140

Casinos want to reward heavy bettors with special perks known as "comps," which often include free rooms, free drinks, or other amenities. The problem in awarding comps is figuring out exactly who are the heavy bettors. One solution is to use the player's chips as an indicator. After all, the more the chips are used, the more the player is playing. Leonard Storch of New York came up with a system for encoding playing chips (by placing optically read messages on the outside of the chip), then monitoring the use of those chips with optical readers placed around the gambling table.

Abstract:

A fully automatic table game player tracking system for Blackjack and other casino games wherein players have individual betting positions on the table is disclosed. An individual B&W CCD chip reading turret is placed inches in front of each player's betting position to scan wagered chips using ambient casino lighting. The turret also has a "comp" light to indicate to the player at the beginning of every hand that his bet was read and credited for his complimentaries (meals, room, entertainment, etc.), thus delivering to the player extra gaming satisfaction every hand. Patterns of repeated coding around the playing chips' peripheral surface represent with light and dark contrasting colors the dollar value and particular casino issuer of the chips. The aesthetically pleasing chip identifying coding patterns are comprised of unique referenceless error controlled self-clocking (n,k) code words, which are repeated around the chip's periphery without space therebetween, for improved efficiency and accuracy no matter the orientation of the wagered chip placed on the table.

I claim:

1. A system for processing information which is represented optically on gambling chips, comprising:

a gaming table having a plurality of player stations each associated with a chip location on the table within which one or more chips to be bet can be placed;

an optical device associated with each of the plurality of chip locations, each optical device being mounted to the table in the vicinity of the chip location with which it is associated facing to receive light reflected from one or more gambling chips at the respective chip location and not facing to receive light from the associated player station; at least one opto-electrical device coupled to the optical devices, the at least one opto-electrical device receiving light provided by the optical devices and providing electrical signals related thereto; and

a programmed processor coupled to the at least one opto-electrical device, the processor being caused by programming to process the electrical signals provided by the at least one opto-electrical device, and thereby process information represented optically on the gambling chips. ∎

Chapter 3

Design Patents for Art & Entertainment

"In our century, art is no longer created by the few or for the few. Rather, art has become integrated into our society's products, and art infuses our homes and lives with qualities once reserved for museums."

Cooper C. Woodring,
"A Designer's View on the Scope of Intellectual Property Protection,"
24 *AIPLA Q. J.* 309 (1996)

A visitor from another planet might wonder why the toothbrush depicted in Illustration 3-1 looks like a telephone. Those of us on planet earth already know the answer—the toothbrush looks like a telephone *because it can*! In today's world a telephone can look like a banana, a radio can look like a football, and a desk lamp can look like the Mighty Hulk cartoon character.

Illustration 3-1

Practical items haven't always had such fanciful appearances, however. Prior to the industrial revolution if you wanted a knife, bowl, saddle, or other useful object, you purchased it from a craftsperson who dutifully merged form and function. Distinguishing the appearance of useful objects became more important in the 20th century, when competing manufacturers realized that that if two products did the same thing and had the same specs, the ultimate buying decision often came down to appearance. As the appearance of industrial products grew in importance so did the need for a system of legal protection for product designs and ornamentation.

This chapter explains that system—design patents—and offers some examples of patented design innovations.

⚠ More information on design patents. To learn how design patents compare to other forms of legal protection and whether a design patent is the right choice for your invention, see Chapters 4 and 5. For instructions on filing a design patent application, see Chapter 8.

A. Design Patent Basics

The first design patent laws in this country, enacted in 1842, were limited to designs for products such as jewelry and furniture. A century later, design patent laws had expanded to protect any novel, nonobvious design or ornamentation for a useful object—for example, the unique appearance of a watch face, running shoe, or credit card.

Design patents are different from utility patents (discussed in Chapter 2) in several ways:

- A design patent is strictly about appearances—that is, it's granted for the ornamental or aesthetic elements of a device; a utility patent is about usefulness—that is, it's granted because of what the invention accomplishes.
- The application process for design patents is much easier than for utility patents. We walk you through the process of filing a design patent application in Chapter 8.
- A design patent lasts only 14 years from the date it's issued; a utility patent is valid for 20 years from the date of filing.
- It's easier to understand what's protected by a design patent because everything that the inventor/artist claims as a right to the design is shown in the drawings. In a utility patent, the protectible elements are described in the claims, which can be difficult to decipher and comprehend.

According to the guidelines furnished to patent examiners, a patentable design should be inseparable from the article to which it is applied—that is, it cannot exist alone merely as a "scheme of surface ornamentation." This seems to preclude registration for two-dimensional items such as computer icons, wallpaper imagery, or a graphic design for note paper. But—as demonstrated by the examples, below—this is not always the case, and various surface ornamentation seems to have achieved design patent protection. As we explained in Chapter 2, patents—whether utility or design—can cover anything you can get away with: If

the patent examiner approves the application then you get a patent. It's that simple.

Regarding the ban on surface ornamentation, consider the following designs:

Illustration 3-2

Illustration 3-2 depicts a design for the ornamental appearance of business paper. The patent is owned by the telephone company SBC, and is used for their telephone bills.

Illustration 3-3

Illustration 3-3 is a design for the ornamental appearance of wallpaper ("Crowd and Field Scene Wallpaper") depicting a crowd.

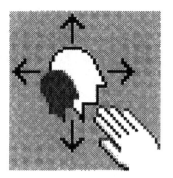

Illustration 3-4

Illustration 3-4 is a design for a computer icon to be used as part of a user interface for a medical playback device.

In order to stop anyone from using, manufacturing, or selling a competing product with a similar design, the design patent owner must prove that an ordinary observer would find the two designs similar. How similar? So similar that the purchaser would be deceived into purchasing one thinking it's the other. If a competitor has a design that is similar but does not contain your novel elements, there's no design patent infringement.

This chapter highlights a few groups of patented designs to show just how broad the design patent category is. The first group includes general art and entertainment concepts such as mobiles, musical instruments, food shapes, architectural designs, sculptures, and fashions. The second group shows patentable designs used for specific products: telephones, toothbrushes, shower caddies, and credit cards.

The designs shown in this chapter are just the tip of the design patent iceberg. Appendix B includes a list of all of the classes used by the USPTO to categorize design patents. A cursory glance will give you an idea of the incredible variety of decorative and ornamental designs that can be protected under design patent law. For example, you will find classes for designs for accordions (D17/3+), Afghan blankets (D06/603), ceremonial robes (D07/739), negligees (D02/718), aquariums, (D30101), candlesticks (D26/9+), hairpins (D28/39+), harmonicas (D17/12), incense burners (D11/131.1), kaleidoscopes (D21/439+), kitchen utensils (D07/368+), lamps (D26), metronomes (D10/43), moccasins (D02/924+), musical chimes (D17/22), pianos (D17/7), quilts (D06/603+), toys (D21/398+), and underwear (D02/700+). In short, any novel, nonobvious decoration or design for a useful object will qualify.

Who's Got the Biggest Portfolios?

Historically, companies with the largest design patent portfolios have products that are functionally indistinguishable from competitors—for example, Reebok and Nike (shoes), Goodyear, Michelin, and Bridgestone (tires), Casio, Sony, Sharp, Seiko, Hitachi, and Toshiba (consumer electronics), Motorola, AT&T, and Nokia (telephones), Kohler and American Standard (plumbing supplies), Colgate-Palmolive and Proctor & Gamble (health and cleaning supplies). Other companies with large portfolios include Rubbermaid, Timex, Black & Decker, and Gillette. This shows the importance of design patents—even though these companies make products that serve the same purpose, the appearance of each company's product distinguishes it form the competition.

⚠️ **Design patents won't work for decorative arts with short commercial life.** Design patents may not be proper for short-shelf-life designs, since applications normally take at least a year or more to process (though there are expedited application procedures, and the USPTO has promised to speed up the process).

B. Design Patents for Art & Entertainment

The design patents shown in the following sections are not tied specifically to consumer products. Instead, many of the designs *are* the product—that is, the function of the device is almost inseparable from the appearance. In other cases, the objects are so inextricably linked with art and entertainment—for example, food, musical instruments, or architecture—that their design is really more than ornamentation; it is an irreplaceable part of the object itself.

1. Mobiles

The mobile was invented by Alexander Calder in 1932 (and named by Calder's friend, the artist Marcel Duchamp). Calder's first mobile consisted of sheets of metal, painted black, white, and primary colors, suspended from wires and rods. His inspiration? The colored rectangles covering the artist Piet Mondrian's studio walls.

Design patents are intended to protect ornamental designs for functional objects. But what is functional? Is beauty or aesthetics functional? Traditionally, the USPTO has maintained that ornamentation and usefulness are two separate attributes. But, as the design patents granted below demonstrate, the USPTO considers kinetic sculpture consisting of parts that move—mobiles—to be functional objects, even though common sense tell us that a purchaser is buying it purely because of its appearance. After all, what function does a mobile have other than to aesthetically please the viewer?

Below are design patent drawings for five kinetic sculptures: a candle chandelier mobile (Illustration 3-5), a desktop mobile (Illustration 3-6), a wind chime (Illustration 3-7), a spiral hanging sculpture (Illustration 3-8), and a futuristic kinetic sculpture (Illustration 3-9).

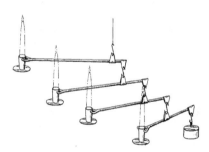

Illustration 3-5

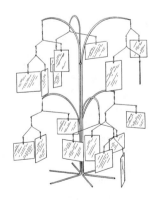

Illustration 3-6

Illustration 3-7

Illustration 3-8

2. Food Shapes

In the 18th century Viennese bakers supposedly shaped dough in a crescent shape—the symbol on the Turkish flag—to signify the defeat of the Turkish army. Croissants are but one example of a culinary obsession—shaped foods. As the design patents in this section demonstrate, food shapes go far beyond animal crackers and Christmas cookies. Modern chefs even try to shape foods so that they look like other foods—see the berry, jalapeno, and popcorn shaped foods, below.

The USPTO devotes an entire class (Class 1) to the visual aspects of food—specifically its shape. Below are images from design patents for food shaped like a heart (Illustration 3-10), popcorn (Illustration 3-11), a royal gingerbread house (Illustration 3-12), a berry (Illustration 3-13), a cactus (Illustration 3-14), a "curly puff" (Illustration 3-15), a donut (Illustration 3-16), a castle turret (Illustration 3-17), a diamond (Illustration 3-18), a jalapeno (Illustration 3-19), America and Africa (Illustration 3-20), a racecar (Illustration 3-21), and a golf tee (Illustration 3-22).

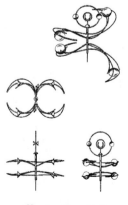

Illustration 3-9

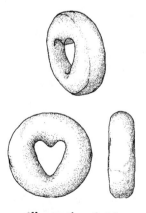

Illustration 3-10

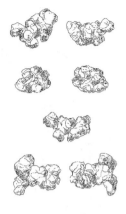

Illustration 3-11

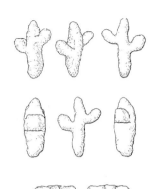

Illustration 3-14

Illustration 3-12

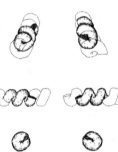

Illustration 3-15

Illustration 3-13

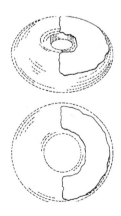

Illustration 3-16

Illustration 3-17

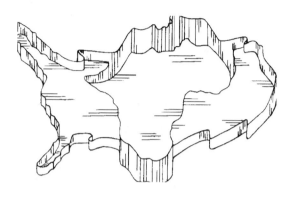

Illustration 3-20

Illustration 3-18

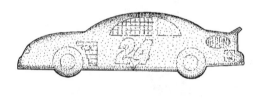
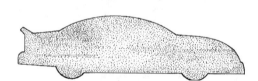

Illustration 3-21

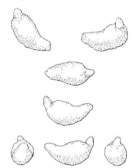

Illustration 3-19

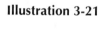
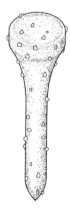

Illustration 3-22

Shaping the Ice Cream Cone

The ice cream cone is an invention that may be subject to both utility and design patent protection. Since the cone functions as an edible container for ice cream it would have been—at the time of invention—suitable subject matter for a utility patent. In fact, in December 1903, the precursor to the ice cream cone, a pastry container that held ice cream, was the subject of a utility patent (U.S. Pat. 746,971). Italo Marchiony, a New York ice cream merchant, invented a mold that made tea-cup-shaped pastries with handles. (Note: popular lore has it that the cone was invented at the 1904 Louisiana Purchase Exposition (World's Fair), when an ice cream merchant merged his goods with a Syrian pastry (Zalabia) available at a nearby booth. But that confection—upon closer historical analysis—is believed to be no more than ice cream wrapped in a waffle, not a cone-shaped container.)

Nowadays, design patents are granted for ice cream cone designs that contain novel shapes, imprinted imagery, or unique waffle patterns—for example, see Illustration 3-17.

3. Architecture

Were the architects of Stonehenge creating a functional structure or simply placing stones in a visually appealing arrangement? Some scholars have argued that Stonehenge's compass-like design permitted its use as an open-air observatory. Others have argued that Stonehenge is purely decorative. In 2003, for example, Canadian researchers concluded that the structure was simply a massive fertility symbol depicting female genitalia.

As we saw in the chapter on utility patents, an architect or inventor can protect building construction elements, building methods, or even the general structure of a new building—for example, the structure of a casino or health resort—with a utility patent. But if the construction format is already known and the designer has created only a new, nonobvious visual appearance, then a design patent can be acquired to protect that visual appearance. (Design patents for buildings are found in class D25.)

As you can imagine, there is considerable overlap between utility and design patents when it comes to floor plans for a new building layout. For example, Illustration 3-23 is for a floor plan for a building where conflict resolution is taught. Below are examples of drawings from several architectural design patents including several house facades (see Illustrations 3-24 through 3-30), a door facade (Illustration 3-31), a retail store facade (Illustration 3-32), a condominium facade (Illustration 3-33), a custom-built house (Illustration 3-34), a house (Illustration 3-35), a bus shelter (Illustration 3-36), and a floor plan (Illustration 3-23).

4. Sculptures

Just as the USPTO treats mobiles as patentable design subject matter (see Section B1), it also devotes an entire class of design patents (Class 11) to sculptures—that is, any three-dimensional artwork typically made of only

Illustration 3-23

Illustration 3-26

Illustration 3-24

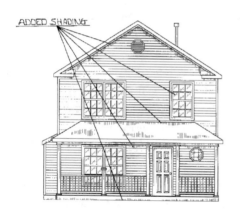

Illustration 3-27

Illustration 3-25

Illustration 3-28

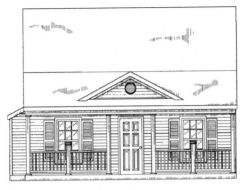

Illustration 3-29

Illustration 3-32

Illustration 3-30

Illustration 3-33

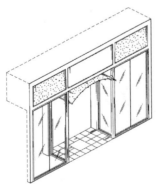

Illustration 3-31

Illustration 3-34

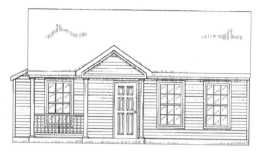

Illustration 3-35

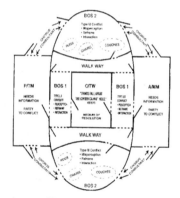

Illustration 3-36

Illustration 3-37

one material. As with mobiles, it's difficult to understand how the function and appearance of the products in this class can be separable especially when the design is as minimal as carving a word into a stone (see Illustration 3-37).

Equally confusing, a family of related sculptures can be protected by acquiring a design patent for each sculpture or by acquiring a utility patent for the entire family (see the utility patent for miniature trees in Illustration 3-38). Below are examples of other Class 11 design patents for a tree sculpture (Illustration 3-39), a sculpture of dancing girls (Illustration 3-40), a plant (Illustration 3-41), a ceramic Zen garden (Illustration 3-42), a chess piece set (Illustration 3-43), a macaw sculpture (Illustration 3-44), an iguana sculpture (Illustration 3-45), a toucan sculpture (Illustration 3-46), a pinecone sculpture (Illustration 3-47), an engraved rock (Illustration 3-37), and a star constellation sculpture (Illustration 3-48).

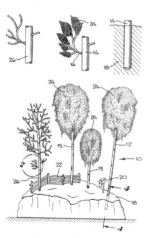

Illustration 3-38

Illustration 3-39

Illustration 3-42

Illustration 3-40

Illustration 3-43

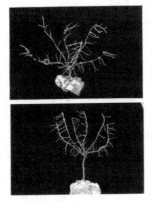

Illustration 3-41

Illustration 3-44

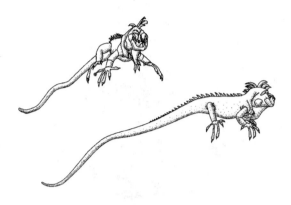

Illustration 3-45

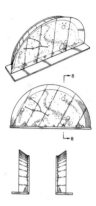

Illustration 3-48

Illustration 3-46

Illustration 3-47

5. Fashion

More than any other field of design, fashion influences the day-to-day appearance of our environment. The colors, shapes, and statements made by our clothing send out decorative, emotional, and social messages. The appearance of our clothing is also tied to the technology of clothing manufacture and materials. Exercise clothing, for example, reflects both a social state of mind (a need to stay fit) and a sense of technology (miracle fabrics and fibers). And of course, the design and appearance of our clothing is also a matter of evolution. "[T]he peignoir became a tea gown and eventually a day dress; the bra and panties became a bikini; the corset prepared the way for the swimsuit; the chemise, earlier worn as a nightshirt or under a corset, became a dress shape; and slip and bustier emerged as evening wear." *Thames and Hudson Dictionary of Fashion and Fashion Designers*, Preface (1986).

As with architecture, fashion can be protected for its function with a utility patent or for its form and appearance with a design patent. The following illustrations demonstrate a few of the designs protected in the fashion design class category, including a panty with mistletoe (Illustration 3-49), a shirt (Illustration 3-50), illuminated clothing (Illustration 3-51), a horned hat (Illustration 3-52), a metal necktie (Illustration 3-53), a butterfly bow (Illustration 3-54), a clothing patch (Illustration 3-55), a knitted garment pattern (Illustration 3-56), a dress (Illustration 3-57), a clothing ensemble (Illustration 3-58), a handbag from Louis Vuitton (Illustration 3-59), leprechaun slippers (Illustration 3-60), a knitted sweater (Illustration 3-61), and a ruffled sock (Illustration 3-62).

Illustration 3-49

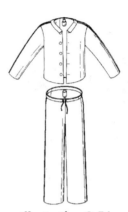

Illustration 3-51

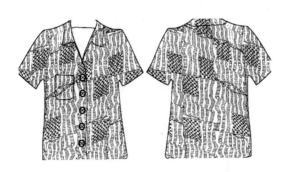

Illustration 3-50

Illustration 3-52

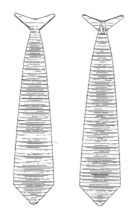

Illustration 3-53

Illustration 3-56

Illustration 3-54

Illustration 3-57

Illustration 3-55

Illustration 3-58

Illustration 3-59

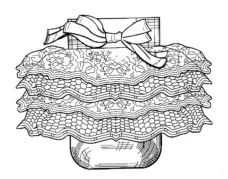

Illustration 3-62

Illustration 3-60

Illustration 3-61

6. Musical Instruments

In Chapter 2, we discussed how acoustic guitars morphed into electric models, which paved the way for the development of rock and pop music. But amplification and great guitar playing aren't enough to satisfy music fans. The appearance of the instruments also matters. One of the first to recognize this trend was guitarist Bo Diddley, whose box-shaped guitar became his signature instrument. Heavy metal guitarists also rely on ornamentation—guitars shaped like machine guns or adorned with flames and satanic ornamentation. The musicians who are most well known for the appearance of their instruments are the members of the Americana rock band, ZZ Top, whose videos feature unusually shaped (and even furry) guitars. The guitarist from the band, Billy Gibbons, acquired three design patents for guitars, one of which is shown below (Illustration 3-63).

The USPTO devotes an entire class of design patents, Class D17, to the ornamentation and design of musical instruments. Any visual improvements to musical instruments that don't affect the acoustics can be protected by a design patent. (Features that affect the sound or the way the instrument functions must be protected by a utility patent.)

Below are images from several musical instrument design patents. We show three guitar designs (Illustration 3-63 through 3-65), a violin (Illustration 3-66), a flugelhorn (Illustration 3-67), a tambourine (Illustration 3-68), a maraca-guiro (Illustration 3-69), a saxophone design (Illustration 3-70), a cello (Illustration 3-71), a mandolin (Illustration 3-72), and a harmonica (Illustration 3-73). Also keep in mind that a musical instrument can be incorporated into the design of a nonmusical product (for example, by embedding a tambourine into the structure of a book; see Illustration 3-74).

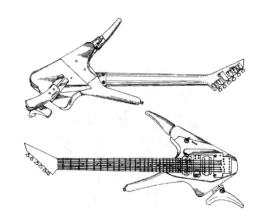

Illustration 3-64

Illustration 3-65

Illustration 3-63

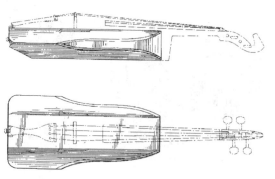

Illustration 3-66

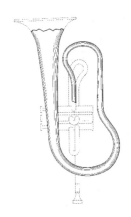

Illustration 3-67

Illustration 3-70

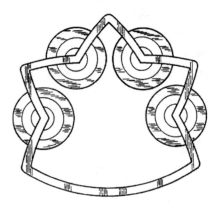

Illustration 3-68

Illustration 3-71

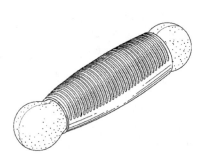

Illustration 3-69

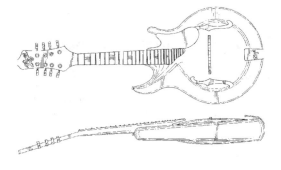

Illustration 3-72

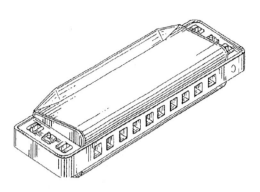

Illustration 3-73

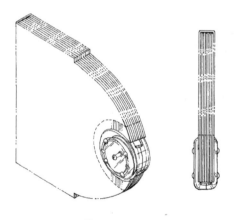

Illustration 3-74

C. Design Patents for Products

In the following sections, we look at five types of products and review a sampling of design patents for each of these products. In some cases (such as the telephone patents), the emphasis is on what might be called industrial design—a merger of engineering

and aesthetics. In other cases (such as the toothbrush), the emphasis is on fanciful or decorative appearances—that is, ornamentation that is easily separable from the function of the device. What all of these products have in common, however, is that their consumer appeal is often strongly influenced by their appearance.

1. Toothbrushes

If it weren't for Wallace Carothers, you might still be brushing your teeth with the neck hairs of the Siberian wild boar—favored for centuries for toothbrush bristles. Once Mr. Carothers invented nylon in 1937, the boar was spared—and the modern toothbrush was perfected. Or almost perfected—there have been over 3,000 utility patents filed for toothbrush inventions since 1965. Although the first electric toothbrush was marketed in 1880, the modern electric model was developed in Switzerland and first introduced in the United States in 1960.

Of course, as your dental hygienist will attest, having a toothbrush and using a toothbrush are two different things. To entice children (and adults) to buy and use toothbrushes, companies have patented hundreds of designs, a few of which are shown below.

As you can see, the toothbrush can conjure up our national pastime (baseball bat: Illustration 3-75), space, the final frontier, (Illustration 3-76), the telephone (Illustration 3-77), the gridiron (Illustration 3-78), marsupials (Illustration 3-79), or even a fanciful creature with glowing eyes (Illustration 3-80).

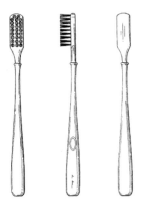

Illustration 3-75

Illustration 3-78

Illustration 3-76

Illustration 3-79

Illustration 3-77

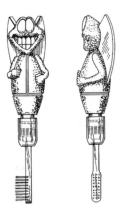

Illustration 3-80

2. Telephones

For most of the 20th century, consumers had very few telephone designs to choose from. From 1914 to 1933, consumers used Bell Telephone's candlestick telephone—a two-piece device. Consumers had a second choice in 1933—the Model No. 3, which combined the transmitter and receiver into one functional unit. A third choice arrived in 1949; the classic Model 500 rotary-dial telephone designed by Henry Dreyfuss and Associates. Ten years later, U.S. consumers got a fourth choice when AT&T offered the "feminine" Princess Phone. (In Europe, designers had already added more artistic flair—for example, the Siemens's innovative one-piece folding push-button *Grillo* Telephone.)

Real choice for U.S. consumers began in the late 1970s, when AT&T further diversified its line (including its Mickey Mouse telephone) and sold the new models at phone stores. Once deregulation hit, however, any company could design, make, and sell telephones, and the floodgates of art, entertainment, and design were unleashed on Bell's device. Soon, there were phones shaped like apples, bananas, Pepsi and Coke cans, Bugs Bunny, L.A. Gear shoes, and Bart Simpson. By 1980, the appearance of the telephone had become just as important to consumers as its function. (For a remarkable collection of novelty phone designs see The Farmer's Novelty Telephone Notebook at www.geocities.com/SoHo/Museum/1192/index.html.)

Below are a few patented approaches to telephone design: Bang & Olafsun's post-modern style (Illustration 3-81), Josh Zeitman's big-buttoned model (Illustration 3-82), Jim Chen's seashell motif (Illustration 3-83), Arthur Wang's triangular shape (Illustration 3-84), Daewoo's upright (Illustration 3-85), Richard Constantine's arched model (Illustration 3-86), and Jodie Fletcher's console style (Illustration 3-87).

Illustration 3-81

Illustration 3-82

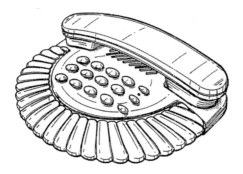

Illustration 3-83

Illustration 3-86

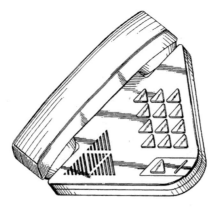

Illustration 3-84

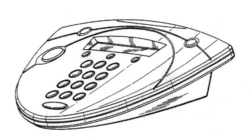

Illustration 3-87

Illustration 3-85

3. Shower Caddies

The concept of the shower caddy is simple enough—a device that can hold all of your bath and shower necessities. And apparently, there is no shortage of design ideas when it comes to shower caddies. The sheer multitude of designs demonstrates that the function of these devices is not limited by any one specific form, which helps prove that the design differences are purely ornamental (and therefore that a design patent—rather than a utility patent—is appropriate).

How many ways can you store shampoo? There's the nautical approach (Illustration 3-88), the feline angle (Illustration 3-89), the fan style (Illustration 3-90), the basic wire design (Illustration 3-91), a variation on the basic design (Illustration 3-92), the metal basket (Illustration 3-93), the jazzy wire fashion (Illustration 3-94), full frontal (Illustration 3-95), industrial (Illustration 3-96), and tubular (Illustration 3-97).

Illustration 3-90

Illustration 3-88

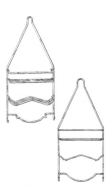

Illustration 3-91

Illustration 3-89

Illustration 3-92

Illustration 3-93

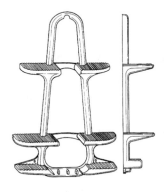

Illustration 3-96

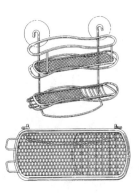

Illustration 3-94

Illustration 3-97

Illustration 3-95

4. Transaction Cards

30 years ago, credit cards featured the logo of the provider—Diner's Club, Visa, or MasterCard —and a splash of background color. Nowadays, financial institutions eager to appeal to "affinity-card" consumers ornament their plastic with thousands of choices ranging from sunsets, puppies, guitars, goldfish, Harley Davidsons, the Starship *Enterprise*, James Bond, Elvis Presley (the "King of Cards"), and even Jesus Christ ("Show the world your love for Jesus Christ, by putting his image on your credit card, only from NextCard Visa").

Credit cards are only one type of "transaction" cards, a category that includes prepaid phone cards, debit cards, and transportation passes. These plastic cards that include graphic design elements have increasingly converted our wallet into art and entertainment galleries. As technology progresses, our wallets will probably become noisy and animated arcades as well.

Below are some transaction card design patents. Some are basic, such as First USA's Transaction Card (Illustration 3-98) and Visa International's (Illustration 3-99). Others break the mold such as Paul Chu's oval card (Illustration 3-100) and Victor Morgante's hole-punched card (Illustration 3-101). Some feature figurative surface ornamentation, such as George Opel's cameo card (Illustration 3-102) or Visa International's eagle (Illustration 3-103).

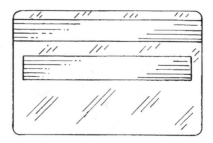

Illustration 3-98

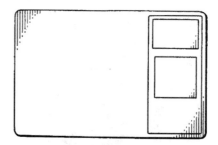

Illustration 3-99

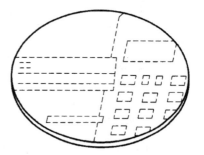

Illustration 3-100

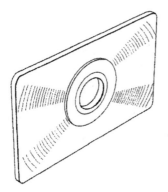

Illustration 3-101

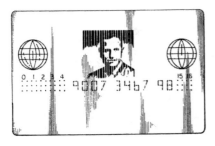

Illustration 3-102

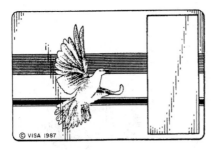

Illustration 3-103

D. Design Patents for Multi-Use Items

You can only get a design patent for a specific combination of design and object. For example, suppose you have a new floral design pattern and want to patent it for use on the surface of a door, the fabric of a couch, and the motif for a dress. Because of an archaic historical quirk, you must apply for three design patents, one for each of these objects. This is a particularly vexing problem nowadays, when designs are commonly applied to multiple objects. There should be a system—similar to that available to trademark owners—for obtaining multiple design patent rights without having to file multiple applications.

A set of U.S. fashion design patents issued to Kim Park, of Seoul, South Korea, illustrates this point. Over the past few years, Park has acquired a number of design patents for a floral design that is applied to a variety of women's undergarments. To date, he has been awarded 20 such patents. A few examples are shown below, including: a body suit (Illustration 3-104), a brassiere (Illustration 3-105), a girdle (Illustration 3-106), a panty (Illustration 3-107), a waistband (Illustration 3-108), and a corset (Illustration 3-109).

Illustration 3-104

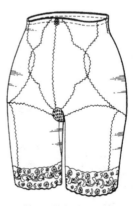

Illustration 3-107

Illustration 3-105

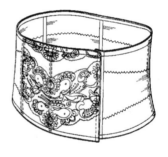

Illustration 3-108

Illustration 3-106

Illustration 3-109

Chapter 4

Traditional Protection for Art & Entertainment

*T*echnology companies (those that own patents) and content companies (those that own copyrights) are often at each other's throats. Consider the Sony Corporation, maker of patented devices that duplicate, broadcast, and store copyrighted content. (Sony certainly believes in patents. In the U.S., alone, the company possesses almost 18,000 patents. During the week that we wrote this chapter the company received 13 utility patents and four design patents.)

Copyright owners often view Sony's patented products as the devil's work. For example, one movie studio characterized the 1976 release of the Betamax SL-7200 video recorder as "a Japanese invasion trampling U.S. copyright laws." (J. Lardner, *Fast Forward: Hollywood, the Japanese and the VCR Wars* (Norton 1987).)

But a funny thing happened to Sony Corporation. In 1988, it bought CBS Records for $2 billion; then one year later, the company bought Columbia and Tri-Star pictures for $3.4 billion. Today, in addition to its core business of selling patented technology like mini disc players, camcorders, televisions, telephones, computers, and CD and DVD players, Sony owns or has interests in copyrighted content from Columbia Tri-Star, Jim Henson Productions, Mandalay Entertainment, Sony Pictures Classics, Sony Metreon Cinema, Sony Signatures (entertainment-related clothes and merchandise), Sony Music, Columbia Records, Epic Records, Columbia-TriStar Television, and other cable and television enterprises. Sony was suddenly flush with both copyrights and patents.

In 2000, the inevitable happened: Sony sued itself. Well, not exactly. But it did change sides as it found itself in the position of a copyright owner battling a technology company. Sony lined up with other record companies as part of the Recording Industry Association of America's (RIAA) assault against Napster, and later against other peer-to-peer file sharing companies and even individual college students.

While Sony attempts to protect the copyrights of Bob Dylan, Korn, Bow-Wow, Yo-Yo Ma, Men in Black, and *Spiderman*, the company also sells to the enemy who must buy the Sony equipment essential for file swapping—MP3 players, CD burners, and Sony Vaio computers. Is it schizophrenic to own both patents and copyrights? Or is it synergy? The answer lies in the changing perception of copyright law.

For artists and entertainers, copyright has traditionally been the favored choice for intellectual property protection. Copyright law is tailored to books, movies, plays, music, art, and other forms of creative expression, and the protection of a copyright lasts for a long, long time—often over a century. Industry lobbyists and special interest groups have sculpted the law to fit each new form of artistic expression. They have also carved out confounding exceptions—for example, the fair use doctrine, (discussed in Section B) which is supposed to protect the public interest by allowing certain limited uses of copyrighted materials.

Copyright not only protects individual works of art; it also prohibits modifications and variations (known as derivatives) of those works. But copyright also has its problems. As the battle over software has demonstrated, there may be cases where some form of patent protection is superior to copyright (see Section C).

In this chapter we look at copyright and other laws that have traditionally protected art and entertainment. By looking at their strengths and weakness we prepare for Chapter 5, where we help analyze whether patents are the right choice for your art and entertainment innovations.

A. Advantages of Copyright

Like a utility or design patent, a copyright gives you two basic rights: You can chase after people who rip off your work and you can earn money by licensing or selling your rights.

If someone uses your copyrighted work without your permission, you can make them stop and perhaps collect a financial payment for the damage they've done. You can take these actions against anyone who, without your permission, copies your work, displays your work, makes photos of it, broadcasts it on television, or makes modifications or variations on it.

You can also make money from your copyright by giving your rights to someone else, either temporarily (a license) or permanently (an assignment). For example, the artists who created Cabbage Patch Dolls earned millions from licensing their creation. In return for letting a company "use" their copyrighted designs, they earned a royalty for each doll sold.

Copyright protection offers a lot of benefits:

- **It's broad.** Copyright protects any original artistic expression—architecture, photography, music, graphic arts, sculpture, motion pictures, plays, video games, computer programs, websites, or dance.

- **The standards are low.** To get a copyright, you don't need to prove novelty or nonobviousness (as you would with a patent); you have to show only that you didn't copy it from another source. And there are no intensive examinations at the copyright office, no comparisons to previous works. Applications are routinely approved except in rare circumstances.

- **It's cheap.** Copyright is free. You get it once the work is fixed—that is, once the ink dries on your paper or the photograph is printed. If you'd like to register your work with the Copyright Office—a prerequisite for filing a lawsuit or acquiring damages for unauthorized use (you must register before the infringement)—the fee is $30. The application is simple to prepare. Visit the copyright office to download the forms (www.copyright.gov).

- **It's fast.** Copyright protection is automatic. There's no waiting for approval from a government bureaucrat. You can create a photograph in the morning and go after someone for infringement that afternoon. Patents take years to acquire—and you can't stop anyone from copying your work until the patent issues.

- **It lasts for a long time.** Copyright protection begins once a work is created and lasts for the life of the author (the person who creates the work) plus 70 years (for works created by a single author). Works made for hire (works prepared by employees and independent contractors, which belong to the employer or hiring firm) are protected for 120 years after their date of creation or 95 years from their first publication, whichever is longer. The same duration of copyright applies whether the work is registered or not.

B. Drawbacks of Copyright

Here are some of the limitations of copyright as compared to patent protection.

- **It doesn't protect useful things.** If your work is functional, you can't get a copyright on it. Under copyright law, books, paintings, movies, photographs, dance, and so on are not considered functional (See "Books Aren't Useful," below.) Because of this limitation, innovations that are protected by utility patents cannot be protected by copyright. (However, there is some overlap between design patents and copyright, as explained below.)

- **It only protects product designs that are "separable."** When art or entertainment is used as part of a useful product's design or packaging, it can be protected by copyright only if it can be physically or conceptually separated from the underlying useful object—that is, the form (the artwork) can be separated from the function (the product). Although the same rules apply to design patents, courts seem to have more difficulty

separating form from function in copyright cases than in design patent cases.

- **You have to disprove independent creation.** Under copyright law you can only stop those who copy your work; you cannot stop someone who independently created the same work. Therefore, in order to stop a competitor, you've got to make like a detective and prove that the competitor had access to your work and copied it—something that's not required under utility or design patent law.

- **You have to prove substantial similarity.** Even if you can show that someone copied your work, you still have to demonstrate that the two works are substantially similar if you want to prove infringement. There are various tests for measuring similarity depending on the subject matter of the work (for example, software, music, or characters) and the laws of the jurisdiction where you bring the case. Showing that similarity is *substantial* can be tough—especially when the rules for similarity aren't consistent. Substantial similarity is also an issue when proving infringement of a design patent.

- **Watch out for fair use.** If you do prove copyright infringement, the alleged infringer has one last ace to play: fair use. This often-unpredictable defense permits copying for purposes of commentary. In other words, the user can copy your work in order to review it, respond to it, or otherwise comment on it. (Although there are defenses to patent infringement, none are equivalent to fair use.)

- **There is no central repository of copyrighted works.** You can search the USPTO database to find out if inventions similar to yours have received patents, but there is no similar central repository of copyrighted works. (The Library of Congress database indexes title and author information, but does not describe content.) Although copies of works are deposited with the Copyright Office, this collection is not maintained (many registered copyrighted works are eventually destroyed) and cannot be searched.

- **Minimalist designs won't get a copyright.** Copyright law frowns upon minimalism, particularly when artwork is used to adorn useful objects. For example, the designs for the bowl with handles in Illustration 4-1 and the glass in Illustration 4-2 are minimal designs that were both granted design patents, but are unlikely to receive protection under copyright.

Illustration 4-2

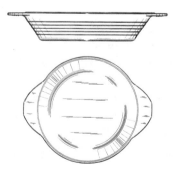

Illustration 4-1

Books Aren't Useful

Under copyright and patent laws, books, paintings, movies, photographs, dance, etc. are not considered functional or useful, even though they dazzle, entertain, and amuse us. The Copyright Act states that a "useful article" is an article having an intrinsic utilitarian function that is not merely to portray the appearance of the article or to convey information. (17 U.S.C. § 101.) The application of the functionality rule may appear arbitrary. Costumes and clothing are considered functional and therefore unregistrable under copyright law. Building designs, however, are apparently not functional, and are therefore registrable. Computer programs are also not considered useful and are therefore suitable subjects for copyright registration. (Computer programs are also suitable subjects for utility patent protection, but under patent law, such programs are considered useful. See Section C, below.)

C. Unresolved Copyright Issues

Some critics of copyright law argue that while patent law is built upon precision—the patent claims specifically define the boundaries of the invention rights—copyright law suffers from ambiguity. (It may be cheap and fast, but it's also out of control.) As we discussed above, there are no bright-line tests in copyright law defining exactly what functionality, substantial similarity, or fair use means in practice. This ambiguity makes it tough to predict how effective copyright will be as a business strategy. Below we have highlighted several additional key issues that add to the copyright confusion. We touch on them briefly here, but you can find more thoughts on each of these issues at the website supporting this book, www.patenting-art.com:

- **The idea/expression dichotomy is difficult to apply.** By law, copyright protects only "expression," not "ideas." (17 U.S.C. § 102.) This principle—known as the "idea/expression dichotomy"—has come to mean that you can get a copyright on a particular way of conveying or representing an idea, but not on the idea itself. For example, you can copyright the film *E.T.* but not the underlying idea of an alien traveling to the United States, befriending a young earthling, and then returning to his planet. Legal efforts to apply this rule—particularly in technology disputes, such as those over computer programs—have resulted in millions of dollars in legal fees. After all, when is the expression separate from the idea? How much expression is required to

flesh out an idea? Doesn't such an approach discriminate against minimalist, conceptual and other postmodern artists? These questions have resulted in confusing and changing judicial tests which only encourage fights over copyright ownership. Until Congress cleans up copyright law, the idea/expression problem will continue to burden judges and copyright litigants around the country.

- **Copyright law doesn't adequately define key concepts such as "original," "work," or "author."** Copyright protection is granted "for original works of authorship fixed in any tangible medium of expression." Sounds simple enough, right? Except that the Copyright Act doesn't define "original," "works," and "author." Though the Act opens with over 40 legislative definitions, there is no explanation of these essential terms. Whenever legislation suffers from this kind of lack of clarity, the next step is always the courtroom. (For example, "Does an author have to be a natural person?" Answer: A corporation or a business entity can be an author but a computer or machine can't be an author.) The imprecision of copyright terminology—though not uncommon in the law—encourages litigation and tends to favor those with the funds to weather a lawsuit. The same terminology issues are not as visible in patent law, where precision is more often the norm.

- **Independent creation is an antiquated concept.** As we noted above, the Copyright Act of 1976 fails to define originality.

However, judges interpret originality as work that is original to the author—that is, it was not copied from someone else. This means that identical works can be created without infringing, as long as the second author never saw the first one. So, copyright owners have a special hurdle to clear: They must prove that the infringer had access to their work. Because millions of works are now accessible on the Web, this issue has become even more muddled. In patent law—with its defined world of prior art—it's much easier to pinpoint who created something and when.

- **Copyright protection lasts much longer than patent protection.** What's the difference between John Grisham and Dean Kamen? About 100 years of legal protection. Grisham writes legal best-sellers; Kamen invented lifesaving devices, including an auto syringe, a dialysis machine, and a mobility device for the disabled (as well as the Segway human transporter). Even assuming that the results of their labors are equally beneficial to society and that both are distinguished in their respective disciplines for mental vigor, it isn't immediately clear why Grisham (or his estate) can stop others from copying his works during his entire life and for 70 years after his death, while Kamen can stop others from copying his inventions for only 17-18 years. Economic indicators have demonstrate that most copyrighted works earn all of their revenue in the first 20 years after publication, which makes the extended duration of copyright even more difficult to defend.

The problems elaborated above—the idea/expression dichotomy, the failure to define terminology, the concept of independent creation, and the disparity in duration of protection—all come to a head in the confusing mess known as software copyright. Approximately three decades ago, U.S. software entrepreneurs, legislators, judges, and lawyers cobbled together a means of protecting software under copyright law. First, they determined that code was a work of authorship—that is, it was not functional and that it was the expression of an idea, not the idea itself—two incredible stretches that provoked great dissension in the famous CONTU (National Commission on New Technological Uses of Copyright Works) hearings that were organized to determine software copyrightability. Second, they determined that operating software—software that controlled computer operations such as DOS and Windows—was protectible, not just application programs such as *Word* or *Photoshop*. Then, to make sure that software could be registered, they categorized it as a literary work, because it consists of letters and numbers. The result has been 30 years of confusing standards and judicial tests, and a general consensus among attorneys that patents are a far superior and more predictable way to protect software.

D. Trademarks & Trade Dress

Copyright and patents aren't the only forms of intellectual protection for art and entertainment. Trademarks and trade dress also protect creative innovations and ideas—in the commercial sphere.

1. Trademarks

Trademarks, in addition to copyrights and patents, are grouped under the umbrella of intellectual property. The owner of a trademark can stop others from using a similar name, image, or other product identifier if it is likely to confuse consumers. In some cases, the owner of a famous trademark can stop others who seek to blur or distort a trademark's value. For example, the Coca-Cola Company was able to stop another company from using a bubble-gum container that mimicked the shape of the famous Coca-Cola bottle.(*Coca-Cola Co. v. Alma-Leo U.S.A., Inc.*) 719 F. Supp. 725 (N.D. Ill. 1989).)

For our purposes, trademarks differ substantially from copyrights and patents in that they don't protect creative works or processes, per se: they protect the names, logos, and other commercial indicia that buyers associate with products. For example, in 1999, the Pepperidge Farm Company, maker of the Goldfish snack cracker, stopped rival Nabisco from selling an orange puffed cheese pet food also molded into the shape of goldfish. (*Nabisco, Inc. v. PF Brands, Inc.*, 50 F. Supp. 2d 188, 192 (S.D. N.Y. 1999).) In that case, neither novelty nor originality was determinative; what mattered was that consumers were likely to be confused and the value of the trademark was diluted.

2. Trade Dress

One exception to this rule is a class of trademarks known as trade dress. Trade dress protection allows a company to stop others from copying the shape and appearance of a product as well as the container and other elements that make up the product's total visual image. Under trade dress law, for example, the owner of the *Cliff's Notes* series could stop a competitor from using the same distinctive black and yellow combination and unique lettering. Trade dress is part of the trademark family because its function is the same—to prevent consumer confusion by protecting the distinctive appearance of a product.

Trade dress won't protect functional features—for example, a distinctive spout on a milk carton. And although you can register trade dress with the USPTO, whether or not you register, you can pursue a competitor with similar trade dress.

3. Using Trademark and Trade Dress to Protect Art and Entertainment

Historically, trade dress has been a low-cost, useful way to stop infringers with similar product designs. And many artists and entertainers have used trade dress and trademark law as an effective tool for protecting product design. In one case, a court allowed an artist to stop others from copying his style—which consisted of specific color patterns and shading, distinctive placement of women (with certain physical attributes) in sitting and reclining positions, and characteristic clothing—under trademark law principles. (*Romm Art Creations, Ltd. v. Simcha Int'l, Inc.*, 786 F. Supp. 1126 (E.D. N.Y. 1992).)

But that was back in the good old days. Most intellectual property experts agree that the power of trade dress shrank dramatically in 2000, when the Supreme Court decided *Wal-Mart Stores, Inc. v. Samara Brothers, Inc.*, (120 S.Ct. 1339 (2000)). Samara created a line of children's clothing that featured one-piece seersucker outfits decorated with appliques of hearts, flowers, fruits, and the like. Wal-Mart authorized another clothing company to copy Samara's designs, then sold the knock-offs at a lower price. Samara sued Wal-Mart and a federal district court ordered Wal-Mart to pay Samara $1.6 million in damages. The Supreme Court eventually overruled that decision, finding that product designs (that is, their shape and configuration), no matter how creative and clever, were not protected under trademark law unless the owner could demonstrate that consumers found the appearance distinctive and associated the product design with one source—a principle known as the "secondary meaning" rule.

After the *Samara* decision, retailers, manufacturers, and catalogue companies declared open season on product designs. Only those companies that can demonstrate secondary meaning—that is, that consumers associate a particular product design with their company—dare to sue for trade dress infringement. It takes time (and money) to prove secondary meaning. For example, one company proved secondary meaning in its lawn furniture designs by showing that it spent $1.2 million advertising the product line, it had gross sales of approximately $5 million, and customers associated the design with the company. If you want to stop someone from copying your product design under trade dress law, you'll need to measure consumer behavior in the marketplace, which can be tricky—and expensive.

After *Samara,* a company seeking to prove that its product design has been infringed under trademark laws, must establish that:

- the product design of the two competing products is confusingly similar, and
- the product design has obtained secondary meaning.

You'll also have to be prepared to defend against any claims that your trade dress is functional—that is, your design's primary purpose is to distinguish your product for consumers. (If your competitor can prove that your design is primarily functional—for example, using iridescent yellow for tennis balls—then you will not be able to assert trade dress rights.)

That's a lot of work for an uncertain outcome. If you had relied on a design patent for protection, you wouldn't have to analyze consumer behavior or provide similar empirical evidence. Design patent infringement is a "much narrower field of inquiry ... a design patentee may prove infringement simply by showing that an ordinary observer would be deceived by reason of another device's ornamental design." (Harry C. Marcus and Mark J. Abate, "Design Patent Infringement

Put to Sea Without Guiding Charts," 22 *AIPLA Q. J.* 135 (1994).)

By themselves, trade dress laws don't provide a powerful strategy for short-term protection of art and entertainment incorporated in product designs. And it can be tough to get protection—for example, a trade dress registration process at the USPTO often takes longer than a design patent application and competitors are more likely to oppose the registration. In most situations, you'll probably be better off choosing a different method of protecting your artistic or entertaining idea.

E. Trade Secrets

In a 1902 article, "The Unmasking of Houdini," a German newspaper accused magician Harry Houdini of a "fraudulent performance." Houdini sued the newspaper for slander but in order to prove that his performance was not a fraud, he was required to publicly reveal a few of his handcuff-opening secrets. Later, Houdini lamented to a friend, "Just imagine, in order to save my honor I had to show how I did it."

Houdini, like all magicians, based his livelihood on secrecy. In legal terms, this type of intellectual property is referred to as a trade secret. A trade secret is any information that both benefits a business commercially and is kept a secret. And since it is maintained as a secret, any legal claims to it are lost—like Houdini's handcuff trick—once public disclosure is made.

Beyond the world of magic, trade secret protection has limited value for artists and entertainers who rely on public reaction and response. It might be suitable for:

- concealing a craft or artistic process—for example, a glazing technique or a makeup formula—that is unknown to other artists
- protecting the plot, title, or characters for an unreleased movie, book, or video game
- keeping secret a marketing or promotional plan—for example the touring sponsors for a superstar performer, or
- preserving contractual relationships—for example, the fact that an author has switched publishers or a film company as switched distributors.

Trade secret protection and patents. The USPTO treats patent applications as confidential, making it possible to apply for a patent and still maintain the underlying information as a trade secret, at least for the first 18 months of the application period. Unless the applicant files a Nonpublication Request at the time of filing and doesn't file for a patent outside the United States, the USPTO will publish the application within 18 months of the filing date. Because a patent application is published by the USPTO, all of the secret information becomes public and the trade secret status of the application is lost. If an applicant files a Nonpublication Request at the time of filing the application, the information in the patent application will become publicly available only if and when a patent is granted.

The key to trade secrecy is that information that qualifies as a trade secret is subject to legal protection only if the owner has taken the necessary steps to preserve secrecy. If you own a secret, you should use reasonable efforts to keep it secret and disclose it only to someone who has signed a nondisclosure agreement. (Although employees have a duty to maintain secrecy, you should also require them to sign nondisclosure agreements.)

It's also important to keep in mind one of the biggest drawbacks of trade secret law when compared to patents—you can only stop someone from using a trade secret if they obtain it by theft, not if they arrive at it independently or reverse engineer your products.

Some activities that the courts will commonly treat as trade secret theft—which means the owner will be afforded some judicial relief, such as damages or an order preventing use of the stolen information—are:

- disclosures by key employees and others occupying positions of trust in violation of their duty of trust toward their employer

- disclosures by employees (current and former) in violation of a nondisclosure agreement entered into with their employer
- disclosures by suppliers, consultants, financial advisors, or others who signed nondisclosure agreements with the trade secret owner, promising not to disclose the information
- industrial espionage, and
- disclosures by any person owing an implied duty to the employer not to make such disclosure, such as directors, corporate officers, and other high-level salaried employees.

When a disclosure is considered wrongful, the courts may also consider use of the information wrongful and issue an order (injunction) preventing its use for a particular period of time.

 For more information on trade secrets, review *Nondisclosure Agreements: Protect Your Trade Secrets & More,* by Richard Stim and Stephen Fishman (Nolo). ■

Should You Apply for a Patent?

Should you seek a patent for your art and entertainment innovation? This chapter will help you answer that question. Section A explains the pros and cons of applying for a utility patent—and the types of inventions for which utility patents are best suited. Section B explains when a design patent might be the way to go. Along the way, we'll also cover other forms of legal protection that you may want to seek instead of—or in addition to—a utility or design patent.

While researching material for this book, we found a great article by Robert S. Katz and Helen Hill Minsker, "Design patent + trademark = better protection?" (*National Law Journal*, May 1, 2000). The article provides factors to consider when you're trying to decide how best to protect a product design. We found this approach so useful that we borrowed from their work and applied it to utility patents as well. We are grateful for their ideas and permission. If you'd like to review their article, you can find it at www.bannerwitcoff.com/articles/bydesign1.pdf.

A. Should You Get a Utility Patent?

Utility patents are potent—which is one reason why we believe in their expanded use for art and entertainment innovations. We also acknowledge, however, that utility patents have drawbacks—they're expensive to obtain and enforce.

In general, utility patents are most effective:
- for art and entertainment inventions that have a commercial life of more than two years
- for popular products within industries where copying is common, and
- in conjunction with other forms of protection, such as design patents, trademark, or copyright protection.

Remember, utility patents protect only the functional features of your invention (how it works and what it does), not its appearance.

EXAMPLE: A design company, Xportal, develops *RocketWriter*, a miniature remote control toy vehicle that can "draw" with the aid of a retracting felt marker. The functional (and potentially patentable) components of the invention are the protruding/retracting mechanism that grips the marker, the mechanism that propels the car, the remote control device, and any novel software or electronics that control the vehicle and the marker.

EXAMPLE: An animation studio, Renada, has developed a digital editing process that is 50% more efficient than existing editing software. The novel and patentable aspect of the software is the unique process by which it removes color and compresses sound, thereby providing a "ghost" editing format.

You Can Choose More Than One

As you review your innovation, remember that it (or its various features) may simultaneously qualify for a utility patent, design patent, copyright, trademark, and trade dress. In other words, you don't have to choose one form of protection to the exclusion of all others. To give you an example of the range of possibilities, consider the Fender Stratocaster guitar in Illustration 5-1.

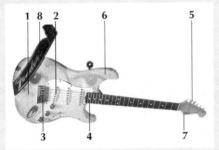

Illustration 5-1

Copyright, trade dress, and design patent law may protect the imagery on the body of the guitar (1). Utility patent law may protect the electronic pickups (2), the bridge that holds the strings (3), the process for making and coating the strings (4), and the tuning knobs (5). Trade dress and design patent law may protect the shape of the guitar (6) (though unlikely in the case of the Stratocaster). Trademark law protects the name and logo of the guitar-maker as emblazoned on the guitar (7) and on merchandise such as the guitar strap (8). (For another example of a legal analysis of an acoustic guitar see Nate Cooper's "Issue Spotting Your Guitar," *Entertainment and Sports Lawyer*, Volume 20, Number 3, Fall 2002.)

Combining legal protections is especially effective for product designs, particularly those that can exist in another medium. For example, a toy or a puppet may lend itself to animation or reproduction on merchandise. In that case, you can use design patent law to effectively halt the copying of the product, and copyright law to stop it from being copied in other mediums.

EXAMPLE: Consider the Frankenstein-style puppet in Illustration 5-2. Imagine that, without the permission of the designers, a movie studio creates an animated series based upon the puppet and sells similar puppets and other merchandise containing the puppet's image. Under design patent law, the designers can stop the manufacture, sale, and distribution of substantially similar puppets. Under copyright law, the company can stop the studio from making the animated series and related merchandise based on the puppet.

Illustration 5-2

EXAMPLE: Lydia has created a process—using a unique set of flexible plastic strips with a hook-and-loop fastener (*a la* Velcro)—to convert fabric into bags and back. For example, she has applied her process to beach towels that convert to beach bags, and then, once at the beach, can be used as a towel. (She also plans to use the process for placemats that convert to lunch bags.) Lydia's process may be the subject of a utility patent.

Of course, creating something functional doesn't automatically qualify your innovation for a utility patent; it must also meet other patent standards, such as novelty and non-obviousness. (These standards are covered in Chapter 1.)

Nonfunctional features—the appearance, packaging, and ornamentation—of your innovation may be protected under design patent laws. We discuss these and related forms of design protection in Section B, below.

If you believe that your idea may be patentable, the questions below can help you decide whether a utility patent is right for you.

- **What is the life expectancy of your invention?** If the estimated commercial life of your innovation is less than two years—based on similar products in similar markets—there's little sense pursuing a utility patent. The USPTO takes 18 to 30 months to process a utility patent application, and you can't stop anyone from infringing until you have the patent. (You can, in some circumstances, collect damages from those who infringe during the patent pending period. See "Publication and 'Patent-Pending' Damages," below.) If you think your invention will have a commercial life of three years or more, then a utility patent may be the right choice.

EXAMPLE: The shelf life for remote control (RC) vehicles is usually two years, one year in the U.S. and one year in Europe and Asia. Xportal's *RocketWriter* is different from typical RCs, however, because it can "draw" with the aid of its retractable marker innovation. Xportal believes the RC may be commercially successful in the "play activity" market—a market in which toys have a longer life. The company foresees a commercial life of at least ten years, which makes the *RocketWriter* a good subject for a utility patent

If you anticipate a lengthy commercial life—more than 20 years—consult with an intellectual property attorney to see if you can combine utility patent protection with other legal rights—for example trademark, trade dress, copyright, or trade secrecy—so that some aspect of your innovation will be protected beyond the term of the patent.

Have You Got Commercial Potential?

Although we haven't included this as a factor in your patentability decision, you should—if you haven't already done so—weigh your chances for commercial success before considering a patent. Most innovators are in love with their creations and presume commercial success. Considering the high mortality rate for products, however, you cannot base your patentability decision on good faith. There are numerous books and online guides that can help you determine commercial potential. For a speedy review, you can usually consider just four factors: cost, competition, ease of use, and future of the market.

EXAMPLE: Renada wants to figure out whether it will turn a profit on its color-coded digital editing software. It analyzes the four factors as follows:

- **Cost.** The price of making and selling the software product (not including marketing costs) is relatively low, because Renada spread development expenses over several third-party animation projects. (In other words, clients paid to use the process as it developed.) In addition, the costs for making and selling the software are low. Downloadable software is an inexpensive form of distribution and CD replication and packaging, even if it includes a cardboard box and manual, is still less than $2.50 per box (at a duplication rate of 10,000 copies).
- **Competition.** There are several video editing programs, but none that directly address the functionality in Renada's program. However, competitors include Adobe, Pinnacle, and Apple (and Microsoft is rumored to be considering a digital editing product). An entrenched playing field makes it more difficult for Renada to break in.
- **Ease of use.** Testing has demonstrated that Renada's program is intuitive for users.
- **Future of the market.** The software industry is in transition. The retail trade channel is disappearing and the national chains are tough to crack (except for high-volume mass market software). On the other hand, digital video hardware and software sales have increased incrementally for five straight years.

Renada concludes that it has product with a low cost of goods and a potential for profit. Unfortunately, the company is uncomfortable about competing against major software companies. Renada executives are inclined to seek a patent but are more likely to sell or license the patented technology than to manufacture and distribute it themselves.

Publication and "Patent-Pending" Damages

You can refer to your invention as "patent pending" during the period between when you file your patent application (or provisional patent application) and when the patent issues. As explained in Chapter 1, an inventor has no patent rights during this pendency period. In other words, an invention that states "patent pending" can be copied freely by anyone. However, many potential infringers won't copy a patent-pending device fearing that a patent will later issue and the money spent on expensive tooling would be wasted.

Although you cannot sue for patent infringement, it is possible to recover for infringements during the pendency period. Patent law requires that the application be published at least 18 months after the application is filed (unless the applicant doesn't plan on seeking foreign patent rights and a nonpublication request is filed). Provided that (a) the application is published and (b) later issues as a patent and (c) the infringer had notice of the publication, the patent owner can recover damages for this post-publication patent-pending period. In addition, the inventor does not have to wait the 18 months and have the application published earlier (15 U.S.C. § 122). Provided that a patent issues for an invention with identical claims, the inventor can recover damages for this earlier post-publication period, as well. (15 U.S.C. § 154).

Patents as Defensive Weapons

When evaluating whether to seek a patent, another issue to consider is whether this is an industry in which companies stockpile patents as defensive tools. Companies in the software, Internet, biotech, and other tech industries commonly use patents as bargaining chips in the patent litigation.

Here's how it works: Company A sells cellular phones and service and is sued by Company B, a competitor, for infringing a patent for converting audio signals. Company A has recently acquired an important manufacturing patent that streamlines cellular phone assembly. Company A offers to license its patent to Company B in return for a license to use Company B's audio signal patent. This business strategy—analogous to the stockpiling of nuclear weapons—is an impetus for some companies to seek patents in emerging technology fields.

- **What is the nature of your competition?** Is this an industry in which competitors routinely copy other innovators? If so, you may need a utility patent to wave in the face of an imitator. If your competitors are likely to be pirates, you should also look to beef up and seek protection for your invention's nonfunctional features through design patents, trade dress, and copyright.

EXAMPLE: The competition among makers of remote control cars is fierce, and

Xportal, designer of the *RocketWriter*, knows that copying is common unless patents—particularly U.S. and Japanese patents—are in place. Therefore, the company has strong motivation to patent its technology, as well as to trademark its name, and seek a design patent for the *RocketWriter*'s appearance.

- **What will it cost to assert your rights?**
  Patent litigators routinely charge $300-$400 an hour. The cost to pursue a patent case through trial depends on the amount at stake, but even you were to seek $1 million in damages (considered a small amount in patent litigation) expect to pay at least $500,000. The median cost for the average patent lawsuit through trial is normally—you might want to sit down for this—several million dollars. Although a small percentage of cases actually go to trial, even pretrial actions can cost $10,000 to $50,000. If you believe your invention is commercial and patentable but you cannot afford to assert your rights, you may want to consider several alternatives. One alternative is to seek investors to fund your lawsuit. Some companies invest in litigation in return for a percentage of the proceeds. In addition, you may be able to find an attorney who will take the infringement case on contingency. Finally, you may choose to license the technology. Under a license, the company that acquires the rights (the licensee) can go after infring-

ers. Having a powerful licensee also deters copying.

EXAMPLE: There's a large market for Lydia's convertible fabric process. Unfortunately, imitators are likely to copy the innovation. Lydia can't afford to go after infringements that surface at Walgreens, K-Mart, and other mass-market merchandisers, so she seeks a company to license her technology instead.

 For more information on the licensing process, review *License Your Invention*, by Richard Stim (Nolo).

- **How difficult is it to acquire a patent?**
  Unlike other types of intellectual property, the patent process is fairly rigorous. Do you have the time and funds to pursue the patent over one or two years? Equally important, are you likely to end up with a broad claim (which gives you a larger net for catching infringers) or a narrow claim that a competitor will be able to design around?

EXAMPLE: Renada, the company with the video editing software, believes that it has a potentially broad patent claim for combining color coding with digital editing in a wide range of implications. The company is concerned, however, that it may have to narrow its claims to avoid stepping on a crowded field of prior art. If narrowing the claims results in a neutered patent, it may not be worth pursuing.

(Though not as powerful as a utility patent, copyright protection for the software is available as a less powerful enforcement tool (see Chapter 4, Section C)).

- **What's your budget?** Will your innovation comprise one patent application or several? Will you seek a utility patent as well as a design patent and trademark registration? You may need to consult with a patent attorney to make sure you choose the protection that is most effective *and* economical.

EXAMPLE: Xportal, the maker of the *RocketWriter,* has developed multiple inventions—including software that will enable a remote control vehicle to write alphanumeric characters. Xportal is in its last month of the fiscal year and is seriously strapped for cash. They decide, after speaking with an attorney, to file one utility patent immediately (using an attorney to file and prosecute a patent application can cost between $5,000 and $10,000) and wait to file the rest—along with trademark and design patent registrations—in six months when the company expects to be in better fiscal health.

- **How much time do you have?** Has more than a year passed since the invention was on sale or in public use? If so, then your innovation cannot qualify for utility patent protection (although other forms of protection might be available for the nonfunctional features of your innovation).

EXAMPLE: Renada, the animation company, has been using its video editing software offsite with clients for almost a year and billing the clients for the use. Renada's patent counsel determines that these uses don't preclude the filing of a patent under the one-year rule (and immediately files the application).

- **Are you an enforcer?** Some companies don't believe in aggressive patent enforcement—they are willing to tolerate some copying rather than pay the costs of enforcement. If your company takes this kind of laissez-faire approach, investing in a utility patent may not be worth the effort.

EXAMPLE: Renada, the animation company, has not been aggressive about enforcing its intellectual property rights. It turns the other cheek when Renada's hit series, *The Vast Beyond,* shows up illegally on peer-to-peer networks. Renada believes that enforcing rights will anger its base of Web-savvy users. Because the company has a cultural bias against aggressive IP enforcement, acquiring a patent may not fit within the company's mandate.

- **Have you anticipated defenses?** If you plan to assert patent rights, you must anticipate any unique defenses that an alleged infringer may raise. For example, do you have clear title to the invention? Are you the sole inventor? If defending

How Effective Are They for Stopping Infringers?

The reason you want to protect your idea in the first place is to stop others from using and profiting from it. So how easy is it to use each type of protection to go after infringers?

Utility Patent: Acquiring a utility patent is the most effective means of stopping an infringer. You can prove literal infringement—that is, that the patented claims cover the infringing device or, in some cases, that the infringing device is essentially equivalent. You don't have to show that the infringer actually copied your work.

Design Patent: To prove infringement of a design patent, you have to show only that your work and the infringer's work are substantially similar—not that the infringer saw and copied your work.

Copyright: To prove copyright infringement, you must prove not only that the infringing work is substantially similar to yours, but also that the infringer had access to your work and copied it. The infringer can claim certain defenses—for example, that the copying fell under the fair use exception, which allows others a limited right to copy for the purpose of commentary. For these reasons, it can be harder to enforce a copyright than a patent.

Trade Dress: To prove infringement of trade dress, you must show that your trade dress has acquired a secondary meaning—that it is distinctive and consumers associate it with your product. You must also show that the infringement is likely to deceive consumers. And a number of defenses are available to infringers, including a fair use defense for noncommercial uses of your trade dress.

Trade Secret: There is no such thing as trade secret infringement. You can only enforce trade secret rights by demonstrating that someone misappropriated your trade secrets—that they acquired them illegally or in violation of a confidentiality agreement.

your utility patent is going to be a problem, there's no sense pursuing one.

EXAMPLE: Jim, one of the inventors of Xportal's *RocketWriter,* claims to have developed the remote controlled retractable pen before he began work at Xportal. He demands a royalty payment in return for an assignment of his rights. Xportal's counsel reviews the matter and determines that Jim's argument is weak, because he had a duty to disclose the invention before he got hired. The company has anticipated this defense and proceeds with the patent.

B. Should You Get a Design Patent?

If your art or entertainment innovation is not functional (or if it has nonfunctional features), you should analyze whether it's worth the effort to acquire a design patent. Although we believe in the expanded use of design patents, we're also realistic; design patents have some disadvantages—they're more expensive to obtain than trademarks or copyrights, and they don't last as long.

In general, design patents are especially effective:

- for popular art and entertainment product designs that have a shelf life of less than 14 years
- in conjunction with either trademark or copyright protection, and
- for popular products within industries where copying is common.

To help you decide whether to apply for a design patent or simply rely on the protection of trademark and copyright law, consider these questions (similar to those for utility patents, in Section A):

- **What is the life expectancy of the design?** If the design's commercial life is less than one year—based on similar product designs—a design patent is probably not worth the effort, because it can take one to two years for the USPTO to issue a design patent. If the design's life is longer than two or three years, a design patent may be ideal. Keep in mind that copyright protection is automatic—once you create the work, you have a copyright—so, if your work qualifies for copyright, you should always consider that as part of your legal arsenal for designs. Trademark law is also especially useful for designs with a very long shelf

life. (For more on copyright and trademark law, see Chapter 4, Section D.)

EXAMPLE: Zooey designed a family of dolls she calls the "Bad Hair Girls." The dolls share similar characteristics—"madugly" hairdos, large eyes, pastel colors, and heads that are larger, in proportion, to the doll bodies. The commercial life of dolls is hard to predict. Some have long lives—for example, Mattel's *Barbie*—while the vast majority disappear after one showing at Toy Fair. Because of its limited 14-year life cycle (and because copyright protection is automatic for the dolls), the design patent does not seem appropriate for her product. Zooey decides to show the dolls to toy companies (under a nondisclosure agreement); if there is sufficient interest, then she'll reconsider whether a design patent makes sense.

- **What is the nature of your competition?** As discussed above, if copying is common within the industry, then you will want to seek the maximum protection—perhaps a combination of design patent, trade dress, and copyright—through overlapping registrations.

EXAMPLE: Ripper Music has designed a device called *Keynote* that combines an ergonomic computer keyboard and a musical keyboard. The company has filed a utility patent for the functional aspects of its hardware and now seeks a design patent for the color and shape of the product design. (It also plans to file a trademark application for the name of the device.)

- **What will it cost to assert your rights?** Of the various forms of protection available for designs, trademarks and trade dress may prove the most expensive to enforce. To win a trademark case, you may have to conduct extensive surveys to prove that your design has achieved secondary meaning (see Chapter 4, Section D). This may be more costly than preparing the evidence for a design patent case.

EXAMPLE: Gratefull Pet Toys has developed a line of dog toys—balls, ropes, kongs, and bones—with a tie-dyed appearance. Faithful's legal counsel has advised the company it will be easier to stop infringers under design patent law than trade dress law. The company weighs that factor against the cost of filing a design patent on each of its six types of toys. It decides to design patents on two of its most popular items, the kong and bone.

- **How difficult will it be to get a design patent (compared to trademark or copyright)?** If your design merges form and function, a design patent may provide a quick means of securing protection. It may prove hard to register the copyright (the Copyright Office may object to the merger of form and function) or protect your design under trade dress laws, if the design lacks the inherent distinctiveness or secondary meaning required. And design patents typically issue in 1½ years, while registering a trademark that isn't distinctive may take many years.

EXAMPLE: Modello, an upscale kitchen equipment company, has designed a coffeemaker titled *Perko,* which combines a retro percolator appearance with a high tech brewing system. The design is virtually unprotectable under copyright law, since it is very difficult to separate—for copyright purposes—the form from the function. The design can be protected with a design patent, however, because it is a novel ornamental appearance for a useful object. (Acquiring trade dress rights will likely take a few years, because the company will have to build up sufficient consumer awareness to demonstrate secondary meaning.)

- **What's your budget?** Will the design fit in a single design patent or trademark application, or will you have to file multiple applications? If money is a factor, you should look to see whether elements of the design require individual or collective protection, and then determine which type of protection is most economical.

EXAMPLE: Zooey's "Bad Hair Girls" all contain similar features, but they also are individually customized. For example, one doll, Beehive Bobby, is a pastel blue doll with a caricature bouffant hairstyle. In order to protect her dolls under design patent law, each of the ten dolls would have to be the subject of a separate application. Zooey reviews the material in this book, determines that if she prepares and files each application the filing fees would total $1,700 ($170 per application). However, if each design patent is granted, she will have to pay a design issue fee $240 per design (an additional $2,400). She doesn't have $4,100 available for design patent protection and decides, instead, to spend $645 for copyright and trademark registrations (at a cost of $300 for copyrights—or $30 per application—and $345 for federal trademark registration for the name "Bad Hair Girls").

• **How much time do you have?** Has more than a year passed since the design was on sale or in public use? If so, then design patent protection is precluded by statute, but trademark and copyright protection may still be available.

EXAMPLE: Frankie's unique rococo eyeglass case design was first offered for sale 13 months ago at the National Crafts Fair. Frankie cannot seek a design patent on that design. However, he can still seek copyright and trade dress protection—see Chapter 4.

• **Has your design acquired distinctiveness?** One advantage of a design patent is that a company can use the design patent's

14 years of exclusivity to develop consumer goodwill—a factor that can then translate into trademark value. At the very least, a company can use the patent to obtain the five years of substantially exclusive use needed to register the trademark on the basis of acquired distinctiveness.

EXAMPLE: Strategic Foods has created a line of snacks entitled Smileys—crackers in the shape of the classic smiley face. Because the smiley face can't be protected under copyright law, the company must consider seeking protection under trade dress and design patent laws. Under trade dress law, the design will have to achieve secondary meaning—consumers will have to associate the design with a Strategic Foods product. That could take as long as five years. In addition, such trade dress cases are often difficult and expensive to win. The company decides to seek a design patent.

• **Are you an enforcer?** If your company takes a laissez-faire approach to copying, investing in a design patent may not be worth the effort.

EXAMPLE: Modello, makers of the upscale coffeemaker *Perko,* sell their wares to a wealthy demographic that prides itself on acquiring status products. For that reason, Modello is accustomed to seeing low-end knockoffs of its designs from mass-market appliance makers. Because of the intense consumer loyalty to the Modello brand, the company rarely pursues infringers and decides not to bother getting a design patent.

- **Have you anticipated defenses?** If you're going to assert legal claims, you'll need to be prepared for possible defenses that an infringer may raise. For example, do you have clear title to your design? Design patents are the most predictable of the three forms of rights, and give rise to the most predictable defenses.

EXAMPLE: Xportal recently learned, after their design patent issued, that a wedge-shaped vehicle, similar to their *RocketWriter* design, was popular with children in the 1920s. Xportal's management is concerned that if the company sues an infringer under design patent law, this prior art will be discovered and invalidate their design patent. As result, they are more likely to emphasize trade dress and copyright enforcement; those two forms of protection would not likely be affected by the existence of a similar vehicle. ■

Part Two

Practice

The Patent Search: Make Sure Your Idea Is New

With this chapter we begin the practical (and less theoretical) portion of this book, providing information for artists and entertainers on patent searching. In Chapter 7, we'll discuss invention documentation; and in Chapters 8 and 9 (and Appendix A), we'll offer background on the process of applying for and acquiring design and utility patents.

Consider these patents for inventions related to art and entertainment:

- U.S. Pat. 4,600,919 (1986) for a method of generating animation by use of a sequence of video frames.
- U.S. Pat. 5,008,804 (1991) for a robotic camera television dolly system in which a motorized dolly carrying a camera rolled freely across a studio floor under computer control.
- U.S. Pat. 5,051,835 (1991) for a system for processing images in digital format for use on theatrical film.
- U.S. Pat. 5,459,529 (1995) for a video image composition system and method that enabled an artist to move an insert cut-out of a foreground image relative to a background image while continuously observing it on the monitor.

What do all of these patents have in common? Ultimately, they were all found invalid. A patent (or more precisely the patent claims) can be invalidated as a result of a lawsuit filed over ownership of the invention or during a reexamination process at the USPTO. Either process starts when another patent owner or a third party submits prior art patents and printed publications in an effort to show that the invention is not truly novel—and therefore, that it should not have been granted a patent. If the courts or the USPTO agree that appropriate prior art exists, the patent claims are kaput. In other words, goodbye to the thousands of dollars invested in these inventions (and their patent applications). What the USPTO giveth, the USPTO can taketh away.

In previous chapters, we talked about the importance of prior art searching. We pointed out that an issued patent—such as the art and entertainment patents listed above—could be rendered worthless if prior art demonstrates that your invention is not novel or nonobvious. And if similar prior art is uncovered during the application process, the patent application will be rejected. If that isn't incentive enough, there's another reason to do a thorough prior art search: to avoid claims of patent infringement. Searching prior art not only turns up ideas and inventions that might prevent you from getting a patent; it also helps you avoid a potential legal disaster. If someone holds an in-force patent for an invention that claims to do the same thing as your invention, your manufacture, use, sale, or offer for sale of the same invention would infringe this patent. And, if you sell your invention knowing someone else has a patent, you may be liable for increased financial damages.

This chapter includes:

- how to find patents on the Internet (Sections A and B)
- how to read the patents you find—and figure out whether an existing patent can

be distinguished from your invention (Section D)

- how to search for other prior art, such as publications or commercial uses of an invention (Section E), and
- how to use a patent searcher to examine records at the USPTO (or examine them yourself) (Section F).

Prior Art Primer

What constitutes prior art to your invention? As discussed in Chapter 1, prior art can come from just about anywhere. It includes all previous developments that are available to the public, such as:

- patents for inventions similar to yours
- publications discussing inventions like yours
- foreign patents for inventions similar to yours
- any commercial sale or use of an invention like yours, and
- any public knowledge or use of a similar invention.

If you're feeling daunted by the thought of wading through all of these documents, take heart. You can start simply by performing a preliminary search using the Internet with its databases of U.S. patents from 1790 to the present and its vast stores of commercial and academic information. If that search doesn't knock out your patent, you can proceed with a more detailed search or you can hire a patent searcher to review files at the USPTO or at engineering libraries.

The Festering *Festo* Decision

In 2002, the Supreme Court decided the *Festo* case (*Festo Corp. v. Shoketsu Kinzoku Kabushiki Co. Ltd.* 122 S. Ct. 1831 (2002)), which put some limits on a patent holder's right to sue infringers. Generally, there are two ways that a patent owner can go after an infringer. One method is to sue for direct or literal infringement. If the claims in your patent fully describe (or "read on") the infringing invention—in other words, the inventions are literally the same—you can sue for direct infringement. The second method is to prove that the two devices, though not identical, are sufficiently equivalent in what they do and how they do it that it's fair to prevent the infringer from using the invention. This second method is called the "doctrine of equivalents."

In the *Festo* case, the U.S. Supreme Court ruled that an if an applicant amended his patent claims during the examination process, then the doctrine of equivalents is presumed not to apply to those amended claims. The exceptions to this rule are if the patent owner can show that the amendment involved a feature that was "unforeseeable at the time of the application" or "for some other reason" could not be included in the original claim. If one of these two exceptions applies, the patent owner can use the doctrine of equivalents. Otherwise, the patent owner can only prove infringement if the devices are literally the same—a much harder showing to make.

How Patent Searchers Do It

Gregory Aharonian, co-author and instigator of this book, works as a patent consultant and patent searcher. His job is to search prior art and find documents that either guarantee patentability or are used to bust (invalidate) patents.

In addition to our how-to explanation about patent searching, it might be helpful to get an idea of how professional searchers work, so Greg answers some common questions here. (Unfamiliar Internet references and patent terminology will be explained throughout this chapter.)

Question: Before the USPTO issues a patent, an examiner will make a prior art search to determine novelty and nonobviousness. If the USPTO has to search prior art before issuing the patent, why should an inventor bother doing the search before filing? Why not wait and see what the USPTO turns up?

Answer: Because patent examiners do not have enough time to do the searching themselves. Examiners tend to do a good job searching patents, but not such a good job finding other types of prior art. There is little value in obtaining a patent if the examiner didn't find some relevant prior art—if you later sue someone for infringing your patent, they can hire someone like me to find that missing prior art and use it to bust your patent.

And the more prior art you cite, the harder it is for people like me to attack your patent—your patent, when it issues, will be perceived to be stronger.

Just as important, if you draft your patent claims without knowing what prior art the examiner might find, you will be forced to amend and narrow your claims if the examiner comes up with something. In most situations, you lose significant enforcement rights when you amend your claims, because of a recent Supreme Court decision called the *Festo* case. (For more information, see "The Festering *Festo* Decision," above.)

The more you know ahead of time, the better your chances of obtaining and enforcing a patent—and the less money you will waste pursuing a patent that will ultimately be invalidated.

Question: If you were an inventor getting ready to file a patent related to art or entertainment, how would you do the patent search? Would you hire a professional or try to do it yourself?

Answer: Spend an hour or two and try searching yourself. It costs you nothing, and you can learn a lot. If you end up finding little to nothing that is relevant (indicating that you might have something patentable), you then might want to hire a professional. Typically, patent lawyers retain and work with searchers on behalf of their clients. There is an advantage in doing the search yourself—you can see how others described their invention, especially variations in their ideas.

For nonpatent prior art, at least do something like a Google search. It is quick, easy,

How Patent Searchers Do It (continued)

and fairly comprehensive. If you live near a university with a good accessible library, go over one afternoon and do a bit of searching. Again, it won't cost you much more than your time.

Question: If you're searching through the PTO records online, do you prefer using keyword searching or searching by class? (Keyword and classification searching are covered in Sections A and B.)

Answer: Most of the time, I do keyword searching. When you have a lot of people doing the classifying, it is hard to maintain consistent quality standards, so the classification system isn't always accurate. On the other hand, the same technology can be described with many different keywords, so classification searching can help you narrow things down if you are intimate with the classification system. One problem is that the classification system evolves over time, and not always in the most optimal ways.

I suspect it is more of a personal preference—with enough experience you can be efficient with either method. Typically, most searchers will use one style, and then finish the search with the other style. Keep in mind that the Americans and Europeans have different classification systems, which you will have to become familiar with if you are doing classification searches.

Question: What are some common mistakes that inventors make when searching for prior art?

Answer: One common mistake is failing to realize that different words can be used to describe the same aspect of a system. For example, consider searching for a device that uses a microprocessor. While "microprocessor" is the commonly used term, other words such as "processor," "controller," and/or "microcontroller" are also used and should be searched. This discourages some people, because they either have to submit multiple queries based on all possible combinations of words, or use one really long search query including all of the words, which takes a lot of time for the search engine to process.

Also, while the PTO databases are in English, there are two kinds of English: American and British. For example, you may have search for both "color" and "colour." Then, there are all of the acronyms, like "CPU" for microprocessor. The U.S. Patent Office should have one of its programmers write a little computer program to intelligently expand search queries, and make the program available on their website.

Question: A few years back, the PTO began publishing patent applications (usually 18 months after the application was filed). How helpful is it to search through these published applications?

Answer: Well, if you are applying for a patent, published patent applications will prevent you from getting a patent just as effectively

How Patent Searchers Do It (continued)

as an issued patent, so it is worthwhile to search published patent applications. Also, because they were submitted quite recently, published patent applications are a better measure of what is going on in research and development.

Not all patent applications result in issued patents, as is sometimes the case with wacky inventions. With published patent applications, you can see some of these rejected inventions, whereas in the past, the patent application remained hidden within PTO files if the patent wasn't granted.

Question: Obviously, the language used in patents is not in the same spellbinding style as a Stephen King novel. For many first-time searchers, this can be a big obstacle. They may find the right patent, only to discover that they can't read it. Any suggestions for deciphering patentese?

Answer: What's confusing about "an elongated nonstraight cylindrical object made of carbon based materials"? OKay, be a baby and use the word "stick." Yes, patent lawyers in the end are lawyers, for whom the lack of clarity is often an effective strategy. The claims have to be logically consistent and structured—and they are ultimately understandable, but you have to spend some time reading patent claims until you get the hang of it. Look for patent claims that are easy to understand, and study them first. Then tackle the more difficult claims. Some of the problems are unintentional—for

example, some Japanese patent claims that appear in the U.S. patents are hard to understand because they were translated from Japanese.

Question: Do you see much difference between the free patent-search databases such as the USPTO's and fee-based online patent databases like Delphion? (Both are discussed in Section A).

Answer: The for-pay databases tend to have more flexible searching capabilities, plus more extensive data analysis features you can apply to groups of patents that you find in a search. For-pay databases also tend to combine the various free patent databases (such as the PTO, EPO, and WIPO patent databases). Some databases, such as Derwent, actually rewrite the patent title and abstract to better reflect the invention, which can make searching more efficient.

But as a good first step for patent searching, the free databases are an excellent way to go.

Question: Do you use any shortcuts when searching for foreign patents or foreign prior art?

Answer: Most of the time, I can meet my patent searching needs with just U.S. patents and prior art. With over 6½ million issued patents, the United States has the largest body of published descriptions of inventions, so you can often find what you need in the U.S. data. But when I do make use of foreign patent data or prior art, my

How Patent Searchers Do It (continued)

search strategies don't change much, except for making allowances for dealing with multiple languages. Searching the large body of Japanese literature tends to be hardest. Most European materials are described or are written in English.

Question: If patent searching is like detective work, what's your style? Do you have a philosophy for uncovering likely suspects?

Answer: Fortunately, most patent searching work has obvious pathways. A patent on a natural language translation computer program will usually be written in the style of engineering papers, and use the standard terminology in the patent abstract and claims. So your initial search strategy is to identify the key concept words used in the patent abstract and claims, and search the online databases using those words. It is easier to do this if you have been doing it for many years like I have, but that's not necessary. The bigger problem for many is that there are few libraries around the country with sufficient amounts of literature in one place to make searching logistically practical—at some point, you have to physically access the conference proceedings or back volumes of journals. The two best areas in the United States are the Boston and San Francisco areas, where, co-incidentally, I have spent all of my life.

Question: You earn your living as a patent searcher. If there is such a thing as a "typical job," what would that be like for you? How does it start? What do you have to do?

Answer: For patent applications, I usually start by searching issued U.S. patents. I like to find ten to 20 relevant patents, which is usually enough to help the lawyer figure out how broadly to scope the patent claims. I then switch over to the nonpatent prior art, and try to find a similar number of papers and articles (though if the prior patents I found come close to the new invention, then all I need is a few more nonpatent prior art items). The trick, at least for me, is to find one good initial reference—a starting point. Usually that initial reference refers to other references, and it grows from there. Doing searches to bust a patent is much the same; I just spend much more time at each step of the search.

What's the 4-1-1?
Deciphering Patent Numbers

Every U.S. patent issued since 1836 has a patent number. For example, patent number 5,996,251 was issued in 1999 for a combination jazz dancing and character/tap dancing shoe (Illustration 6-1) and patent number 6,276,523 was issued for a "Compact Disc Container" (Illustration 6-2). In patent disputes, judges and attorneys refer to each patent by the last three digits of the registration (for example, the "251 patent"). Patents issued before 1836 did not have numbers—they are referred to by the name of the inventor. A patent number that is preceded by the letter "D" (for example, D455,885) signifies a design patent (in this case, the design for a cremation urn lid).

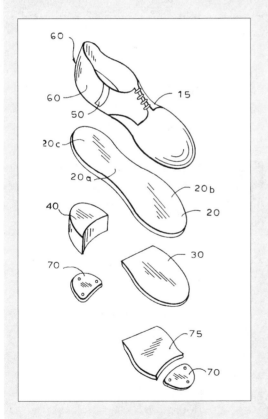

Illustration 6-1

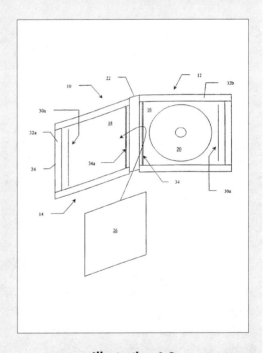

Illustration 6-2

⚠️ **Even the most thorough search may not uncover all prior art.** Whether you do it yourself or hire a competent searcher, there are limitations to every search. You can never expect to uncover 100% of the prior art because you may not have access to some pending patent applications, foreign patents, or nonpatent references. Even at the USPTO headquarters in Alexandria, Virginia, some prior art may be missing or on loan—and therefore unavailable to you or the searcher you hire, even if you show up in person.

📖 **For More Information on Patent Searching.** For a comprehensive discussion about patent searching, read *Patent Searching Made Easy,* by David Hitchcock (Nolo).

A. Patent Searching on the Web

Let's look at some tips and strategies for online patent searching for an art or entertainment invention. We recommend starting your prior-art search by reviewing previously issued U.S. patents and published U.S. patent applications.

Keep in mind that most of these tips—particularly those relating to keyword searches—are intended for searching utility patents, not design patents. That's because design patents don't contain much writing; they usually include only a title and drawings. So, your keyword search will retrieve a design patent only if the keyword is in the title of the design patent. (You'll find tips for searching for design patents in Section D, below.)

1. Find the Right Words

Before you start your search, analyze your invention carefully. What words would you use to describe it? Try to come up with a broad list of words commonly used to describe similar inventions. To succeed in your patent search, you'll have to figure out which words and phrases are most likely to appear in the patents. For example, if you invented an artificial rainmaking machine, you may not find it under "artificial" or "rainmaking"; the patents covering this topic may instead refer to it as "rainfall simulation." A broad arsenal of search words will allow you to use trial and error to find the patents you need—and to work around words that have multiple meanings or are used to describe a wide range of inventions.

 You can speed the process of finding search terms by using a thesaurus or a flip dictionary. You can find these resources online at, for example, Merriam-Webster.com (www.m-w.com), Dictionary.com (www.dictionary.com), or YourDictionary.com (www.yourdictionary.com).

EXAMPLE: Here are some search terms we gathered for three of the inventions discussed in chapter 2:
- Terms for a hand rest for an artist's easel: (U.S. Pat. 6,565,059): hand, rest, control, brush, easel, and canvas.
- Terms for the Super Soaker toy squirt gun (U.S. Pat. 4,591,071):

squirt, gun, water, pistol, compress, and nozzle.

- Terms for the method of marking your place in a digital audiobook (or "indicating when a predetermined location has been encountered in stored data") (U.S. Pat 5,872,712): book, audio book, audiobook, audible, bookmark, digital, download, locate, locator, mark, and marker.

2. Search for Free ... Or for a Fee

At the USPTO website (www.uspto.gov) (Illustration 6-3), you can search a vast database of patents, including all previously granted U.S. patents, for free. Most of the older patents (from 1790 to 1975) have been scanned as digital illustrations. Although you can read them, you can't search the text for keywords. However, you can search the text of U.S. patents issued after 1975. You can also extend your search of U.S. patents back to the 1920s for free at the EPO's (European Patent Office) website (http://ep.espacenet.com). This site also provides a searchable database for many foreign patents.

You can search the front page and claims of U.S. patents for free at the Delphion site (www.delphion.com). However, to access more patent information at Delphion or to access published applications or international patents, you'll have to pay an access fee.

Another fee-based service is Micropatent (www.micropatent.com), which offers the unique capability to conduct full-text searches of U.S. patents back to 1836. However, the Micropatent historic database (pre-1976) has been assembled through optical character recognition of patent documents, so it contains many errors and incomprehensible words.

Derwent (www.derwent.com), another popular fee-based patent database, provides U.S. and international patents from the USPTO, WIPO (World Intellectual Property Organization), EPO, and Japanese and German patent offices. Derwent provides value-added information—they rewrite patent titles and abstracts in language that more clearly describes the invention, which makes it easier to find relevant patents.

Keep in mind that many of these searching services are priced for patent lawyers and corporations. An artist or inventor with limited resources may find the fees astronomical. Before you break your bank paying for a fee-based service, make sure to thoroughly exhaust the free services at the USPTO.

3. Keep Track of Prior Art

It may seem obvious, but we'll say it anyway: You have to keep track of what you find. Set up a word processing document or a spreadsheet that includes the patent numbers and a summary of each similar invention you come across. If possible, make this document part of your inventor's notebook (Chapter 7 explains how to create and maintain an inventor's notebook).

You should also make copies of all relevant prior art that you find. You can copy pertinent sections from any USPTO patent issued after 1975 by using your computer's "copy" and "paste" features. You can download and save a

Illustration 6-3

complete patent by clicking "File" and "Save As" in your Internet browser (for example, Internet Explorer) while the patent is onscreen. The patent will be saved as an HTML file—a code that you can read by clicking on the file or opening it in Internet Explorer.

You can get a PDF (Portable Document Format as used in Adobe Acrobat) of a patent at the PatentFetcher website. If you enter the U.S. patent number or the serial number of a published patent application, you can view and download a PDF of the patent or application. (The site comes in two versions—a faster fee-based version and a slower free version.) You may also order patents directly from the USPTO. Click "Add To Shopping

Cart" when viewing any patent on the USPTO website, then follow the instructions to pay by credit card. The patent will be emailed to you. You can mail-order a paper copy of a patent. Send your request to Commissioner of Patents and Trademarks, Washington, DC 20231, and enclose the patent numbers and a check. You can find out how much to send by checking the Fee Schedule at the USPTO website.

You may also want to try Patent Hunter, a software program from Patent Wizard (www .patent-hunter.com) that provides a helpful method of downloading and organizing prior-art patents. Once you type the patent number into Patent Hunter's search engine, the program will download it from the USPTO website (you must be connected to the Internet), place it in a file on your computer, and organize it in an easy-to-use list. The patent you download will be an image file—which means that you cannot copy text from it. (Patent Hunter also provides search capabilities with its own intuitive versions of the basic and advanced searches offered by the USPTO.)

4. Read Before You Write

If you're not familiar with the look and feel of patents, you may be surprised by their rigorous, mystifying style. But don't let the perplexing arcana put you off; the more patents you read, the more familiar you will become with their structure and language. This will help you search more efficiently, because you'll know which fields of the patent—for example, the abstract or specification—are most likely to be relevant. (For more on reading patents, see Section D, below.)

5. A Picture Is Worth a Thousand Words

Sometimes, you may find it more helpful to view patent drawings than to read the text of the patent. At the USPTO website, you can see all of the drawings for a particular patent by clicking "Images" while you are viewing it. If the drawing doesn't appear after you click, you may need to download free software known as a "TIFF-viewer." One place to get it is AlternaTIFF (www.alternatiff.com). You can also view the drawings by downloading a PDF (for free) via the PatentFetcher website (see Section 2, above).

6. Look Beyond Valid Patents

Keep in mind that you're not just searching for valid U.S. patents. Expired patents, current patent applications, foreign patents, and nonpatented inventions are all valid forms of prior art. You can find tips for locating them in Section E.

7. Search the Internet and More at a PTDL

The USPTO has designated several Patent and Trademark Deposit Libraries (PTDLs) throughout the country to house copies of U.S. patents and patent and trademark materials and to make them available to the public at no cost. Most of these PTDLs provide some sort of Internet or computer access to the USPTO's patent databases. At some PTDLs—for example the Sunnyvale Center for Innovation, Invention, and Ideas (www.sci3.com)—extensive searching resources are available. Librarians will even perform customized patent searches for a reasonable price. You can find out more about each PTDL's features by checking the USPTO website or calling the respective library.

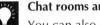 **Chat rooms and other Internet resources.** You can also obtain prior art information by communicating with others at chat rooms and forums hosted by invention and patent sites such as the Patent Café (www.patentcafe.com). Chat rooms can provide information about locating prior art and finding patent searchers. They also give you a place to post queries or ask others directly whether they know of any relevant prior art.

B. Searching the USPTO Website

This section explains how to search the USPTO website for prior art. There are two ways to structure your search:

- Search the patent index and classification system. The USPTO categorizes all inventions using a system of classes and subclasses. Once you locate the appropriate class and subclass for your invention, you can find similar prior-art patents in the same class/subclass. (Throughout this book, we will use numbers separated by a slash as a shorthand for class/subclasses. For example, 2/144 refers to Class 2, Subclass 144.) We explain how to conduct this type of search in Section 1, below.

EXAMPLE: A patent examiner seeking to identify prior art for a doll would start with Class 446 (Amusement Devices: Toys). The examiner could review subclasses for dolls such as aquatic dolls (446/156), sleeping (or horizontal) dolls (446/345), dolls with moving eyes (446/346), talking, crying (sound-making) dolls (446/297), or inflatable (simulation of an animate being) dolls (446/226). By examining patents grouped in these subclasses, the examiner can determine whether any prior art may preclude granting a patent or force the inventor to narrow the patent claims.

- Use keywords and other indicia to search the USPTO Patent Database. In addition to searching by classification, you can also search the vast collection of patents directly. This method allows you to look for matches based upon search terms and other criteria. You will find more information on this method of searching in Section 2, below.

EXAMPLE: Imagine you invented a guitar tuning peg. Someone tells you that a rival inventor from South Carolina had patented a similar peg a few years earlier. You can ask the search engine to find all patents that have the words "tuning and peg" in the abstract and were filed by an inventor from South Carolina.

Some searchers start with a keyword and move to the classification system. In some cases, the inventor starts with class and narrows that down with keywords. You are more likely to get on the right track if you use the classification index. This system will help you avoid getting sidetracked by numerous patents that have little or peripheral relation to your invention.

1. Search by Classification

The USPTO categorizes every patent application or patent in a class and a subclass.

EXAMPLE 1: Imagine you invented a jet-propelled toy. The USPTO would categorize your application in Class 446/187 if it was a jet-propelled balloon, Class 446/163 for a jet–propelled aquatic toy, or perhaps 446/221 if it was simply a jet-propelled toy that didn't fall into either of these categories.

EXAMPLE 2: Imagine you invented a board game, *Art Biz*, that teaches players the business of selling fine art. The USPTO would categorize it in Class 273 (Amusement Devices; Games) and Subclass 236 (Board games, pieces or boards).

Check Our Index First!

To save you some time, we've already trolled the thousands of classifications at the USPTO site and picked all of the ones that we thought might encompass inventions related to art and entertainment. Our index is not foolproof—we may have missed a few classes—but it's the only comprehensive art & entertainment patent classification available, so check it out (in Appendix B at the end of this book) before starting your classification search.

a. Finding the Right Class and Subclass for Your Invention

To search using the USPTO classification system, follow these seven steps.

Skip these steps if you know of a specific patent. You can bypass these steps for finding the class/subclass if you know of a patented invention that is very similar to yours. You can locate that patent using the search methods described in Section 2—for example, searching by the name of the invention, inventor, or company that owns the patent. Once you find the patent, you can see how the USPTO categorized it.

1. Find the patent classification home page. Start at the USPTO home page (www.uspto.gov). Click "Patents." Click "Guidance, Tools & Manuals." Choose "Manual of Patent Classification." This will take you to the patent classification home page. (See Illustration 6-4.)

2. On the right side of the page you will see "B. U.S. Manual of Classification." Click the drop-down menu next to "Look in" and choose "Index to Classification."

3. Type in a keyword. To locate the class for your invention, type in your broadest keyword. For example, "saxophone" in the case of a saxophone accessory, "doll" in the case of a crying doll, or "easel" in the case of a folding easel. You can type in more than one word—for example, "crying doll"—but you must also select the appropriate drop-down menu choice: "Any Word" (which will find any class that contains either word) or "All Words" (which will only find classes that contain every word in your list).

4. Examine your results and determine your class. When you click on any of the search results, you will be directed to a class/subclass index page that contains your search term. Finding your search term on a particular result page is simple—use the "Find on This Page" feature in your Internet browser. (In Internet Explorer, click "Edit," then "Find on this Page.")

Class to subclass. When you start by searching for class, you may be directed to the proper subclass as well. For example, imagine you had invented a "sheet music page

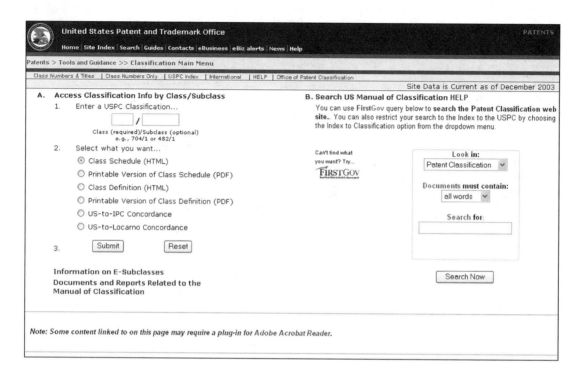

Illustration 6-4

turner," a device that turns pages of sheet music. You searched the index of classification for two words, music and turner. That directs you to several choices including the correct class and subclass: 84/521. (Class 84 is for "Music." Subclass 521 is for "music leaf turner.")

5. Examine the class and its definition. Click on the class number to see how the class is defined.

   EXAMPLE: When we click on Class 84, we are taken to a page with the name of the class, MUSIC, and all of its subclasses.

6. Find your subclass. Once you get to the page that lists your class and its subclasses, you need to find the correct subclass. To do this, use the "Find on This Page" feature in your Internet browser (described in Step 4) and type in some of your alternate search terms until you locate an appropriate subclass.

7. Look for more than one class/subclass. We recommend that you continue searching and checking the results of your initial index search until you find every class/subclass combination that might encompass your invention.

Finding Foreign Equivalent Classifications

If you want to search through international patent databases, you'll need to use the international classification system known as the IPC (the International Patent Classification). Once you know the U.S. classification, you can easily locate the IPC equivalent at the Patent Classification Home Page (Illustration 6-4). Type in the appropriate class/subclass and you will be directed to the appropriate IPC concordance. (Although the Locarno Concordance, also listed on the Web page, may sound like the right place to look, it is not relevant for our purposes. It lists only classifications for designs, not inventions.)

b. Use the Class/Subclass to Find Prior-Art Patents

Once you've categorized your invention by potential class/subclass, you're ready to locate relevant prior art by plunging into the vast databases of existing and expired U.S. patents.

Follow these steps to complete your class/subclass searching.

1. Start at the patent searching home page. Click on "Patents: Search" on the USPTO home page. Choose "Quick Search" under "Patent Grants" (on the left side of the Web page).
2. Search for patents by class/subclass. On the "Quick Search" page, set the "Select Years" drop-down menu to "All Years."

Type in the class/subclass you want to search.

EXAMPLE: You invented a marionette with internal lights and translucent material. You want all marionette patents (Class/Subclass 446/363), so you type "446/363" next to Term 1. In Field 1, you select "Current U.S. Classification." When you click the "Search" button, you are directed to a page with a list of patents, including a phantom marionette (U.S. Pat. 5,030,162), a marionette bird (U.S. Pat. 4,048,749), and an invisible marionette (consisting only of a pair of feet) (U.S. Pat. 4,253,270).

3. Read and save relevant patents. If you have trouble reading and understanding patents, review Section D. It gets easier with practice: the more you read, the easier it becomes.

Which patents are relevant? You should look closely at any patent or document that demonstrates an important similarity to your invention and the way it works. In the case of a bird-shaped marionette with translucent qualities, relevant patents would deal with toy figures, puppets, and marionettes that have unique viewing qualities—for example, they are illuminated, transparent, or made of materials that affect the appearance of the figure. Keep in mind that you are not just seeking prior art that defeats your invention; you're also seeking prior art that you can distinguish from your invention. If you can show that a relevant prior-art patent is somehow different from your invention, you should cite the patent to the USPTO in a document known as an Information Disclosure Statement. You should submit this document either with your regular patent application or within three months after filing your regular patent application.

4. Check "References Cited." The good news for patent searchers is that a relevant prior-art patent will likely lead to additional prior art. Check the "References Cited" portion of the prior-art patent for leads to other inventions.

> **EXAMPLE:** The phantom marionette patent described in the previous example leads to other classes that are also relevant for our marionette invention—for example, Classes 446/361 (Toys/flaccid support or manipulator), 446/360 (Toys/Relatively movable striking platform), and 446/83 (Toys/Toy theater including movable figure).

When searching for class/subclass at the USPTO, you are directed from classes to their definitions to subclasses and then to patents. This may seem like one big mass of information, but it's derived from three print publications that are available at the USPTO, PTDLs, and some public libraries. These books are:

- *Index to the U.S. Patent Classification.* This book offers an alphabetical list of possible subject areas of invention, together with the appropriate class and subclass.
- *Manual of Classification.* This publication lists all classes numerically, including the

subclasses under each class. After locating the class and subclass numbers, you can use the *Manual of Classification* to find other, closely related classes and subclasses.

- *Classification Definitions.* Here you will find definitions for every class and subclass in the *Manual of Classification*. At the end of each subclass definition, cross-references give you additional places to look that correspond to that subclass.

2. Searching the Patent Database by Keywords

In some circumstances, you may want to search for patents using criteria other than class/subclass. For example, it makes more sense to search by keywords if:

- you want to find patents filed by a particular inventor
- you want to find a patent by its number
- you want to find all of the patents owned by a certain company, or
- you want to look up a particular invention to determine its class/subclass.

The USPTO's main search page allows you to perform three types of searches: "Quick Search," "Advanced Search," or "Patent Number Search."

a. Start With "Quick Search"

Start out using "Quick Search." It's comprehensive and easy to learn—and you can search two fields at once. "Advanced Search" accesses the same information and permits you to search more than two fields at once.

Unfortunately, "Advanced Search" requires considerable trial and error for first-time users.

Click "Search Patents" on the USPTO home page to get to "Quick Search." Click "Quick Search" under "Patent Grants." If you want to search published patent applications instead, click "Quick Search" on the right side of the Web page.

Searching Published Patent Applications

Most regular patent applications are published 18 months after filing. If an application is not published, that means either that the application was filed within the last 18 months or that the inventor submitted, at the time of filing, a Nonpublication Request stating that the inventor will not be filing the application outside the U.S.

You can search all applications published since March 15, 2001 at the USPTO website. To search published applications, start your search on the right side of the USPTO searching Web page titled "Patent Applications." Search using the criteria and methods described in this chapter.

Design patents, plant patents, and provisional patent applications are not published and therefore won't show up in your search.

---

b. "Quick Search" Features

When you use "Quick Search," you select criteria that set the parameters for your search, including:

- **Fields.** Fields are different types of patent information—for example, "Inventor Name," "Application Date," "Abstract," "Title," or "Inventor City." You can also find an explanation of each field at the USPTO website. If you don't know which field to choose, select "All Fields."
- **Terms.** Terms are the words, names, dates, or numbers that you type into the blank spaces.

EXAMPLE: You invented a software animation program and the resulting imagery reminds you of movies such as *Finding Nemo* and *Toy Story*, created by the Pixar company. You'd like to see the patents issued to Pixar. Choose "Assignee Name" (the company that owns the patent is the assignee) as Field 1 and type in "Pixar" as Term 1. You will recover several patents, including Pixar's U.S. Pat. 6,300,960 (Realistic surface simulation in computer animation) and U.S. Pat 5,771,109 (Method and apparatus for digitizing films using a stroboscopic scanning system).

- **Connectors.** When you search by more than one field criterion, you must choose one of three ways to connect your choices—AND, OR, and AND NOT. (You can use AND NOT to avoid getting certain patents.) Connectors are a good way to narrow down your search.

EXAMPLE: You invented an amusement car that you believe can be used at a theme park such as Disney World. You'd like to see if the Disney company has already patented a similar device. You want all Disney patents with the word "car" in the abstract. You choose "Assignee Name" as Field 1 and type in "Disney" as Term 1. Choose the connector "AND." Then choose "Title" as Field 2 and type in "car" as Term 2. (You may also want to repeat this search and type in "vehicle" for Term 2 or use "Abstract" for Field 2. Both of these will further broaden your results.).

- **Years.** Here you select the range of years for which you wish to seek patents. Keep in mind that if you select "All Years," you cannot search through the text—except for the title of the patent—of pre-1976 patents. You can read those patents, but you can't search them at the USPTO. (The easiest way to locate old patents is by typing in their patent number in a Patent Number Search.)

C. Design Patent Searching

Searching for design patents is a little trickier than searching for utility patents. Most online searching is accomplished by searching text, and design patents have very little text; they're primarily drawings. If you're searching for prior-art design patents, the suggestions in this section will help.

1. Keyword Searching

Because design patents have very little text, searching by keyword as described in Section B2 will work for a design patent only if the keyword is in the title or if you are searching by some other aspect of the patent, such as the designer or assignee.

You can try this method using the "Search Patents" feature on the USPTO home page. Use the "Quick Search" feature. In "Quick Search," you set two criteria. In one box, type a term that will help identify similar design patents (for example, "quilt" or "denim"); in the second search box, type in the letter "D" and set the drop-down menu for "Patent Number" (to let the search engine know you are only seeking design patents). This short-cut approach is not as effective as the method described below, but it may help you get started or quickly locate the classification for your goods.

To see images of any patent, open the patent onscreen by clicking the patent number, then clicking "Images" (it's boxed near the top of the page). If the drawing doesn't appear after you click, you may need to download a TIFF-viewer (as described in Section A5).

2. Finding the Right Class and Subclass for Your Design

Bypass these steps for finding the class/ subclass if you know of a patented design that is similar to yours. You can locate that patent using the search methods described in Section B, above—for example, searching by name of the design, inventor, or assignee (the company that owns the patent). Once you find the patent, you can see how the USPTO categorized it.

1. Find the patent classification home page. Start at the USPTO home page (www.uspto.gov). Click "Patents." Click "Guidance, Tools & Manuals." Choose "Manual of Patent Classification." This will take you to the patent classification home page.

2. Select "Index to Classification." Click the drop-down menu next to "Look in" and choose "Index to Classification."

3. Type in a keyword. To locate the class for your design, type in a broad keyword that might describe your class of goods. For example, "jewelry" or "pottery" will work as keywords. You can type in more than one word at a time—for example, "glass bead"—but you must also select the appropriate drop-down menu choice: "Any Word" (which will find any class that contains either word) or "All Words" (which will only find classes that contain every word in your list).

4. Examine your results and determine your class. Your search will take you to an alphabetically organized class/subclass index page that contains your search term. If you type in "jewelry," for example, you would be taken to a list of patent items starting with the letter "J." (Finding your search term on a particular result page is simple—use the "Find on This Page" feature in your Internet browser. In Internet Explorer, click "Edit," then "Find on this Page.") Under Jewelry, you'll find a list of jewelry items, such as bracelets, finger rings, and lockets. Many of these have classifications that begin with the letter "D." These are design classifications for jewelry. D11 appears quite often, which tells you that it's probably a major class for jewelry items. Keep in mind that you are only looking for classes that start with the letter "D"—those that don't are for utility patents.

5. Examine the class and its definition. Click the class number to see how the class is defined and to make sure it's suitable for your design. For example, if you click D11, you will see that it includes a wide range of possible subclasses.

6. Find your subclass. Once you get to the page that lists your class and its subclasses, you need to find the correct subclass. Review the list until you find an accurate class/subclass.

7. Look for more than one class/subclass. We recommend that you continue searching and checking the results of your initial index search to make sure that you've come up with every relevant class/subclass.

3. Use the Class/Subclass to Find Prior Art

Once you've categorized your design by potential class/subclass, you're ready to locate relevant prior art by looking into the vast databases of existing and expired U.S. design patents.

Follow these steps to complete your class/subclass searching.

1. Start at the patent searching home page. Under "Patents," click "Search" on the USPTO home page. Choose "Quick Search" under "Patent Grants" (on the left side of the Web page).

2. Search for patents by class/subclass. On the "Quick Search" page, set the Select Years drop-down menu to "All Years." Type in the class/subclass you want to search, and set the drop-down menu for "Current U.S. Classification."

3. Read and save relevant patents. Copy or download the information from the Web page and save the patent on your computer.

D. Reading and Distinguishing Patents

Once you've found a few patents, you'll face a daunting task—reading them. To start you on the right course, this section provides some tips on deciphering patents.

Patents generally include several written sections:

- the specification
- the abstract, and
- the claims.

In order to read and understand a patent, you need to be able to identify these sections and tell them apart. Unfortunately, this is easier said than done—patents don't always include headings to let you know where one section stops and another starts.

1. The Specification

The specification explains how to make and use the invention—and how it can be distinguished from the prior art. The specification consists of:

- **A title.** The inventor provides a short, simple summary of the invention—for example, "Ergonomic guitar strap."
- **The field of the invention.** Here the inventor explains what the invention does —for example, "This invention generally relates to straps for holding a guitar or other object. More particularly the invention relates to a strap that extends over both shoulders of a guitar player."
- **A criticism of the prior art.** The inventor describes the prior art and how the invention is distinguishable. (This helps to establish the invention's novelty and nonobviousness.)
- **"Objects and Advantages"** of the invention. The "objects" describe what the invention accomplishes and the "advantages" describe the superior qualities of the invention.
- **Description of the drawings.** Here, the inventor provides a brief explanation for each of the figures or views of the patent drawings.
- **A detailed description of the invention and how it works.** This is the heart of the specification. Here, the inventor describes the invention's structure and explains its performance. After naming and numbering each element of the invention, the inventor describes the action of the invention's parts.
- **Any additional ramifications** that are not important enough to show in the drawing. Here, an inventor might include, for example, alternative ways that an invention can be used or put together.

Finding the Who, What, Where, and When

You don't have to know how to read a patent to find basic data such as the title, inventor's name, address, patent filing date, patent issue date, or referenced patents. You can find these pieces of information on the front page of the patent. Search for them using either the "Quick Search" or "Advanced Search" described in Section B2.

2. Abstract

The abstract—a concise, one-paragraph summary of the structure, nature, and purpose of the invention—may prove the most helpful portion of the patent. The abstract helps you quickly get right to the heart of the invention: what it does and how it works. Below is an abstract for the Disney Company's U.S. Pat 5,989,126 (Water raft amusement ride including a device for spinning a circular water raft)

ABSTRACT:

An amusement water ride is provided including a water course for carrying one or more circular water rafts. The water course is provided with at least one downhill section for accelerating the water rafts into a splash point. A spin mechanism is provided near the top of the downhill section for imparting a spin to the water rafts as they move past the spin mechanism. The spin mechanism includes a movement retarding surface along one wall of the water course and a movement expediting surface along an opposite wall of the water course. The movement retarding surface is provided with a high friction coating which retards sliding movement in a downstream direction of the surface of the raft which contacts the movement retarding surface, and induces rotation of the raft and movement towards the opposite wall. As the raft rotates into contact with the movement expediting surface it encounters no frictional resistance, and the spin is accelerated by the force of gravity acting on the mass of the raft as it moves downhill. The spinning raft increases thrill and introduces uncertainty among the passengers regarding who will be in a position to be splashed when the raft hits the splash zone.

3. Claims

Although they are not always logically consistent and structured, patent claims are ultimately understandable. As suggested at the beginning of the chapter, your best approach is to look for patent claims that are easy to understand and study them first.

As explained in Chapter 1, patent claims establish the legal boundaries or scope of an invention. They are the standard by which patent rights are measured. When a patent owner sues for infringement, the owner contends that someone has made, used, sold, offered for sale, or imported an invention that has all of the elements of one claim or that closely fits the description of the invention contained in the claims. (In patent terms, the infringing invention is said to be "reading on the claims.") In this manner, claims function like the boundaries in a deed for real estate—everything within them belongs to the owner.

You face a few challenges when you examine patent claims. First, you have to figure out how to decipher them. Claims follow strict requirements: they are sentence fragments, always start with an initial capital letter, contain one period, and don't include any quotation marks or parentheses (except in mathematical or chemical formulas).

Another challenge may arise if you're not sure what claims you plan to make for your invention. This type of uncertainty can make it difficult to determine whether your invention infringes the claims in another patent. The structure of patent claims only adds to this confusion. There are two types of claims: independent and dependent claims. The independent claim is written as broadly as possible. It's followed by successively narrower claims designed to specifically recite the invention's unique features (the dependent claims). These dependent claims incorporate the independent claims but act to diversify your patent's coverage. If your independent claim is your main "recipe," the independent claims are variations that provide a diverse menu for stopping infringers.

Chapter 2 includes many examples of patent claims. You may not have to read patent claims when making your prior-art search. Usually, the claims simply repeat—in a more convoluted style—the information in the specification and drawings.

> EXAMPLE: Compare the abstract for U.S. Pat. 5,989,126, above with the first claim of the patent. As you will see, you can

often acquire the basic claims information by reading the abstract and specification.

What is claimed is:

1. A spin mechanism for use with an amusement ride including one or more circular water rafts constrained within a water course having a floor and upstanding walls for containing and directing a flow of water for carrying said water rafts, the spin mechanism comprising:

a movement retarding means adapted to be interactive with a surface of the water raft for retarding the movement past of said water raft, said movement retarding means mounted to a first wall of the watercourse; and,

a movement expediting means adapted to be interactive with the surface of the water raft for permitting free movement past of the water raft, the movement expediting means mounted to a second wall of the watercourse opposite said first wall;

said movement retarding means adapted to be extended a sufficient distance into the watercourse towards said movement expediting means to force a passing water raft into contact with the movement expediting means.

The specification and the drawings often contain more information about the invention than the claims do, because the claims only describe what is being protected—for example, you might describe many features of a musical instrument but only seek protection of the instrument's mouthpiece. For that reason, reading the specification is sometimes the best approach for purposes of patent art searching.

A patent examiner is primarily interested in whether your invention has been described in prior-art documents (examiners say that these documents "anticipate" your invention), not whether your invention infringes an in-force patent. Therefore, it is the prior art itself, not the claims, against which your invention will be judged.

⚠ **Need help sorting out patent claims?** If you feel overwhelmed by patent claims issues, seek assistance from a patent attorney or a patent agent. You can find more detailed information on patent claims in *Patent It Yourself*, by David Pressman (Nolo).

4. Reading a Patent and Distinguishing Prior Art

As you read about previous inventions, you should begin thinking about how you can distinguish your ideas from the prior art. You can do this by taking notes on each patent to explain how your invention differs physically—for example, it has a different shape, size, or parts. You should also explain how your invention provides superior results—for example, your invention is faster, cleaner, more efficient, less expensive or more versatile.

Below is an example of how prior art was distinguished for the hand rest for an artist's easel (U.S. Pat. 6,565,059) discussed in Chapter 2.

EXAMPLE: Distinguishing prior art for hand rest for an artist's easel (U.S. Pat. 6,565,059)

Other types of hand rest devices are also known in the art. For example, U.S. Pat. 5,141,198 to Marion E. Hoyt discloses an apparatus for steadying one's arm at an easel and use thereof. However, the Hoyt '198 patent provides only a single point of origin for the arc of the hand rest member such that the hand rest member is at an uncomfortable angle for some portions of the canvas, and has the further drawback of not providing a means of ensuring that some part of the hand rest member will not drag against the artist's work if accidentally dropped.

U.S. Pat. 3,815,856 to Angelo J. Cortimilia discloses a hand rest attachment for artist's easel that enables the artist to rest and steady his hand. However, the Cortimilia '856 patent applies only to floor easels and makes no provision for tabletop easels. Additionally, since the Cortimilia '856 device is affixed to the easel with several fasteners, it is not easily attached or detached from the easel for multiple uses on the same piece of work. Thereby, the artist would be forced to either paint with the device interfering with his workspace or take several minutes to attach and detach the device with each use.

Similarly, U.S. Pat. 5,765,791 to Raymond R. Givonetti discloses a hand rest for an easel that provides a palm rest within which the artist's hand rests. However, the Givonetti '791 patent does not provide for free movement of the hand along the support member, and the device must be remounted if the arc defined by the initial placement does not cover the area within which the artist desires to work.

Likewise, U.S. Pat. 5,299,772 to Michael S. Weber discloses multifunctional tools for artists that provide a hand bridge upon which the hand can be rested. The Weber '772 patent is similar to the previously described maulstick device, with a hand bridge pivotally mounted on the frame of a canvas. However, the Weber '772 device allows only three positions in which the hand bridge may reside, and has the further drawback of supporting the distal end of the hand bridge against the canvas.

U.S. Pat. 5,172,883 to Acop J. Amirian discloses an artist's tool which enables the artist to rest his hand while painting a canvas. The Amirian '883 device has a horizontal support that can be vertically adjusted and a vertical support which can be horizontally adjusted. However, the Amirian '883 device is designed such that it can be used on only one type and or size of easel. This device can not easily be removed from the easel and placed on another easel of a different size and construction.

Lastly, U.S. Pat. Des. 376,618 to Tommy N. Hix discloses an ornamental design for a hand rest, presumably to be used in conjunction with an artist's easel. However, the Hix '618 patent does not provide any means of attachment to an easel, and has the additional deficiency of only allowing motion in a horizontal plane.

E. Finding Nonpatent Prior Art

To search for prior art beyond U.S. patents, your best place to start is the Internet. There, you'll find a massive storehouse of non-patented prior art. Here are some tips that will help you sift through countless Web pages to find the information you need.

- **Check online stores.** If your idea is commercial, you may find similar inventions already for sale in an online store or outlet.

EXAMPLE: Imagine you invented a multi-track recording device that can connect to a computer. You want to review prior art that is currently available for sale. By typing "multi track" (or "multitrack") into the search engine at the Musician's Friend website (www.musiciansfriend.com), you will find many patented and unpatented multitrack recorders that connect to computers.

- **Embrace Google.com.** Search engines come and go, but none seems to perform as consistently and efficiently as Google .com (www.google.com). In addition to providing links to relevant websites, Google provides thumbnail illustrations culled from the search terms as well as news group commentary on the search terms. For more advanced searches using multiple fields and connectors, try Google's "Advanced Search Features." If you are a heavy Google user, download the Google Toolbar (found at Google .com), so you won't have to keep returning to the Google home page to perform each search.

- **Try NorthernLight.com.** In addition to Google, we recommend using NorthernLight.com (www.northernlight .com). This search engine digs into private collections of articles for reasonable fees ($3 or less per article).

- **Use a master search engine.** In addition to individual search engines such as Google, there are master search engines like Copernic (www.copernic.com) or Dogpile (www.dogpile.com) that search using several individual search engines simultaneously.

- **Search foreign patents.** You can search a worldwide network of patents for free. At sites such as Espacenet.com (http://ep.espacenet.com), you can search the abstracts and titles of 30 million worldwide documents in English. In addition, you can search the full text of the resources at the World Intellectual Property Office (WIPO) and the European Patent Office in the original language.

- **Check the Thomas Register.** The Thomas Register (www.thomas register.com) can enhance your prior-art searching by providing you with images and text from thousands of company catalogs as well as providing websites, CAD imagery (computer-assisted drawings), and other product information.

Beyond the Internet: Hitting the Stacks

Much as we love the Internet for finding nonpatented prior art, a thorough search requires that you—or a professional searcher—visit the stacks of a local university engineering library (or similar institution) to research scientific data that may not exist online. Keep in mind that any printed publication, in any language, that was published before your date of invention is prior art to your invention. That includes technical specifications, owner's manuals, user's manuals, Web pages, textbooks, business plans, case studies, magazine articles, or any other printed publications. A visit to an engineering library, such as the Research Library at Getty Museum, may be essential to conduct a thorough prior-art search.

F. After the Preliminary Search

Once you've completed your preliminary search and reviewed your prior art, you must decide whether to proceed with a more thorough search. If you are concerned that the prior art you have uncovered could defeat your patent, you may want to put off filing for a patent until you get a professional opinion from a lawyer (at a cost of about

$250-$350 an hour). If you are not sure whether the prior art poses a threat to your invention, or you may want to hire a professional searcher or perform a more extensive search yourself. We explain these options below.

1. Hiring a Patent Searcher

Professional patent searchers come in two flavors: those who are licensed to practice before the USPTO (these patent attorneys and agents are known as registered representatives) and those who are not licensed, known as lay searchers. Registered representatives have passed a USPTO test demonstrating their knowledge of patent law. Lay searchers—who are usually knowledgeable in one or two fields of invention—charge less, often half of what registered representatives charge.

Fees for patent searchers range from $100 to $500 for lay searchers, and from $300 and $1,200 for searches by registered representatives. These fees don't include an opinion on patentability—that is, the searcher will not provide an opinion as to whether the USPTO will issue a patent. Only registered representatives are allowed to give you an opinion on patentability—lay searchers have to keep their opinions to themselves. Some patent searchers charge a flat fee; others charge by the hour. If you plan to do some of the work yourself, you'll save money by requesting hourly billing.

You can locate patent searchers in the Yellow Pages of local telephone directories. You can also use Internet search engines (for example, Google.com or NorthernLight.com) —look under "Patent Searchers." All registered representatives are listed at the USPTO website. (To find the list, click the drop-down menu entitled "Select a Search Collection" at the USPTO home page. Then choose "Patent Attorneys and Agents.") Keep in mind that the attorney or agent will either have to travel to the USPTO or hire an associate to make the search—this means that it may not make financial sense to hire a searcher from your home town, depending on where you live.

You'll need to give your searcher a lot of information about your invention, including:

- a description of the invention
- drawings
- information about the class/subclass, if known
- identification of the invention's novel features, and
- any required deadlines.

When you use a patent attorney or agent, requesting a search will not compromise the status of your invention as a trade secret. By law, your conversation with a registered representative is considered a confidential communication. This is not the case with an unlicensed searcher, however. If you use a lay searcher, you should ask your searcher to sign a nondisclosure agreement.

The *Official Gazette*

The USPTO puts out a weekly publication called the *Official Gazette for Patents*, which lists pertinent bibliographic data, the abstract, and one figure or drawing for every patent issued that week. You can view this publication online at the PTO website; PTDLs and some other public libraries maintain copies of the *Official Gazette for Patents* in print or on microfiche. If the drawing and claim in the *Official Gazette* look relevant, go to the actual patent online.

2. Searching at the USPTO

You can also try doing your own more thorough search—but only if you're willing to take a trip to the USPTO's new location in Alexandria, Virginia. The advantage of searching at the USPTO is that you have access to copies of all U.S. patents arranged according to their classifications. The public can access patent paper files without charge and staff members often assist you in locating appropriate files and reference materials. In addition to patent copies, the USPTO search facilities maintain a variety of reference materials including manuals, indices, dictionaries, reference publications, and *Official Gazettes*.

Beware however, the USPTO is in the process of getting rid of its paper materials. Over time, many paper files and patents will be scanned and replaced by digital copies, only. Similarly, new copies of the *Official Gazette* (OG) are available in digital format only (published each Tuesday). The OG announces patents being issued and trademarks being registered or published for opposition. Volumes relating specifically to patents or trademarks are available in the corresponding search facility. ■

Chapter 7

Document Your Invention

*P*rior to the 16th century, artists' ability to draw and sketch was limited by the scarcity of paper. The shortage ended, however, when thousands of garments—belonging to the victims of the Great Plague—were converted into paper. The sudden abundance of this basic commodity didn't just open up the world of drawing; it also led to a much larger and more inclusive use—documentation. Once paper was available, for example, Leonard da Vinci was able to create and maintain volumes of notebooks— all witness to his ideas, sketches, thoughts, and innovations.

Although he considered himself an artist first and foremost, Da Vinci's notebooks also documented brilliant technological prophecies —he sketched submarines and helicopters centuries before they were perfected, and had groundbreaking observations in engineering, anatomy, and ballistics.

Perhaps even more impressive than his prophecies and inventions was the methodology he used within his notebooks—the way he documented, verified, and authenticated his innovations. His notebooks enabled the reader to understand, make, and use his inventions. By combining textual descriptions and detailed drawings, he pioneered a universally adopted system of documentation that we now refer to as the inventor's notebook.

In this chapter, we discuss documentation —the key to acquiring and protecting patent rights. As an artist, entertainer, or innovator, you are probably somewhat familiar with methods of memorializing your ideas. What we discuss here is basically a more formal— but equally important—method of preserving your ideas.

Using the same tools as Da Vinci—words and drawings that demonstrate how to make and use your invention—you can prove that you invented your great idea, and show the USPTO and future inventors exactly what that great idea is. Equally important, using a documentation system known as the Provisional Patent Application, you can preserve your place in line at the USPTO for one year without running up the expenses associated with filing a patent application.

Documentation is important for three reasons:

- **It memorializes your invention's conception and reduction to practice.** Conception is the mental part of inventing—how an invention is formulated or a problem is solved. Reduction to practice refers to the inventor's ability to demonstrate that the invention works for its intended purpose. Reduction to practice can be accomplished by actual reduction to practice (actually building and testing the invention and keeping track of the progress in an inventor's notebook) or by constructive reduction to practice (preparing a patent application or Provisional Patent Application that shows how to make and use the invention and demonstrates that it works). Documenting conception and reduction to practice can also help defeat prior art.

- **It shows you are the owner of the invention.** Documentation establishes who is the first and true inventor and prevents confusion as to ownership rights. Documentation assists in proving ownership, for example, when two inventors simultaneously and independently conceive of an invention, or when several people are working on the same problem together. If you work with others on your invention, your notebook can help document each person's contributions. This evidence may help defeat claims by others that they are co-inventors who should share ownership of your invention. If you are an employee, you can use documentation (such as an inventor's notebook) to show that your invention was not developed during your hours of employment and that you did not use employer resources or knowledge. This evidence will help you prove that you—not your employer— own the invention and are entitled to the patent.

- **If necessary, it may help you defeat a patent owner who claims you are an infringer.** Documentation can also save you from bogus claims of patent infringement. If you are sued by a patent owner and you can demonstrate that your allegedly infringing invention was publicly available and known prior to the patent owner's date of invention, you may be able to invalidate the patent (and thereby defeat any claim of patent infringement).

Documentation Can Defeat Prior Art

Maintaining dates of conception and reduction to practice can help defeat prior art. A prior-art reference is any patent, other publication, or prior public knowledge or use of an invention that casts doubt on the originality of your invention. A prior-art reference has an effective date—usually its publication date, or, if it is a U.S. patent, the filing date. You can prevent a patent examiner from using a prior-art reference against your patent application if you can show either that:

- you built and tested the invention or filed a Provisional Patent Application (PPA) (see Section C) prior to the reference's effective date, or
- you conceived of the invention prior to the reference's effective date, and were diligent in building and testing the invention or filing a PPA or regular patent application up through the reference's effective date. The application must be filed within a year after the date of any publication or the issue date of any patent.

What Is Your Date of Invention?

The U.S. follows the "first to invent" rule. If there is a dispute between you and another inventor, the person with the earliest date of invention gets the patent. The patent laws establish your date of invention as either:

- the date when you "reduced your invention to practice"—that is, the date on which you could prove that it actually worked, or
- the date you conceived of your invention, as long as you diligently reduced it to practice soon after.

Don't Use the "Post Office Patent." There's a myth that you can document conception by mailing a description of the invention to yourself by certified (or registered) mail and keeping the sealed envelope. The PTO's Board of Appeals and Patent Interferences has ruled that such "Post Office Patents" have little legal value.

This chapter focuses on two overlapping forms of documentation, both used as part of the patent process:

- Informal documentation—for example, your notes, records, and informal drawings authenticating your invention process (usually maintained in an inventor's notebook). We discuss how to maintain an inventor's notebook in Section A.
- Formal documentation prepared for USPTO filings—for example, your provisional patent application (an abbreviated version of a regular patent application that can preserve your place in line at the USPTO) and your regular patent application and formal drawings. In Section B, we'll discuss invention drawings; Section C explains how to prepare and complete a Provisional Patent Application.

The most formal record of your documentation—a regular utility patent application—is beyond the scope of this chapter. In Chapter 9, we'll discuss the basic requirements for preparing and filing a utility patent.

A. Inventor's Notebook

The most reliable and useful way to document your art and entertainment invention is to use a permanently bound notebook with the pages consecutively numbered, usually known as an inventor's notebook. In addition to protecting your patent rights and helping demonstrate ownership of the invention (as well as helping you feel like a *real* inventor), the inventor's notebook can be used to prove to the IRS that you are engaged in a business rather than a hobby, which affects how you are taxed and what you can deduct from any income you earn from your inventing activities. On the practical side, your notebook will help you monitor your invention's progress and determine what remains to be done.

Engineering and laboratory supply stores sell these notebooks with lines at the bottom of each page for signatures and signature dates of the inventor and the witnesses. A standard crackle-finish school notebook is

Documentation: Courses of Action

How you use the various methods of documentation discussed in this chapter depend on your invention, your timing (when you plan on making a public announcement about your invention), and your finances. Generally, there are three strategies for documenting your invention:

- **Rely on your notebook and trade secrecy.** This is the least expensive method of documenting and protecting an invention. You record and witness your invention in a notebook, and maintain the secrecy of your invention by use of confidentiality and nondisclosure agreements.
- **File for a patent.** If money is no object and you're on the verge of selling or licensing your product or design, you should consider preparing a utility or design patent by yourself or consult with a patent attorney or patent agent about pursuing a patent. An attorney or patent agent can help you decide whether the invention is patentable and prepare the patent application.
- **File a Provisional Patent Application.** If you're not sure when (or even if) you'll offer your invention for sale, you can prepare a Provisional Patent Application, a document that preserves your place in line at the patent office. (Provisional Patent Applications are covered in Section C, below.)

You do not need to think of these as mutually exclusive approaches. For example, you can maintain a notebook and secrecy, file a Provisional Patent Application, *and* file for a patent in succession, depending on your invention plans and finances.

also suitable, provided that the inventor numbers all of the pages consecutively, and has each page or each invention description dated, signed, and witnessed.

The main purposes of the inventor's notebook are to establish the date you conceived your art and entertainment invention and to show that you were diligent about reducing it to practice. You do this by writing in your notebook all the pertinent facts about your work on your invention—including:

- a functional description of the invention— that is, an explanation of what it does and how it works
- a structural description of the invention— that is, a static description of how the invention is constructed
- descriptions of all experiments related to your invention (these should be detailed enough to allow someone else to replicate the experiment—for example, list the equipment you used and the methods and conditions of the experiment)
- calculations
- test results—both successes and failures
- sketches of the invention (these don't need to conform to special patent application rules)

- how your invention differs from previous similar inventions, and
- if other people are working on the invention with you, their identities and roles in the invention process.

1. Entering Information in the Notebook

To avoid disputes about the accuracy or truthfulness of your notebook, follow these simple rules:

- Use a bound notebook (either softcover or hardcover) so that pages can't easily be removed or inserted.
- List your name and address on the front of the notebook.
- Make all entries in nonerasable ink; use the same pen for a whole page.
- Leave the first few pages of the notebook blank so you can use them later as a table of contents.
- Date the first entry in the upper right-hand corner of the page and fully describe the idea for your invention. If you've already spent time working on your invention, summarize the work you've done. Also, record the date you conceived the invention, the names of people with whom you've discussed your idea, and any tests or experiments you've performed.
- Write legibly.
- Make regular entries in chronological order—preferably every day you work on your invention.
- Date and sign every page. Never back-date a page.

- Use the past tense ("I did") when you're writing about work that has actually been performed; use the future tense ("I will do") to describe work not yet done.
- Describe your work clearly and concisely; don't use jargon.
- Never erase or "white out" mistakes. To correct an entry, draw a line though it and then make a new entry. Be sure to initial the changes.
- Don't leave any blank pages or large blank spaces in the notebook. Write from one edge of the page to the other and fill each page from top to bottom. Fill in blank areas with one or two diagonal lines.
- If you use a computer to take notes, make drawings, or store data, print your documents and have them dated, signed, and witnessed. Then paste them into your notebook. You should refer to the pasted material by handwritten entries in the notebook—this helps show the material wasn't added after the fact.
- Paste photographs, drawings, and other material that can't be directly signed and witnessed into your notebook. Write a caption for the material that briefly describes it (for example, "photo of saxophone stand in use on stage") and draw a line from the caption to the pasted material.
- Make at least one entry every month, so it doesn't look like you've abandoned your invention.
- Each page should be signed and dated by at least one, and preferably two, witnesses (see Section A2, below).

- Keep your notebook in a safe place. You don't need to put it in a bank safe deposit box, but at least lock it in a desk drawer.

2. Witnessing Your Notebook

Each entry in your inventor's notebook should be witnessed. This means you must ask someone to read the page, sign it, and date it. If you ever need to use your notebook as evidence in court, this same person can testify that the entry in your notebook was made on the date stated and has not subsequently been altered or forged.

You can use one witness, but it's best to have two. This gives you a better chance of having a witness available—perhaps years later—to testify in court. And two witnesses who say the same thing are more convincing than one.

Not just anybody can serve as your witnesses. First, the people you pick must be disinterested—that is, they won't benefit financially or in any other way from your invention. This means you can't use your spouse or other family members, investors, or co-inventors as witnesses. A knowledgeable friend or colleague might make a good candidate. In addition, your witnesses must actually be able to read and understand the entries. If your invention is quite simple, any intelligent, disinterested person can serve as a witness. But if the invention is complex, you must use witnesses who have the scientific and/or technical background necessary to understand what you're doing.

The following phrase (or one similar to it) should appear before the witnesses' signatures: "The above confidential information was read and understood by me on (date)." Neither the witnesses' signatures nor your signature need to be notarized.

If getting every page of your notebook witnessed is too difficult, make sure that the pages showing your conception of the invention and any building and testing you do are witnessed. These are the key entries in the notebook for patent purposes.

B. Invention Drawings

If you and your loved ones were competing on *Family Feud* and the category was "Invention Artist," chances are good that you could score by naming Rube Goldberg, whose cartoons depict contraptions that use maximum effort to produce minimal results. (See cartoon below.) Regardless of their comic value, each element of a Rube Goldberg contrivance is clearly drawn and labeled with a letter or number that corresponds to accompanying explanatory text. This method gives the viewer excellent instructions on how to make and use each Rube Goldberg invention.

We use the term "drawing" to refer to any illustration of your invention, whether a line drawing, a flowchart, a schematic, or a photograph. Drawings communicate far more effectively than words—if you don't believe this, imagine trying to understand how a Rube Goldberg invention works just by reading the text—and will help you accurately describe how to build and use your invention.

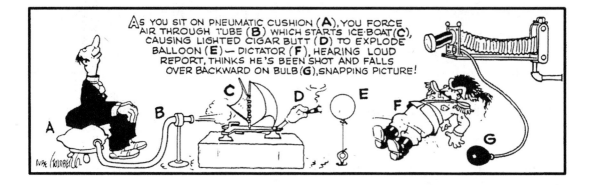

Documenting Conception: The PTO's Disclosure Document Program

Even if you don't use a lab notebook or don't want to rely on witnesses, you can document the conception of an invention by filing a special signed document under the PTO's Disclosure Document Program (DDP). The primary advantage of the DDP is that an inventor doesn't need witnesses to provide credible evidence of the date of conception—you just have to file the document. The disadvantage is that the PTO will destroy your disclosure document after two years unless you file for a patent based on the disclosure. For this reason, many inventors prefer to document conception using a lab notebook instead of the DDP.

To file a DDP, the inventor sends the signed document, a cover letter, a check for the fee (currently $10), and a stamped return receipt postcard to the PTO. The procedures and form for filing a disclosure document are provided in David Pressman's *Patent It Yourself* (Nolo).

Unfortunately, the DDP is often used as the basis of invention scams in which disreputable organizations prey on inventors. Their ads may describe a "special government program" whereby the Patent Office will record and preserve any invention for a nominal fee. The organization charges several hundred dollars to file a disclosure document, a procedure that the inventor could manage for $10. Despite what these scams claim, the DDP does not "secure priority," "reserve rights," or take advantage of a "grace period" for two years. Keep in mind that the DDP is not a substitute for filing a Provisional Patent Application. The DDP documents only conception. The Provisional Patent Application documents reduction to practice.

If you're using an inventor's notebook or filing a Provisional Patent Application, you can prepare and use informal invention drawings. These are easy-to-prepare sketches that should complement (and definitely should not contradict) your written explanation of how to make and use your invention. If you are filing a design patent or utility patent application, you will need to furnish more formal drawings, often prepared by a patent draftsperson.

For help preparing patent drawings, read *How to Make Patent Drawings,* by Jack Lo and David Pressman (Nolo).

Whether you use rudimentary sketches or professionally drafted drawings, you should organize and label your drawings according to traditional patent drawing rules, discussed below. These drawing rules are most suitable for mechanical devices or processes. If you are seeking to patent a business process or software process, that may be best illustrated by a flowchart or other form of drawing, as described in Section B5.

1. The View

As you may have noticed from the invention illustrations in previous chapters, patent drawings commonly depict inventions in different views or figures—for example, top views, side views, or disassembled ("exploded") views. You should use as many views as necessary to demonstrate your invention, including all of its potential versions or embodiments. Each view provides another way of "seeing" the invention. Each view is given a discrete figure number (abbreviated as "Fig" in patent law). For example, the inventor of a device that functions as a travel bag and soundproofing device for a saxophone used the views seen in Illustration 7-1.

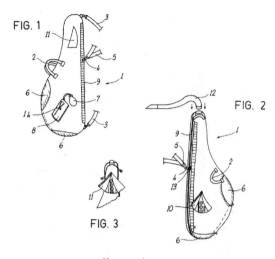

Illustration 7-1

When you create your informal drawings, label each figure consecutively in Arabic numerals—for example Fig 1, Fig 2, Fig 3—and arrange the figures in numerical order on your drawing sheets. Use letters only as suffixes after the numbers, if you want to group several related views together—for example, Fig 1A, Fig 1B, Fig 2A, Fig 2B, and so on.

Here are a few tips that will help you decide which views to include:

- In order to show the internal workings of your invention, you may use an exploded view (Illustration 7-2), in which the parts of the invention are separated but shown in relation to each other.

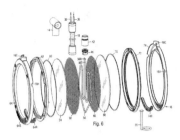

Illustration 7-2

- You may also use views that are not drawings in the traditional sense, such as schematics or flowcharts (see Section B5, below).
- Perspective views (in which you can see several angles and sides of your invention at once) are often more illustrative than straight-on side or top views.
- Show hidden lines by using broken (dashed) lines instead of straight lines (Illustration 7-3).

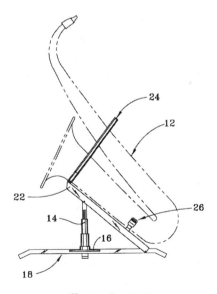

Illustration 7-3

- You do not need to show features that are prior art. For example, if you have invented a decoding system for a sub-woofer enclosed in a traditional speaker cabinet, you do not need to include the speaker cabinet in your drawings unless it is essential for understanding your invention.
- If you're reducing or enlarging the dimensions of your invention, be sure that the parts are in scale—that is, reduced or enlarged in the same proportion.

2. Drawing Sheets

When preparing drawings, place each figure on a separate piece of paper or, if you are entering it in your inventor's notebook, on a separate page. (Each of these sheets is known as a "drawing sheet.") Label and number each separate figure. Number each drawing sheet on the top using a fraction in which the numerator is the number of the drawing sheet and the denominator is the total number of drawing sheets (for example 1/4, 2/4, 3/4, etc.). If you have only one drawing sheet, you do not need to number it.

Here are some tips for creating drawing sheets:

- Use the same size paper for all of your drawing sheets.
- Include a margin of approximately one inch all around each drawing sheet (don't frame the margin with a line; leave it invisible).
- You can group two or more figures on a drawing sheet of 8½ by 11 paper, as long as the page doesn't look crowded.

• Portray each view in an upright position, large enough so that the parts can be seen clearly. Don't connect figures on a drawing sheet (except for electrical waveforms, which may be connected with dashed lines to show relative timing).

3. Identify the Invention Components and Give Each a Number

Use reference numbers and letters to identify the parts or elements of your invention. We recommend that you conform to the official numbering rules used for regular patent applications. Doing so will help you save time if you decide to apply for a regular patent.

The general rule is that every part you will mention or explain in your application should be numbered. The point of the reference number is to help the reader understand what you're talking about when you describe your invention. Here are some tips for labeling:

- Start with a number higher than the number of your highest Fig number, so the reference numbers won't be confused with your figure numbers.
- Number the parts consecutively in even numbers—for example, 10, 12, 14—so that you can insert consecutive odd numbers later if necessary.
- Use the same number with suffix letters to associate and distinguish related parts—for example, "the machine has a left lever 10L and a right lever 10R."
- Write numbers near the part but, if possible, outside the boundaries of the drawing (for example, in Illustration 7-4, the artist was able to keep all of the

reference numbers outside of the drawing with the exception of 14, 23, and 24).

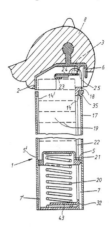

Illustration 7-4

- Don't write a number across a line.
- Don't forget to number parts or items that are used in connection with your invention. For example, the inventor of a tie with concealed pockets must describe the types of items—credit cards, bills, paper—that can be concealed in the invention. (See Illustration 7-5.)

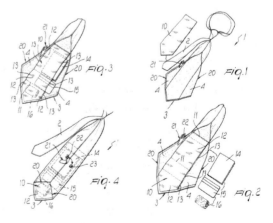

Illustration 7-5

4. Getting Started

You have two related goals when preparing your drawings: (1) to illustrate how to make and use your invention, and (2) to visually represent every element of your invention for which you intend to claim patent rights. In a sense, these goals serve the same purpose. As writer/inventor David Lindsay puts it, "In the end, the whole shebang has to look like something that functions."

You want to show how your invention achieves its result, so your views should demonstrate the steps in your process or the procedure for using your device. Your first step is to imagine the potential views needed to illustrate your invention. You can accomplish this in two ways: (1) if you have a prototype, take pictures of it and organize the photos in order of the steps of operation, or (2) if you don't have a prototype, start with a series of elemental drawings (stick figures are fine). Once you have an idea which views you will need, choose a plan of attack based on your artistic skills, the nature of your invention, and your progress in modeling the invention. Here are your options for creating reliable informal drawings:

⚠️ **Formal drawings are required for a regular patent application.** This chapter explains how to prepare informal invention drawings—drawings that accurately describe your invention but may not meet the standards required when filing a regular patent application with the USPTO. You may use informal drawings in your inventor's notebook, as part of your

Provisional Patent Application, or for any other purpose other than the filing of a regular patent application. (They are particularly helpful when pitching your idea or as rough sketches for someone who must prepare formal drawings.) You must file formal drawings prior to examination of your regular patent applications.

- If you're an inventor who can draw: If you have drawing skills, render drawings of your invention accurately in terms of perspective and proportion. To get started, examine formal drawings for patented inventions similar to yours and create drawings that track their perspective and content. Don't worry about providing the same level of craftsmanship as a professional draftsperson; as long as you provide accurate representations, you'll do just fine.
- If you have a prototype but you can't draw: If you have a prototype but you don't have drawing skills, we recommend that you take photos of the invention and either use the photographs as your informal drawings or create informal drawings by tracing the photographs.
- If you don't have a prototype and you can't draw: If you find yourself with neither drawing skills nor a prototype, you'll need to consider bringing in some technological aids or outside help. For example, you could (a) hire a prototype maker to prepare a three-dimensional model of your invention, then proceed through the steps above; (b) hire an artist to create drawings (you describe it,

then the artist draws it); or (c) draw your invention using a software program or clip art images.

- If you need more than illustrations: If you think you'll need schematics, flow-charts, tables, or graphics other than figurative drawings, review Section 5, below. You can probably create a credible flow chart or table manually or with the aid of a computer. Schematics for electrical inventions may prove trickier—depending on your skill, you may need professional assistance.

5. Flowcharts and Schematics

Nonfigurative patent drawings, such as flow-charts, electrical schematics, and tables, can be used to illustrate inventions as diverse as chemical compounds, business methods, electric circuits, and software. We explain the basics for creating flowcharts depicting software inventions, but we don't provide step-by-step explanations for preparing schematics and tables; if you are designing software or are an electrical engineer, you probably already know how to prepare these more technical drawings. You can find suitable assistance by examining similar inventions.

a. Flowcharts

A flowchart can help you illustrate graphically the steps in a process or program. Each element in the process is represented by an icon or symbol such as a circle, rectangle, or diamond. The user follows the flow of the

process, indicated by arrows and lines. In Illustration 7-6, an inventor uses a flowchart to illustrate an Internet-based advertising scheme. In Illustration 7-7, the inventor of the fashion patent discussed in Chapter 2 uses a simple flowchart to demonstrate the steps of acquiring personal fashion information.

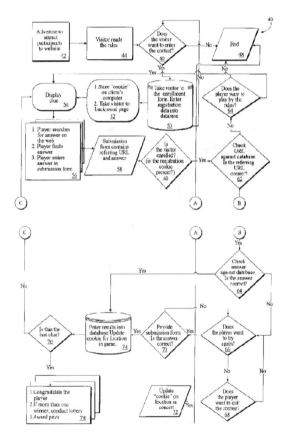

Illustration 7-6

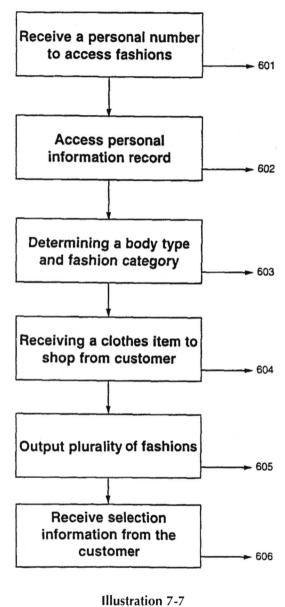

Receive a personal number to access fashions → 601

Access personal information record → 602

Determining a body type and fashion category → 603

Receiving a clothes item to shop from customer → 604

Output plurality of fashions → 605

Receive selection information from the customer → 606

Illustration 7-7

Tips for Creating a Flowchart

Here are some tips that will help you create a streamlined flowchart:

- Avoid using too many different shapes in your chart—if you find yourself having to resort to trapezoids and rhombuses, your viewers are not going to be able to follow your process.
- If necessary, break your process into separate steps, each with its own flow-chart.
- If blocks are connected, label them as one figure; if not, label them as separate figures.
- Ask a friend to review the chart and give you some feedback—is it easy to follow? Is it legible?

If you'd like to learn more about preparing flowcharts, read *Flow Charts, Plain & Simple,* by Joiner Associates (Oriel, Inc.).

b. Software Inventions: Flow Charts or Computer Code?

In order to provide the "best mode" (the inventor's preferred method) of making and using software inventions, programmers must reveal as much as possible about their inventions. The disclosure must be "full, clear, concise, and exact." (35 U.S.C. § 112.) You can do this with:

- a well-drafted flowchart that provides enough details to allow a reasonably skilled programmer to write the invention

- a combination of a well-drafted flow-chart and a printed copy of the program code, preferably in object code format, or
- a printed copy of the source code.

Program code may be the clearest and most exact way to divulge a software program. However, if you include program code in a regular patent application, then devious infringers can copy the code once the patent application is published.

C. The Provisional Patent Application

The independent artist or entertainer who creates an innovation may feel insecure within the world of patents. Acquiring a patent sounds good on paper, but the reality of it is frightening when you have to pull thousands of dollars out of a savings account to pursue your goal. Is there any way to lower the risk while preserving your patent rights? Yes, thanks to a law signed into effect in 1995, you can use an effective, fast, and relatively cheap procedure—the Provisional Patent Application—to safeguard your place in line at the USPTO until you file a regular patent application.

A Provisional Patent Application consists of text and drawings that describe how to make and use your invention. It's a short document—often only five to ten pages—written in plain English, not the arcane language associated with regular patent applications. In fact, if you've written a technical article that accurately describes how to make and use your

invention, you can submit that as part of your application. You do not need to hire a draftsperson to prepare formal drawings; you can furnish informal drawings as long as they (in conjunction with your written statement) show how to make and use your invention. As soon as you send the description, the drawings, and a cover sheet to the USPTO by Express Mail (along with the fee—$80 as of publication of this book), you establish an effective filing date for your invention and can use the term "patent pending" on your invention—at least for 12 months from the filing date.

At the end of this chapter we provide an example of Provisional Patent Application for a doll that simulates tears using LEDs.

The doll Provisional Patent Application described above is from *Patent Pending in 24 Hours* (Nolo), a guide to preparing Provisional Patent Applications written by attorneys Richard Stim and David Pressman. For more information on preparing a Provisional Patent Application consult *Patent Pending in 24 Hours,* or *Patent It Yourself (*Nolo), by David Pressman.

A Provisional Patent Application will not, by itself, get you a patent. In order to patent your invention and obtain some of the benefits listed above, you must file a regular patent application (a more complex document) and the patent must be approved by the USPTO. The Provisional Patent Application is a simple, inexpensive strategy to preserve your rights while you decide whether to file for a regular patent. But if you want that patent, you will have to file a regular application within a year after you file your Provisional Application.

What If You Don't File Your Regular Application on Time?

You won't automatically lose your patent rights if you fail to file a regular patent application within a year after you file the provisional application. But you will lose the benefits described in this section—for example, the earlier filing date, and the right to claim "patent pending" status. You can still file a regular patent and acquire patent rights to your invention, as long as you did not publish information about your invention or offer it for sale more than a year before you file the regular patent application.

1. Advantages

Filing a Provisional Patent Application confers a number of advantages:

- **Opportunity to assess commercial potential.** Once you file the Provisional Patent Application, you will have one year to assess the commercial potential of your invention before you have to prepare a patent application. That should be enough time to figure out whether your idea will be a moneymaker—and, therefore, whether it's worth the expense of filing a regular patent application.
- **Patent pending notice.** There's a certain cachet to labeling your invention "patent pending" or "patent applied for," labels

you may use once you file a Provisional Patent Application. Keep in mind, however, that marking your invention "patent pending" doesn't give you any patent rights. You cannot stop anyone from copying, selling, or using your invention during this period. Patent rights—the ability to stop others from infringing—do not kick in until after your regular patent application is approved.

- **Prove reduction to practice without building and testing your invention.** You don't have to build a prototype to "reduce to practice" your invention. (Neither the Wright Brothers nor Alexander Graham Bell had successfully demonstrated their inventions when they applied for their groundbreaking patents.) You can prove constructive reduction to practice by completing the informal documentation required to file a Provisional Patent Application (or the more formal documentation required for a regular patent application). If you do a constructive reduction to practice, your date of invention is the date you filed your provisional or regular patent application.

There is a potential downside to using the Provisional Patent Application for constructive reduction to practice. Without a working prototype, you may not be able to convince others to license and manufacture your invention. If you really want to market your invention, you will have to create a prototype eventually. Even if you've already built and tested a working model of your invention, you can still file a Provisional Patent Application to claim the other benefits described in this chapter (or you can file a regular patent application to obtain the patent).

- **Establish an official United States patent application filing date for the invention.** Filing a Provisional Patent Application gives you an official patent filing date. As explained above, the USPTO awards patents to the first to invent, not the first to file a patent application. But don't let this rule lull you into complacency—if you want a patent, you should get to the patent office as early as possible. According to many patent experts, the first person to file at the USPTO will often win the battle over who was first to invent something (known as "priority"). The filing date is also important for another reason: If your patent later issues, it becomes part of the prior art against which other patent applications are judged. Other inventors who try to patent the same invention must prove that they invented their creation before you filed your Provisional Patent Application.

- **Your application is preserved in confidence.** The Provisional Patent Application guards your secrecy while preserving your rights at the USPTO. Nobody at the USPTO will read your Provisional Patent Application unless (1) you file a regular application within 12 months, and (2) a dispute arises as to your rights. Otherwise, the Provisional Patent Application will sit safely tucked away in a file cabinet. If you file a regular patent application, the USPTO

will treat that application with secrecy for the first 18 months of the examining process. Approximately 18 months after you file your regular patent application, the USPTO will publish your patent (unless you requested nonpublication at the time you filed). Publication can be a good thing. It paves the way for you to sue later (after you get your patent) for infringements that occurred after the patent is published. On the other hand, it can be a bad thing if your secrets are released, but your patent isn't granted.

- **The expiration date of your patent is extended, if the USPTO later approves your application.** Your patent ends 20 years after the date you file your regular patent application. However, you don't get 20 years of patent rights. Because the USPTO takes one or two years to complete the examination, and because you don't get any rights until the patent actually issues, most patent owners will only have 17 to 18 years of patent rights. Filing a Provisional Patent Application can stop the clock for at least a year on patent examination. Your 20-year term starts from the date you file your regular patent application, not your Provisional Patent Application. So your patent rights, if the patent issues, end one year later than they would have if you filed a regular patent application instead of a Provisional.

- **Benefits for foreign applicants.** Inventors living outside the U.S. can benefit from filing a Provisional Patent Application because, unlike a regular patent application (that must be filed in English), a Provisional Patent Application can be filed in any language. Like their U.S. counterparts, foreign inventors can obtain the earliest possible prior art date—the date against which competing patent applications will be judged. Also, if the foreign inventor files the Provisional Patent Application and the home country patent application at the same time, the foreign inventor—like the U.S. inventor—can preserve ownership rights in the U.S. and extend the life of the U.S. patent, as described above.

2. Disadvantages

Before you sharpen your pencil and get down to work on your Provisional Patent Application, there are some potential drawbacks you should be aware of.

- **Inaccuracy will undo your protection.** If your Provisional Application is inaccurate, you can't count on it for any of the purposes described in this section—an early filing date, proof of invention, or constructive reduction to practice. Leaving out an element of your invention or failing to explain all of the operating elements could be fatal inaccuracies. Other inaccuracies include using faulty supporting data or drawings that don't match the written description.
- **Modifications require a new Provisional Application.** If you modify the manner in which your invention operates or add any new technical information that was not in the Provisional Application (known as "new matter"), you cannot rely on the Provisional Patent Application. You can file a new Provisional Application that reflects these changes. Adding, subtracting, or modifying parts, or changing the structure or operation of the parts, would qualify as a modification. Your previously filed Provisional Patent Application will not protect these new developments.
- **You must file foreign patent claims within a year.** If you fail to file for foreign patent protection within one year of your Provisional Patent Application filing date, you must file patent applications in any countries in which you seek patent protection. If you don't, you will lose any claim to use your U.S. filing date in foreign countries. If you miss the one-year deadline, you can still file in foreign countries (as long as you have not sold, publicly used, or published your invention before the foreign filing date), but you must claim a later filing date. This could be a problem if, during the period between your U.S. and foreign filing, someone else filed for a similar invention. Because the U.S. accounts for one-quarter to one-third of all sales for most patented inventions, many inventors are not interested in pursuing foreign patent rights. However, if you think that a foreign manufacturer may want licensing rights, it's generally a good idea to preserve your foreign patent rights.

3. Basic Principles for Drafting a Provisional Patent Application

If you want to file a Provisional Patent Application, we recommend that you:

- hire a patent attorney or patent agent
- read either *Patent Pending in 24 Hours* or *Patent It Yourself*, both from Nolo, or
- try a software program such as Nolo's *Patent Pending Now!*

To give you an idea of what you're in for, we've described some of the basics below. Although no formal style or format is required, the easiest way to prepare a Provisional Patent Application is to track some of the elements required for a regular patent application. Because your goal is to explain how to make and use your invention, the important questions you will need to answer are:

- What are the objects and advantages of your invention?
- What are the parts or components of your invention?
- How do the parts or components connect or interact?
- How does the invention achieve its result?
- Are there alternative ways that your invention can achieve its result?

Keep your drawings handy. Before drafting a Provisional Patent Application, prepare drawings providing visual representations of your invention. You'll need these drawings in front of you when you draft your application. For more information on preparing drawings for a Provisional Patent Application, consult *Patent Pending in 24 Hours,* by attorneys Richard Stim and David Pressman, or *How to Make Patent Drawings,* by Jack Lo and David Pressman, both published by Nolo.

a. What Are the Objects and Advantages of Your Invention?

To file for a provisional or regular patent, you'll need to be able to describe what your invention accomplishes—or in patent terminology, the "objects" of your invention.

For example, Clinton Runyon patented a stand for holding a saxophone (see Illustration 7-3). Three objects of his invention would be:

- to provide a wind instrument stand especially for saxophones, which prevents accidental rotation of the instrument relative to the instrument's support members
- to provide a stable and portable instrument stand that is both lightweight and collapsible, and
- to provide a stand that can connect to multiple stands and adapt for use with multiple instruments.

You don't have to draft your answer using the term "objects." Instead, summarize them informally in the opening statement of your provisional patent application.

EXAMPLE: If a Provisional Patent Application were prepared for the saxophone stand described above, it might introduce the objects as follows:

"I invented a stable and portable instrument stand that is both lightweight and collapsible and is especially well suited for wind instruments, particularly saxophones. The stand prevents the accidental rotation of the instrument relative to the instrument's support members. The stand can be connected to multiple stands and those stands can be adapted for use with multiple instruments."

The advantages of your invention are the qualities that make it superior to the prior art. You are not required to include your invention's advantages in your Provisional Patent Application, but it helps to distinguish and explain your invention. In some ways, your advantages will overlap with your objects. For example, the object of your invention may be to provide a stable instrument stand, which is also one of its advantages. That's fine. Provisional and regular patent applications include quite a lot of repetition and overlap from section to section.

b. What Are the Components of Your Invention and How Do They Interact?

One necessary element of a Provisional Patent Application is a "static description" of your invention. Basically, that's a description of the parts and how they interact, but not how the invention operates as a unit. In other words, you must describe each part of your invention and how it interacts or connects to all adjacent parts, a little bit like the text of a model airplane kit. For example, here is the first paragraph of a description for a device

that dispenses Pez candy tablets. (See Illustration 7-4.)

> **EXAMPLE:** Portion of static description (U.S. Pat. 4,966,305)
>
> *The tablet dispenser 1 essentially consists of the sleeve 17, the magazine 18 which is axially displaceable inside the sleeve 17 and which holds the tablets 19 indicated by means of a dashed line, and the slide 21 which is subjected to a force by the spring 20 impresses the tablets 19 against the upper end or dispensing end of the tablet dispenser 1. The spring 20 is supported on the base of the magazine 18 which possesses, on its rear, a slot 22 through which a lug of the slide 21 passes and which is open continuously along its front to permit insertion of the stack of tablets when the magazine 18 is pulled upward. The lugs 5, of the slide 21 engage the grooves 7, of the sleeve 17, which terminate before the upper end of the sleeve 17.*

Here are a few tips for drafting your description:

- If you are describing the parts in a process, explain them in order. If you are describing a machine, start from the bottom and work your way up or start from the outside and work your way inside, if that makes sense.
- Start with the main parts, then describe the components of each main part, if possible.
- Insert the reference number after the part name and don't use parentheses—

for example, "above the handle 12 is a lever 10."

- Provide a reference number for every significant part—and don't describe a part unless you give it a reference number.
- Describe the relationship between interconnecting parts—for example, "lever 10 is joined to handle 12 with a hinge 6."
- Avoid using technical language, if possible. If you do use a technical term, define it for the reader.
- The first time you describe a part, use an indefinite article such "a" or "an." For example, "A wiener-receiving bin 12 is attached." After you have introduced the part, use "the." For example, "wieners 16 then drop into the wiener-receiving bin 12." (You don't need to use "the" for parts with a number or with multiple parts. For example, "Lever 10 is connected to horizontal arms.")

Prepare a List of Your Reference Numbers

As you prepare your static description, you may find it helpful to make a list of all the reference numbers you use and the corresponding parts. This list will help you keep your names and numbers straight. You do not need to include it with your provisional patent application, but you will refer to it often as you create your list of components and describe their interaction.

---

c. How Does the Invention Achieve Its Result?

In this portion of your application, you have to get down to brass tacks and describe how your invention actually works. For example, if your goal is to create a guitar tuner or a new method of creating perspective, you must explain how someone can build and operate the tuner or use your process for creating perspective.

EXAMPLE: For some saxophone players, it's not enough to blow your own horn. You may also want to quickly send off a few notes on your electronic musical keyboard as well. So Frank K. Catalano, Jr., invented an electronic musical keyboard attachment for a saxophone.

Mr. Catalano described how to use his invention as follows.

"To install and remove the electronic musical keyboard attachment 72 from the saxophone containing the resilient mounting pad 38, rod 60 is pressed into the sleeve 58, compressing spring 62, which makes all of the openings in the unit in alignment. The mounting pins 78, 80, and 82, are inserted into holes 52, 54, and 56, and the slideable rod 60 is released, compressing spring 62 and locking the notches 88 against the mounting pins 78, 80, and 82. To quickly remove the electronic musical keyboard attachment 72 from the resilient mounting pad 38, a handle 68 of slideable rod 60 is depressed

and compresses spring 62. This disengages the notches 88 from the mounting pins 78, 80, and 82, thus allowing nearly instant removal. To allow quick access to the operation of the slideable rod 60, the slideable rod 60 is elongated and extends slightly above the bell 22, thus making it readily accessible for nearly instant removal or attachment of the electronic musical keyboard attachment 72. When a player blows through the mouthpiece 2b, the reed causes a column of air produced in the second tube member 2 and the straight tube member 1 to vibrate, and the tone thus produced is changed depending upon the fingering. Plots X1 of FIG. 4 show variation of the pitch of the tone produced by the saxophone shown in FIG. 3, and plots X2 stand for variation of pitch of the tone produced by the prior art saxophone."

d. What Are Alternative Ways That Your Invention Can Achieve Its Result?

Although it's not required, it's a good idea to describe alternative ways that your invention can be used or assembled. For example, in the keyboard/saxophone patent described in the previous section, the inventor chose a resilient mounting pad for the keyboard. The inventor noted, alternatively, that "The resilient mounting pad 38 may be replaced by a simple metal or rigid plastic rectangular sheet that could be spring-mounted or magnetized on to the mounting posts 30, 32, and 34."

These variations are referred to as "alternative embodiments." It's important to include every significant alternative embodiment for your invention—doing so will broaden the potential reach of any resulting patent. Under new decisions by the federal patent courts, a court may hold that someone who sells or makes a variation of your invention has not infringed your patent's claims, unless the variation is described in your specification. You can also focus more closely on—and describe in greater detail—one particular alternative.

e. Putting It All Together

There is no one correct style for writing a Provisional Patent Application. Your goal is to assemble your answers to the questions in this chapter into a readable narrative form.

Just as there is no fixed style for a Provisional Patent Application, there is also no fixed length. Your goal is to clearly explain how to make and use your invention. The number of words and tone you use to achieve that goal is up to you.

Here are a few tips to help you get started:

- **Be yourself.** Think of your specification as a letter that you might send to a colleague or relative, not to a patent examiner. In other words, use conversational first-person style, not legalese. For example, "I invented a rotating light socket," not "I hereby enclose my provisional patent application for the rotating light socket invention described herein."
- **Use bulleted lists.** You will notice that the Provisional Patent Applications at the end of this chapter use bulleted lists

to explain alternative embodiments and to distinguish the invention from the prior art. These lists help the reader by clarifying points and breaking up large chunks of text.

- **If you have already written a technical article describing your invention, include that article with your draft.** You might even be able to use that article (or a revised form of it) as your application, as long as it provides the information described in this chapter.
- **Have a friend or colleague review your draft**—then listen with an open mind to any criticisms of content and style. Make sure the reader agrees that you have given enough detail to allow someone with ordinary skill in the field of your invention to make and use it from your drawings and explanation.
- **ALWAYS compare your draft with other patents in your field,** to make sure your language and drawings conform to the style of similarly patented inventions.
- **ALWAYS use the spell check feature of your word processing program.**
- **Include a footer on every page** indicating your name, the name of your invention, the page number, and the total number of pages included in your application.
- **If you can't tell whether you have properly prepared your Provisional Patent Application, consult an attorney**
- **Never say anything negative about your invention,** no matter how candid you want to be. Always stress the positive aspects of your invention. *Wrong*: "My

Fig 2 embodiment didn't work as fast as the embodiment in Fig 3." *Right*: "Fig 3 embodiment operates faster, while my Fig 2 embodiment is more economical."

Documenting Your Claims

As we explained in Chapter 1, claims define your patent rights. However, as you can see from the many examples of claims in Chapter 2, it's no easy task to draft patent claims. Furthermore, you don't have to include claims in a Provisional Patent Application.

Generally we recommend against drafting your own claims unless you've familiarized yourself with the tricky art of claims drafting. (David Pressman's book, *Patent It Yourself* (Nolo), explains how to draft claims.) If you're working with a patent attorney, your lawyer will provide advice on this issue. One of the sample Provisional Patent Applications at the end of this chapter includes a claim, and the other doesn't.

4. Packaging and Mailing Your Provisional Patent Application

Once you've drafted your drawings and Provisional Patent Application, you can file it with the USPTO. If you have doubts about whether you have properly prepared your Provisional Patent Application, consult an attorney.

You must also submit a Provisional Patent Application (PTO Form SB0016), which you can download from the USPTO website at www.uspto.gov. Click "Patents" and then, under "Patenting," click "Forms." Currently, the filing fee is $80. Regardless of how you pay your fee—check, credit card, or money order—you will need to complete the USPTO's Fee Transmittal Form (SB0017). You can also download Form SB0017 from the USPTO website. On the top of the form, indicate whether you are claiming "small entity status" (you're eligible unless you have assigned, licensed, or transferred your invention to a for-profit company with more than 500 employees). Indicate your method of payment and, under "Fee Calculation," write in the amount of your fee. Sign and date the form.

If you are paying by check, make your check out to Commissioner for Patents. If you are paying by credit card, you'll need to complete the USPTO's Form 2038, which you can download from the USPTO website.

Finally, if you want to acquire the fastest filing date, we recommend using U.S. Express Mail. (Another advantage of using Express Mail is that if the Post Office loses your application, you can still claim your original filing date—but only if you saved the original mailing receipt.) Obtain a U.S. Express Mail envelope and label from your local post office. Address your package to:

Mail Stop Provisional Patent Application
Commissioner for Patents
P.O. Box 1450
Alexandria, VA 22313-1450

Include a return postcard with every document you send to the USPTO. Write your mailing address on the front of the postcard. On the back write:

> Provisional Patent Application of [*your name or names*] for [*title of invention*], consisting of [*number of pages*] pages of specification, [*number of pages*] drawing sheets, and filing fee of $[*insert amount of filing fee*] received today: _____

If you failed to include something in your package, the USPTO's Office of Initial Patent Examination will send you a letter telling you what to do and what fees you will be charged for the error. Supply what is needed, following the instructions in the letter.

D. Provisional Patent Application for a Method of Simulating Tears in a Doll

To give you an idea of how you can document your invention using a Provisional Patent Application, we've borrowed an example from *Patent Pending in 24 Hours* (Nolo) for a doll that simulates tears using LED lights.

Provisional Patent Application for a Method of Simulating Tears in a Doll

I have invented a method of simulating tears in dolls using linear groups of blinking light-emitting diodes (LEDs). These linear groups of LEDS are affixed to the doll's eyelids and extend downward on the doll's cheek. A battery-powered microchip controls the LEDs, causing the lights to blink in a pattern that simulates falling tears. The microchip can be triggered by either a sensor that detects external stimuli such as audio, movement, or by an on/off switch.

Dolls have been produced in the past that simulate crying. These dolls—for example, the Tiny Tears™ doll produced by the Ideal Company in the 1950s—have been very popular with children who enjoy role-playing. As Fusi and Jensen stated in their Tearing Eye Doll patent (Pat. 4,900,287, 1990), "Playacting performs an important role in child development, and the most effective dolls are those which simulate reality. This is why dolls which produce crying sounds are appealing, and why dolls capable of tearing also satisfy a child's need for verisimilitude."

In the past, crying dolls have relied on two concepts, ejecting water from the baby's eyes or emitting crying sounds. The Tiny Tears doll, for example, ejected water when the child placed the doll horizontally. The problems with water excretion systems are that they:

- are capable of leaking

- require refilling

- often corrode the internal working parts

- include numerous internal parts such as nozzles, reservoirs, tubing, and pumps, and

- can create a play hazard.

The problems with dolls that simulate crying sounds are that they:

- may startle or frighten a young child, and

- may create alarm in adults unaware that the sound is coming from a doll.

My method of simulating tears is preferable over previous tearing dolls because it emits light instead of water or sound. In addition to avoiding the mess, hazard, and annoyance of previous methods, the small glow from the LEDs simulation provides the advantage of comforting a child using the doll in a darkened bedroom.

I've included four drawing sheets.

FIG. 1 is an elevated front view of a doll embodying the invention.

FIG. 2 is an internal view of the inside of the doll's head.

FIG. 3 is a flowchart indicating the steps in turning the simulation on and off.

FIG. 4 is another elevated front view of the doll embodying an alternate version of the invention featuring multiple LED tear simulations.

The components of my invention are:

- a toy doll 10 consisting of a doll's head 12 and body 14 contoured with human characteristics and including a cavity 16 in the doll's head for placement of elements

- LEDs 18 extending in linear groups downward from the doll's eye 20

- an LED microchip controller 22 that directs on, off, frequency, and order of blinking lights

- a battery 24 to power the microchip and LEDs

- a motion sensor 26 (or sound sensor 28) to direct the microchip controller to turn on, off, or otherwise control the blinking LEDs, and

- an ON/OFF switch 30.

The method or arrangement of wiring or connecting the above electronic components and mounting them in a doll will be well known to those with ordinary skill in the electronic and mechanical arts. Microchip controller 22 is a standardized chip, having a ROM with a suitable embedded program (PROM) arranged to cause it to perform the functions indicated.

Specifically, the microchip when triggered, will light each LED for a .5 second period in a repeating 1, 2, 3 sequence.

My doll achieves its result as follows: Extending from the doll's eye 20 are three LEDs 18 affixed or embedded in the face of doll 10; these simulate the path of a falling tear drop. LEDs 18 are connected to a controlling microchip 22 and battery 24 located in a cavity 16 within the doll's head 12. The controlling microchip 22 is connected to a motion sensor 26 or sound sensor 28 affixed in head 12 and to a manual on/off switch 30. The microchip is a simple electronic distributor which illuminates the LEDs in sequence as in Table 1 as follows:

Table 1 indicates the sequence and timing of the on times of the three LEDs as the light "moves" downward from the doll's eye. The sequence repeats until halted by motion or audio sensor or by on-off switch.

Table 1			
	LED 1 on	LED 2 on	LED 3 on
Time 1 (start)	X		
Time 2 (.5 sec. later)		X	
Time 3 (.5 sec. later)			X

The user may, if desired, simply turn the tear simulation on or off by pressing the switch 30 affixed to doll's head 12 or body 14. When the child uses switch 30, microchip controller 22 is directed to begin or stop the moving light sequence. Sensors 26 and 28 may also be used to turn on and off the moving light sequence. For example, controller 22 may be directed to turn on the LED tear simulation after a short period of inactivity—for example, the child has put the doll down. Subsequent motion—for example, the child picking up the doll—would turn off the tear simulation.

Alternatively, a sound sensor 28 may be programmed to turn off the lights—for example, the sensor is triggered by the sound of the child comforting the doll. Finally a timer, embedded on the microchip controller will turn off the timer after an extended period of inactivity.

There are many alternative ways that my crying doll using simulating lights can be implemented:

- Instead of a doll, it is also possible that the crying simulation can be implemented with a life-sized mannequin (e.g., as used in store displays), with plush toys, or with puppets.

- The doll may also include sound effects that accompany the tear simulation, for example the sound of crying.

- The battery or source of the power may vary and can include disposable, long-life, or rechargeable batteries.

- The LEDs may be all one color, e.g., white, or they may be more fanciful or whimsical as embodied in a series of colored lights.

- Instead of LEDs, the moving lights may be created with laser diodes, OLEDs, passive-matrix or active-matrix liquid crystal displays, or other non-heating low power electric lighting sources.

- The shape of each LED may be so as to create a teardrop appearance or other fanciful shape that amuses or stimulates a child.

- The linear LEDS may extend in any number of combinations on the doll's face (see Fig. 4), e.g., one strip from each eye, several strips from each eye, or strips down the front of the cheek while the doll is upright or down the sides of the cheek while the doll is in a horizontal position.

- Alternate timings may also be proposed, for example—different time separations between each LED.

- Table 2 indicates a pattern than can also be used for left and right doll eyes. This delayed timing sequence—in which one eye appears to shed a tear drop after the other can be manipulated in innumerable ways—for example, one eye might not commence until after .3, .4, .5, or .6 second from when the other eye began its LED simulation.

	L1 on	L2 on	L3 on	R1 on	R2 on	R3 on
Table 3						
Time 1 (start)	X					
Time 2 (.5 sec. later)		X		X		
Time 3 (.5 sec. later)			X		X	
Time 4 (.5 sec. later)						X

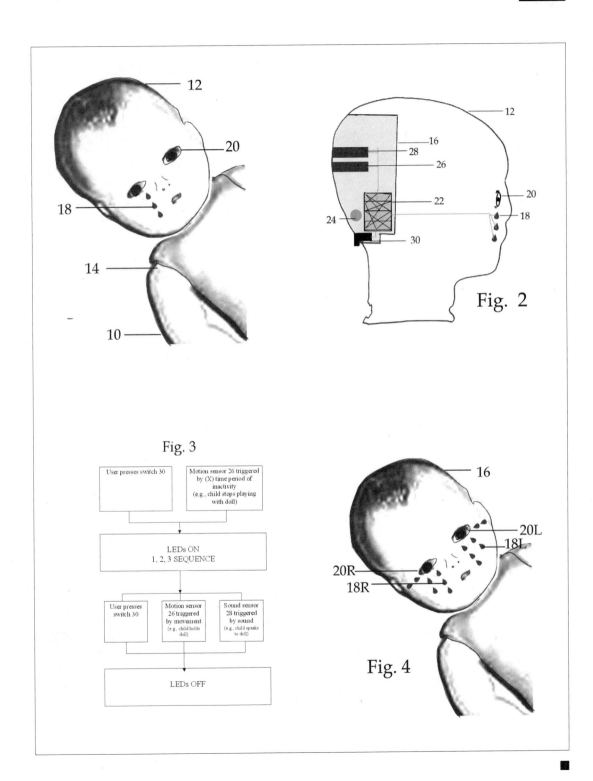

Fig. 2

Fig. 3

User presses switch 30	Motion sensor 26 triggered by (X) time period of inactivity (e.g., child stops playing with doll)

LEDs ON
1, 2, 3 SEQUENCE

User presses switch 30	Motion sensor 26 triggered by movement (e.g., child holds doll)	Sound sensor 28 triggered by sound (e.g., child speaks to doll)

LEDs OFF

Fig. 4

Chapter 8

How to File a Design Patent Application

*D*esign patents protect virtually any new and nonobvious ornamentation of a useful object, from the flickering icon on your computer screen to the shape of your MP3 player. But despite this breadth of coverage and the legal advantages of patent protection, design patents have an "image problem" in the intellectual property world. One of the reasons for this black sheep status is indifference. As one attorney stated, "The potential using public, for the most part, ignores the system. The problem creates a degenerative circle: because few pay sufficient attention to the [design patent] system, an even lesser number envision its true potential." (W. Thompson, "U.S. Design Protection: Discussion of Status and Suggested Proposals," 24 *AIPLA Q. J.* 393, 395 (1996).)

As the influence of art and entertainment in product design increases—and it *must* in a world of otherwise similar products—the use of design patents as a legal remedy will likely expand as well.

In this chapter we cover:

- the standards for design patents, and
- how to file a design patent.

Appendix A explains what happens to a design patent application after the USPTO receives it—in other words, the examination process.

Read this chapter only if you want a design patent. This chapter focuses on the "how to" aspects of filing a design patent—that is, we provide the standards and procedures required for acquiring design patent rights. If you're not interested in pursing a design patent, skip this chapter.

A. Design Patent Standards

This section explains the standards for design patents—this is what you will have to demonstrate to the USPTO if you want to get patent protection. If you're convinced that your design qualifies, proceed to Section B, which describes how to prepare an application.

There are three requirements to get a design patent. The design must be:

- new and original
- nonobvious, and
- an ornamental design for a useful article of manufacture.

1. New and Original: Imitation Is Not Flattery

As every designer knows, there are concepts—for example, the idea of a sectional sofa—and there are designs—the particular appearance of *your* sectional sofa. To be new (also referred to as "novelty"), a design must differ from all previous product designs (known as the "prior art"). You don't have to come up with a new concept, only a new design.

A design must also be original, which means that it has to do more than simply imitate what already exists. A design that simulates a well-known object—for example, a paperweight replica of the Empire State Building—is not considered to be original. The design must be the result of "industry, effort, genius, or expense." (*Smith v. Whitman*, 148 U.S. 674 (1893).)

It's generally not considered original to depict something naturally occurring, but this standard is interpreted loosely. For example, a design patent for a model of a human baby was invalidated (*In re Smith*, 77 F.2d 514 (CCPA 1935)), but the designers of replica female breasts on beads were granted a design patent and successfully enforced it against competitors (*Superior Merchandise v. M.G.I. Wholesale,* 52 U.S.P.Q. 2d 1935 (E.D. La. 1999).)

What Is Prior Art?

For purposes of a design patent, prior art includes:

- any design used on a useful object in public use or on sale in the U.S. for more than one year before the filing date of your design patent application
- anything that was publicly known or used by others in the U.S. before the date your design was created
- anything that was made or built in the U.S. by another person before the date your design was created
- any work that was the subject of a prior design patent, issued more than one year before the filing date of your design patent or any time before the date your design was created, or
- any work that was published more than one year before the filing date of your design patent or any time before the date your design was created.

2. Nonobviousness

If your design would be considered obvious by others in your field, the USPTO will reject your design patent application. As is true of the novelty standard, a design concept may be obvious while the actual design is not. For example, Spiro Agnew—the late vice-president, famous for such alliterations as "nattering nabobs of negativism"—was depicted in caricature on the face of a watch. Although the concept of caricature was obvious, the particular design was not.

Is Nonobviousness Nonsense?

If you find the nonobvious standard for designs confusing, you're not alone. There aren't too many clear standards for determining when a design is obvious and when it's not, which means that individual patent examiners—and judges, if someone files an infringement lawsuit—have a lot of leeway in making these decisions. There have been periodic attempts to change the law, but the standard remains for now, in all its murky glory.

It doesn't necessarily take great originality or craftsmanship to create a nonobvious design; sometimes, it requires only the ability to visualize things a little differently. For example, you can demonstrate nonobviousness by:

- using a familiar form in an unfamiliar medium—such as the use of a floral pattern as a candle holder (see Illustration 8-1)

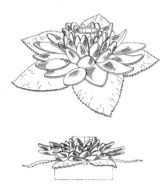

Illustration 8-1

- making a slight change to an existing design that produces a striking visual effect—such as alternating the position of hearts on a wedding ring (see Illustration 8-2)

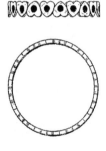

Illustration 8-2

- omitting a visual element commonly associated with similar designs—such as the waterbed design in Illustration 8-3, which is distinguishable by the absence of visible seams on the top and sides of the mattress, or

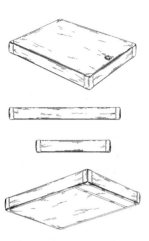

Illustration 8-3

- juxtaposing elements in a way that creates an unexpected visual statement—such as embedding a poker chip in the bottom of a shot glass (see Illustration 8-4).

Illustration 8-4

Your design will be more likely to meet the "nonobvious" test if:

- it has enjoyed commercial success

- it has a visual appearance that's un-expected
- others have copied the design
- the design has been praised by others in the field
- others have tried but failed to achieve the same result, or
- you created a design that others said could not be done.

It is possible for a design to be new and obvious at the same time. For example, a court determined that a design for an alcohol server that was shaped like an intravenous dispenser ("Combined Stand and Container for Storing Liquids" in Illustration 8-5) was new —no such design had been used for serving alcohol—but it was obvious and therefore not patentable. (*Neo-Art, Inc. v. Hawkeye Distilled Products, Co.,* 654 F. Supp. 90 (C.D. Cal. 1987), *aff'd,* 12 U.S.P.Q. 1572 (CAFC 1989).)

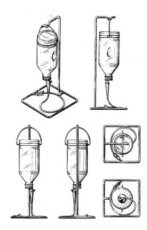

Illustration 8-5

The difference between novelty and non-obviousness is this: A design is novelty if no one has previously made a similar design, while a design is nonobvious if no one has even considered making the design. In practical terms, though, the two standards often overlap—and lack of prior art becomes the measure of both nonobviousness and novelty.

3. Ornamental Design for an Article of Manufacture

For patent purposes, "design" refers to the visual and reproducible appearance of products. As the *Manual of Patent Examination Procedure* (MPEP) puts it, design "is the appearance presented by the article which creates an impression through the eye upon the mind of the observer" (MPEP § 1542). In other words, it's the way that a product looks.

There are three types of protectible product designs:

- shape and proportions—for example, a Mickey Mouse telephone
- surface ornamentation—for example, a Keith Haring Swatch watch, or
- a combination of shape and surface ornamentation—for example, an Air Jordan sports shoe.

In addition, a design "must be a definite, preconceived thing, capable of reproduction and not merely the chance result of a method" (MPEP § 1502). For example, a randomly changing laser light pattern could not be protected, but a water fountain display—the combined appearance of the water and the underlying sculpture—is protectible.

Patent examiners are instructed that a "design is inseparable from the article to which it is applied and cannot exist alone merely as surface ornamentation" (MPEP § 1502). But as the inventions in Chapter 3 demonstrate, designs can live separately as a scheme of surface ornamentation. For example, wallpapers and posters can be protected under design patent law. What the standard really means is that the design patent owner cannot stop others when the surface ornamentation is "separated" from the useful article for which it was registered (for example, a lunchbox) and reproduced on another useful article (like a knapsack).

To be patentable, a design must be "primarily ornamental." This means that the claimed design cannot be dictated by the article's function. If a variety of designs could achieve the same function, the design is ornamental.

To be ornamental, the design should also be visible during normal intended use or at some other commercially important time—for example, at the time of sale or in an advertisement. Designs for articles that would be hidden intermittently—for example lingerie, garment hangers, tent pegs, and inner soles for shoes—may still acquire design patents.

Finally, a design patent can be granted only if the design is embodied on an article of manufacture—a term that encompasses anything made "by the hands of man" from raw materials, whether literally by hand or by machinery or by art. (*In re Hruby*, 373 F.2d 997 (CCPA 1967).) Although the term "article of manufacture" is broad and includes everything from computer icons to wallpaper, it is not meant to include paintings, silk screens, photographs, or separable two-dimensional surface ornamentation, such as decals. How-

ever, this distinction is difficult to pin down. For example, a roof shingle that mimics the appearance of wood shingles (and fools the eye into believing that a two-dimensional product is a three-dimensional product) is protectible despite its "separable" surface ornamentation and similarity to naturally occurring objects." (*National Presto Industries Inc. v. Dazey Corp.*, 18 U.S.P.Q.2d 1113, 1116 (N.D. Ill. 1990), *aff'd*, 949 F.2d 402 (Fed. Cir. 1991).) Finally, a design can be patented even if it's only a portion of the article—for example, the shank of a drill bit.

Beware the One-Year Deadline

You cannot get a design patent if you wait more than a year after the design was publicly available to file your patent application. After one year following a sale, offer for sale, public or commercial use, or public knowledge about your design, that design will no longer be considered novel by the USPTO. If the USPTO is unaware of the public sale or use and issues a design patent, the patent will be declared invalid if someone can later show that the design was publicly shown or sold. Therefore, the clock starts ticking once you post your design on your website, show your design at a show, or print postcards with the design.

If you miss the one-year cutoff date, you can no longer seek patent protection for your design. However, you may still be able to protect it under other legal principles, such as copyright or trade dress laws.

4. Stopping Infringers Under Design Patent Law

Under design patent law, if a competitor copies your patented design and you want to put a stop to it, you need to prove that an ordinary observer would find the two designs so similar as to be deceived into purchasing one thinking it's the other. In other words, consumers must be deceived by your competitor's design. This standard applies to the whole design, not merely to specific elements. The standard is also not limited to what is visible at the point of sale. Instead, the court will consider the visible appearance of the design as claimed in the patent drawings.

You get a design patent only if you come up with something new. It naturally follows that you can stop others from copying only whatever it is that makes your design "new." If a competitor has a design that is similar but does not contain your novel elements, there's no design patent infringement.

If you win a design patent case, the infringer is liable for "his total profit." (35 U.S.C. § 289.) In addition, the court can award you a reasonable royalty along with interest and costs. And the court may increase the damages up to three times the amount found or assessed. (35 U.S.C. § 284.) In one case, an inventor, Jan Coyle, won a jury verdict of $33 million dollars, and the infringer paid another $10 million to settle the case, rather than having to face the possibility of triple damages as provided for by the statute. As in trademark and copyright cases, courts may award reasonable attorney fees to the prevailing party in a patent infringement lawsuit.

B. Filing a Design Patent

Preparing and filing a design patent is fairly simple—especially when compared to preparing and filing a utility patent. If you're a self-starter with a do-it-yourself mindset, you can, with a bit of work, prepare your own design patent application and save anywhere from $500 to $1,000. Below, we present basic instructions for preparing a design patent application. If you would like more information, read *Patent It Yourself,* by David Pressman (Nolo), or read and download the design patent information provided at the USPTO website, www.uspto.gov. Even if you prepare the rest of the application yourself, however, you may need to hire a patent draftsperson to create professional drawings.

If you're not the do-it-yourself type, you can always hire an attorney or patent agent to review and analyze your design and advise you on whether pursuing a design patent is worthwhile. The attorney or agent can prepare the application. If there is a problem at the USPTO—for example, an examiner challenges your application—the attorney or agent can respond and keep the application on track.

If you don't want to do it all yourself, you'll have to pay between $750 and $1,500 for:

- an attorney to draft the application
- a patent draftsperson to create the drawings, and
- the filing fee (currently $170); (also, note that if your design patent is granted you will have to pay an additional $240 for a design patent issue fee).

Unless you pay for expedited processing of your application, you will have to wait one to two years for your design patent, and you cannot use it to stop others from copying your design until the patent has been granted. (The USPTO has indicated that it will place design patents on a faster track than utility patents, which can take two to three years.) Design patents automatically expire 14 years after they're issued, and you cannot renew them.

As the inventor, only you have the right to apply for the patent. (For historical reasons, the USPTO often refers to the designer as the inventor and to the design as the invention.) Even if you signed away your rights to someone else or you were employed to create the design, you must still be listed as the inventor and sign the application. However, the issued patent application will indicate that your rights have been assigned. If someone else contributes to a new, nonobvious element of your design (see Sections A1 and A2, above), that person is a co-inventor, and the two of you should reach an agreement as to ownership of the patent.

If you're employed to create designs, your employer may own rights in any resulting design patents. Who owns the design depends on the contents of your employment agreement, your employer's policies, whether you used your employer's time and resources to create the design, and state laws regarding employee ownership rights.

For more on employer ownership of invention and design rights, see *Inventor's Guide to Law and Taxes,* by Stephen Fishman (Nolo).

The design patent application consists of:
- the "specification"—a short written document describing your design
- drawing(s) showing the appearance of your design
- the Design Patent Application Transmittal —a cover sheet that accompanies your application
- the Declaration—an oath provided by the designer
- the Fee Application Transmittal Form, and
- a fee (currently $170).

Who's Examining Your Design?

In an article about design patents a few years ago, a former UPSTO official detailed the academic degrees of the design examiners. There were nine architects, six examiners with degrees in fine arts, three with interior design degrees, four with industrial design degrees, four with degrees in clothing and textile design, two with degrees in journalism, and one with a degree in sociology.

1. The Specification

The specification is quite simple to prepare. We've provided a sample one for a table design (Illustration 8-6), created by designer Andrew Bergman, in Section 10, below.

The elements of the specification are fairly straightforward. Here's a quick breakdown:
- **Preamble**—one or two boilerplate sentences announcing that you're seeking a design patent.

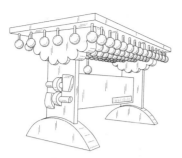

Illustration 8-6

- **Specification**—the place to introduce your design by name. A basic title such as "glass bowl," "puppet," or "steel table" will work best.
- **Cross References to Related Applications** —here, you indicate whether you have filed a previous design patent application to which this one is related.
- **Statement Regarding Federally Sponsored R & D**—indicate here whether the design was prepared under a government grant or as part of government research.
- **Description of the Figure(s) of the Drawings**—describe the view presented in each of the drawing sheets.
- **Feature Description**—provide a short description of your design; for example, "My candle is characterized by a pinwheel effect that gradually slopes outward."

2. Drawings

As you can see from the drawings in this chapter and in Chapter 3, design patent drawings are technical and stylized. Each element—for example, stippling (use of dots), linear shading (use of lines), and distinctive patterns (for indicating colors)—has a special

Talking About Copyright in Your Design Patent

Some patent attorneys have begun mentioning the work's copyright in the design patent application. The purpose of this statement is to alert the public that although it is okay to copy the drawings for purposes of design patent law, the drawings may not be copied for purposes unrelated to the patent. Arguably, a notice like this may help an inventor demonstrate that someone who copied the design after seeing the warning was a willful infringer subject to steeper copyright penalties. However, these notices have not yet been tested in a lawsuit. What's more, the design patent owner retains these rights regardless of whether they are expressly "reserved" by a written warning. For these reasons, we think these warning labels are probably just unnecessary legal verbiage.

If you want to provide a statement like this just in case, add the following language after your feature description: "A portion of the disclosure of this patent document contains material to which a claim for copyright is made. The copyright owner has no objection to the facsimile reproduction by anyone of the patent document or the patent disclosure as it appears in the Patent and Trademark Office patent file or records, but reserves all other copyright rights whatsoever."

meaning. You are allowed to provide informal drawings, such as rough sketches or photographs, with your design patent application, but no one will examine your application until you provide formal drawings similar to those shown in this chapter. To avoid delay, we recommend that you provide formal drawings in the first place. (The only time you should furnish informal drawings is when you are in a hurry to obtain an early filing date but haven't had a chance to draft the drawings.) For information on the difference between formal and informal drawings, see Chapter 7, Section B.

With a little drawing skill or computer graphics knowledge, you can prepare formal drawings for your design patent application. In their book *How to Make Patent Drawings Yourself* (Nolo), David Pressman and Jack Lo explain how to prepare these drawings using computer software or pen and ink. One chapter is devoted solely to design patent drawing rules. If you prefer to have a professional draft your drawings, you can accomplish this relatively inexpensively (about $80 per drawing sheet; each sheet may contain one or two figures). You can find a suitable patent draftsperson by typing "patent drawing" in your Internet search engine. A good list of draftspeople is also provided at the Pipers website, www.piperpat.co.nz/resource/drawings.html.

Designs are commonly depicted in different views—for example, top views, side views, or disassembled views. You should present as many views as are necessary to demonstrate your design. Each view provides another way of "seeing" the design. Each view is given a discrete figure number (abbreviated as "Fig" in patent law).

Keep in mind that the design patent *only* protects what is disclosed in the drawings. If you later change the design substantially, you can't protect it unless you apply for a new design patent.

3. The Design Patent Application Transmittal

You must submit a cover sheet with your design patent application. The USPTO has prepared one that we recommend you use. A sample is shown below. To obtain this form, go to the USPTO home page at www.uspto.gov, and click "Patents" on the left side of the screen. Click "Forms," then follow the instructions to download Form SB0018. You must have a copy of Adobe Acrobat on your computer to download this PDF form. Save the form to your computer. That way, you can use it again without connecting to the Internet.

The cover sheet is a "fillable" PDF form, which means that you can enter (but not save) information onto the form using a current version of Adobe Acrobat. If you don't have the technology to fill in the form on your computer, print out a copy of the form and fill in the blanks using a typewriter or pen.

Here's the information you'll need to supply:

- **First Named Inventor.** At the top of the form, there's a box for the First Named Inventor. Fill in the name of one of the designers.
- **Title.** In this section, provide your design title as indicated in your specification.
- **Express Mail Label Number.** Copy this number from the Express Mail label (the

bottom page). You don't have to use U.S. Express Mail. If you wish, or if you're not in the United States, you can mail your design patent application by regular mail or by an overnight express service such as Federal Express. However, any document sent by Express Mail that includes the Express Mail Number on the cover letter will be considered received on the day you mail it. (37 C.F.R. § 1.10.)

- **Application Elements.** Check the "Fee Transmittal Form" box and check "Applicant claims small entity status." (You have small entity status if you are an independent designer, or if the company that owns the design is a nonprofit, or a for-profit company with 500 or fewer employees.) Check the "Specification" box and indicate how many pages you're sending in the box to the right. Check the "Drawings" box and indicate the number of drawing sheets in the box to the right.
- **Oath or Declaration.** Check the "Newly executed" box. You will include a separate declaration.
- **Application Data Sheet.** Do not check this box. (An Application Data Sheet is a voluntary submission that includes additional information about you and your design—there's no need to bother with it.)
- **Accompanying Application Parts.** With the exception of the "Return Receipt Postcard," these choices will probably not apply to you.
- **Correspondence Address.** Provide an address where the USPTO can send correspondence regarding your design.

If you have a USPTO Customer Number (many law firms and corporations do), mark the box and provide the number, or use a bar code sticker. Otherwise, mark the box "Correspondence address below" and write the name of the individual or company that should receive mail from the USPTO. If you fail to include something in your package, the PTO's Office of Preliminary Examination will send you a letter telling you what to do and what fees you will be charged for the error. Supply what is needed, following the instructions in the letter.

4. Declaration

The declaration, Form SB/01, is a two-page form that you can download from the USPTO website. Check the box "Declaration Submitted With Initial Filing" and provide the title of your design. On page 2, list the designers and their addresses. Sign the declaration where it is marked "Inventor's Signature."

5. Fee Transmittal

The Fee Transmittal, Form SB/17, is a one-page form that you can download from the USPTO website. Indicate your method of payment. Your choices are:

- **Check or money order.** If you pay by check or money order, mark this box and include a check payable to Commissioner for Patents.
- **Deposit account number.** Disregard this box unless you maintain a deposit account at the USPTO.

- **Payment by credit card.** If you want to pay by credit card, check this box and download and complete the additional required form (Form 2038: Credit Card Payment Form and Instructions). You cannot fill out Form 2038 on your computer; you'll need to print it and complete it by hand or typewriter. In the box titled "Description of Request and Payment Information" (in the section called Request and Payment Information), write Design Patent Application Fee. Leave the rest of this section blank. The remainder of Form 2038 is easy to complete—instructions are provided when you download the form.

In the box marked "Fee Calculation," write the fee (currently $170) in the box next to "Design filing fee." At the bottom of the form, provide your name, your telephone number, and the date. Sign the form on the indicated line.

6. Return Postcard

It's important to include a return postcard with your application (and with every other document you send to the USPTO). Once you get it back, tape it into your file. The postcard will be your permanent record that your application was received. (Your U.S. Express Mail tracking information and cancelled check also provide useful evidence of receipt—tape these into your file as well.)

Write your mailing address on the front of the postcard. On the back, write:

Design patent application of [*your name or names*] for [*title of design*] consisting of [*number of*] pages of specification, [*number of*] drawing sheets, and filing fee of $_____ received today: [*date*].

7. Mailing

Assemble your documents as follows:
1. Design application transmittal form
2. Fee transmittal form
3. Application data sheet (if any)
4. Specification
5. Drawings or photographs
6. Executed oath or declaration.

Address your package to:

Mail Stop Designs—United States Patent and Trademark Office
Commissioner for Patents
P.O. Box 1450
Alexandria, VA 22313-1450

Speeding Your Design Patent Application

If you're in a hurry, are especially concerned that your design will be stolen, or can afford the hefty fee, you can pay a "Rocket Docket" fee to have your design patent application expedited. Currently, this adds $900 to the regular $170 fee. Unfortunately, the USPTO doesn't make clear exactly how much time your money will buy you. For information on the Rocket Docket procedure, its benefits, and current fees, check the USPTO website.

Enclose your materials and take the Express Mail to the Post Office. Don't deposit the envelope in a regular or even an Express Mail mailbox—if you do, you won't immediately receive the Express Mail receipt. Instead, take the Express Mail directly to the Post Office and ask the clerk to date-stamp your copy.

8. If Problems Arise With Your Application

In a perfect world, your design application will sail through the examination process and you will, within 18 to 24 months, receive a notice that it's been approved. However, things don't always go this smoothly. An examiner may object to your application—for example, by claiming that your design isn't novel or ornamental (see Section A, above, for information on the standards your patent must meet). It's beyond the scope of this book to advise you how to respond to examiner notices. If you run into a problem and want to handle it on your own, read David Pressman's *Patent It Yourself* (Nolo). Although the book primarily deals with utility patents, it provides a lot of helpful information on design patents and offers a thorough explanation of the USPTO examination process—including suggestions on responding to examiner objections.

9. Marking the Design Patent Number

Once you acquire a design patent, you must mark your design work with your design patent number. (You'll receive this number when the USPTO grants your patent.) Any placement is suitable, as long as the number can be located by an ordinary user.

Failing to include the notice could cost you money if you later sue an infringer—even if you win. For example, when the Nike company sued Wal-Mart for design patent infringement, the court ruled that Nike was not entitled to a portion of Wal-Mart's profits or statutory damages (damages fixed by law) if Wal-Mart could prove that Nike had failed to mark the design patent number on one of its shoe designs. (*Nike, Inc. v. Wal-Mart Stores*, 138 F.3d 1437 (E.D. Va. 1998).)

10. Putting It All Together: Our Application for the "I Cannot Tell a Lie" Table

To demonstrate the ease with which a design patent application can be prepared, we've assembled an application for the table shown in Illustration 8-6. The fanciful table, inspired by George Washington's legendary cherry tree chopping incident, was designed by crafts artist Andrew Bergman of New Jersey.

Andrew supplied us with photographs, which we forwarded to patent agent Jack Lo. He imported them into a graphic program and then used that as the basis for drawing the four figures shown here.

We combined the drawings with the application (shown below) and the completed versions of the required PTO forms, and assembled these documents with the fee. We sent the complete package by Express Mail to the USPTO.

Design Patent Application—Drawings

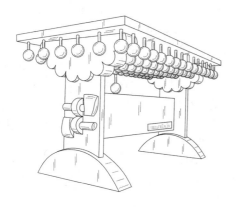

Figure 1

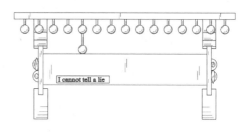

Figure 2

Figure 3

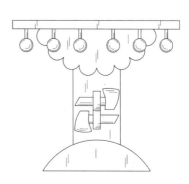

Figure 4

Design Patent Application—Preamble, Specification, and Claim

Mail Stop Designs—United States Patent and Trademark Office
Commissioner for Patents
P.O. Box 1450
Alexandria, VA 22313-1450

PREAMBLE:

The petitioner whose signature appears on the declaration attached respectfully requests that Letters Patent be granted to such petitioner for the new and original design set forth in the specification.

SPECIFICATION:

Petitioner has invented a new, original, and ornamental design for a table entitled "I Cannot Tell a Lie Table," of which the following is a specification. Reference is made to the accompanying drawings which form a part hereof, the figures of which are described below.

CROSS-REFERENCE TO RELATED APPLICATIONS: None

STATEMENT REGARDING FEDERALLY SPONSORED RESEARCH: None

DRAWING FIGURES:

Fig. 1 is a perspective view of my new table design

Fig. 2. is a right side view of my new table design

Fig. 3. is a top view of my new table design

Fig. 4 is a left end view of my new table design

FEATURE DESCRIPTION: My table design is characterized by wooden hatchets, hanging wooden cherries, and the written expression "I cannot tell a lie."

CLAIM: I (We) Claim:

The ornamental design for a table as shown and described.

Express Mail Label # EU121293846US

Date of Deposit: 2004 _____

How to File a Utility Patent Application

*E*very day, hundreds of USPS Express Mail envelopes containing utility patent applications are delivered to the USPTO mailroom in Virginia. Approximately half of these applications will be rejected by patent examiners or abandoned by the applicants. Of the remaining 50%—for which patents are granted—less than 3% will ever be commercialized. In other words, only one or two out of every 100 packages delivered to the USPTO will ever result in a commercial product or process.

Despite these formidable odds, the applications keep pouring in because inventors and companies believe that they cannot risk *not* filing. Their invention may be the next big thing or it may be the "defensive" patent a company needs to keep another patent lawsuit away. And what if someone else gets to the patent office first?

In preceding chapters we explained what a utility patent protects (Chapters 1 and 2) and how to search to determine whether your art or entertainment invention is novel and nonobvious (Chapter 6). We also explained how to document your invention if you decide that you want to apply for a utility patent (Chapter 7). So, you're familiar with the advantages of having a patent and the standards by which patent applications are judged. But there's one last piece of information you need before deciding whether to seek a utility patent: How do you get one?

In this chapter, we'll explain what's inside the utility patent application package and how the application is prepared. (In Appendix A, we'll discuss how an application is shepherded through the USPTO—a process

known as "prosecution.") Most applications for utility patents are remarkably similar. They contain a collection of paperwork (see Appendix A) including filing fees, USPTO payment and application forms, drawings of the invention, and a written document that provides a description of the invention, the invention claims, and other required details.

There are two basic paths for filing a utility patent application—pay a professional or learn how to do it yourself. In this chapter, we'll help you decide which option is best for you.

It's beyond the scope of this book to give you step-by-step advice for drafting the elements of a utility patent application—that is, the specification and claims. The process is covered in detail in *Patent It Yourself*, by David Pressman (Nolo). Instead we'll summarize the requirements and try to give you a practical idea of the process, so you can decide whether you want to go forward—and if so, whether you want to proceed on your own or with the help of a professional.

A. Anatomy of a Patent Application

If you opened a typical utility patent application package at the USPTO mailroom, it would contain the following:

- **Transmittal Form.** The Transmittal Form (PTO/SB/05, see Illustration 9-1) serves as a cover letter for the application. It describes what is being filed, the names of inventors, the number of pages, the fee, and other information used by the

PTO/SB/05 (08-03)
Approved for use through 07/31/2006. OMB 0651-0032
U.S. Patent and Trademark Office. U.S. DEPARTMENT OF COMMERCE
Under the Paperwork Reduction Act of 1995, no persons are required to respond to a collection of information unless it displays a valid OMB control number.

UTILITY PATENT APPLICATION TRANSMITTAL

(Only for new nonprovisional applications under 37 CFR 1.53(b))

Attorney Docket No.	
First Inventor	
Title	
Express Mail Label No.	

APPLICATION ELEMENTS
See MPEP chapter 600 concerning utility patent application contents.

ADDRESS TO: Mail Stop Patent Application
Commissioner for Patents
P.O. Box 1450
Alexandria VA 22313-1450

1. ☐ Fee Transmittal Form (e.g., PTO/SB/17)
   (Submit an original and a duplicate for fee processing)
2. ☐ Applicant claims small entity status. See 37 CFR 1.27.
3. ☐ Specification [Total Pages_____]
   (preferred arrangement set forth below)
   - Descriptive title of the invention
   - Cross Reference to Related Applications
   - Statement Regarding Fed sponsored R & D
   - Reference to sequence listing, a table, or a computer program listing appendix
   - Background of the Invention
   - Brief Summary of the Invention
   - Brief Description of the Drawings *(if filed)*
   - Detailed Description
   - Claim(s)
   - Abstract of the Disclosure
4. ☐ Drawing(s) (35 U.S.C. 113) [Total Sheets_____]
5. Oath or Declaration [Total Sheets_____]
   a. ☐ Newly executed (original or copy)
   b. ☐ Copy from a prior application (37 CFR 1.63(d))
      (for continuation/divisional with Box 18 completed)
      i. ☐ DELETION OF INVENTOR(S)
         Signed statement attached deleting inventor(s) name in the prior application, see 37 CFR 1.63(d)(2) and 1.33(b).
6. ☐ Application Data Sheet. See 37 CFR 1.76

7. ☐ CD-ROM or CD-R in duplicate, large table or Computer Program *(Appendix)*
8. Nucleotide and/or Amino Acid Sequence Submission *(if applicable, all necessary)*
   a. ☐ Computer Readable Form (CRF)
   b. Specification Sequence Listing on:
      i. ☐ CD-ROM or CD-R (2 copies); or
      ii. ☐ Paper
   c. ☐ Statements verifying identity of above copies

ACCOMPANYING APPLICATION PARTS
9. ☐ Assignment Papers (cover sheet & document(s))
10. ☐ 37 CFR 3.73(b) Statement   ☐ Power of Attorney *(when there is an assignee)*
11. ☐ English Translation Document *(if applicable)*
12. ☐ Information Disclosure Statement (IDS)/PTO-1449   ☐ Copies of IDS Citations
13. ☐ Preliminary Amendment
14. ☐ Return Receipt Postcard (MPEP 503) *(Should be specifically itemized)*
15. ☐ Certified Copy of Priority Document(s) *(if foreign priority is claimed)*
16. ☐ Nonpublication Request under 35 U.S.C. 122 (b)(2)(B)(i). Applicant must attach form PTO/SB/35 or its equivalent.
17. ☐ Other: ....

18. If a CONTINUING APPLICATION, *check appropriate box, and supply the requisite information below and in the first sentence of the specification following the title, or in an Application Data Sheet under 37 CFR 1.76:*

☐ Continuation   ☐ Divisional   ☐ Continuation-in-part (CIP)   of prior application No.: ....

Prior application information: Examiner _____   Art Unit: _____
For CONTINUATION OF DIVISIONAL APPS only; The entire disclosure of the prior application, from which an oath or declaration is supplied under Box 5b, is considered a part of the disclosure of the accompanying continuation or divisional application and is hereby incorporated by reference. The incorporation can only be relied upon when a portion has been inadvertently omitted from the submitted application parts.

19. CORRESPONDENCE ADDRESS

☐ Customer Number: _____   **OR** ☐ Correspondence address below

Name	
Address	
City	State	Zip Code
Country	Telephone	Fax
Name (Print/Type)		Registration No. (Attorney/Agent)
Signature		Date

This collection of information is required by 37 CFR 1.53(b). The information is required to obtain or retain a benefit by the public which is to file (and by the USPTO to process) an application. Confidentiality is governed by 35 U.S.C. 122 and 37 CFR 1.14. This collection is estimated to take 12 minutes to complete, including gathering, preparing, and submitting the completed application form to the USPTO. Time will vary depending upon the individual case. Any comments on the amount of time you require to complete this form and/or suggestions for reducing this burden, should be sent to the Chief Information Officer, U.S. Patent and Trademark Office, U.S. Department of Commerce, P.O. Box 1450, Alexandria, VA 22313-1450. DO NOT SEND FEES OR COMPLETED FORMS TO THIS ADDRESS. **SEND TO: Mail Stop Patent Application, Commissioner for Patents, P.O. Box 1450, Alexandria, VA 22313-1450.**
If you need assistance in completing the form, call 1-800-PTO-9199 and select option 2.

Illustration 9-1

USPTO to categorize the filing. All of the inventors must sign the transmittal form. (All of the USPTO forms required for an application are downloadable from the USPTO website, at www.uspto.gov.)

- **Fee Transmittal Form.** This form (PTO/SB/17, see Illustration 9-2) provides information about your fee, including whether you are claiming Small Entity Status. (Most inventors claim this reduced fee status unless they have transferred their invention rights to a for-profit business with more than 500 employees.)

- **Credit Card Transmittal Form.** You must complete this additional form (PTO/SB/2038, see Illustration 9-3) if you are paying by credit card.

- **Fee.** You can pay by personal check, money order, or credit card. Currently, the basic filing fee is $385 for small entities. (There is also an issue fee of $665 if the patent is granted). The fee depends on several variables, including the number of independent and dependent claims, whether the applicant qualifies for Small Entity Status, and whether an assignment is being filed (transferring rights from the inventor to another entity). You can review current filing fees at the USPTO website.

- **Patent Application Declaration (PAD).** The PAD (PTO/SB/01, see Illustrations 9-4a and 9-4b) certifies the accuracy of the statements in the application—in other words, that you are telling the truth.

- **Drawings.** Patent drawings (also known as "drawing sheets") are visual representations of the invention that must be included with the application, if necessary to explain the invention. Throughout this book, we've included examples of patent drawings. The drawings must show every feature recited in the claims. There are strict standards for patent drawings as to materials, size, form, symbols, and shading. To give you a rough idea of how to prepare patent drawings, we describe the process for creating informal drawings in Chapter 7, Section B. If you're adept at drawing or comfortable using computer drawing programs, you can prepare your own formal drawings. (For more information, read *How to Make Patent Drawings Yourself,* by Jack Lo and David Pressman (Nolo).) If you'd prefer to have a patent draftsperson prepare the drawings, you can expect to pay between $75 to $150 per drawing sheet.

You can find patent drawing services with an Internet search (try terms such as "patent drawings" or "patent services"). You can also locate a collection of patent drawing services at Piper Patents, www.piperpat.co.nz/resource/drawings/html.

- **The Specification.** This document will make up the bulk of your application. It describes the invention so that someone knowledgeable in the field of the invention can make and use it without any further experimenting. It also discloses the "best mode" of creating and using the invention. In other words, the specification is a statement that explains the

PTO/SB/17 (08-03)
Approved for use through 07/31/2006. OMB 0651-0032
U.S. Patent and Trademark Office; U.S. DEPARTMENT OF COMMERCE
Under the Paperwork Reduction Act of 1995, no persons are required to respond to a collection of information unless it displays a valid OMB control number.

FEE TRANSMITTAL
for FY 2003
Effective 01/01/2003. Patent fees are subject to annual revision.

☐ Applicant claims small entity status. See 37 CFR 1.27

TOTAL AMOUNT OF PAYMENT   ($)

Complete if Known

Application Number	
Filing Date	
First Named Inventor	
Examiner Name	
Art Unit	
Attorney Docket No.	

METHOD OF PAYMENT (check all that apply)

☐ Check   ☐ Credit card   ☐ Money Order   ☐ Other   ☐ None

☐ Deposit Account:

Deposit Account Number

Deposit Account Name

The Director is authorized to: (check all that apply)
☐ Charge fee(s) indicated below   ☐ Credit any overpayments
☐ Charge any additional fee(s) during the pendency of this application
☐ Charge fee(s) indicated below, **except for the filing fee**
to the above-identified deposit account.

FEE CALCULATION

1. BASIC FILING FEE

Large Entity Fee Code	Fee ($)	Small Entity Fee Code	Fee ($)	Fee Description	Fee Paid
1001	750	2001	375	Utility filing fee	
1002	330	2002	165	Design filing fee	
1003	520	2003	260	Plant filing fee	
1004	750	2004	375	Reissue filing fee	
1005	160	2005	80	Provisional filing fee	

SUBTOTAL (1) ($)

2. EXTRA CLAIM FEES FOR UTILITY AND REISSUE

	Extra Claims	Fee from below	Fee Paid
Total Claims	-20** =	X	=
Independent Claims	- 3** =	X	=
Multiple Dependent		X	=

Large Entity Fee Code	Fee ($)	Small Entity Fee Code	Fee ($)	Fee Description
1202	18	2202	9	Claims in excess of 20
1201	84	2201	42	Independent claims in excess of 3
1203	280	2203	140	Multiple dependent claim, if not paid
1204	84	2204	42	** Reissue independent claims over original patent
1205	18	2205	9	** Reissue claims in excess of 20 and over original patent

SUBTOTAL (2) ($)
**or number previously paid, if greater; For Reissues, see above

FEE CALCULATION (continued)

3. ADDITIONAL FEES

Large Entity Fee Code	Fee ($)	Small Entity Fee Code	Fee ($)	Fee Description	Fee Paid
1051	130	2051	65	Surcharge - late filing fee or oath	
1052	50	2052	25	Surcharge - late provisional filing fee or cover sheet	
1053	130	1053	130	Non-English specification	
1812	2,520	1812	2,520	For filing a request for ex parte reexamination	
1804	920*	1804	920*	Requesting publication of SIR prior to Examiner action	
1805	1,840*	1805	1,840*	Requesting publication of SIR after Examiner action	
1251	110	2251	55	Extension for reply within first month	
1252	410	2252	205	Extension for reply within second month	
1253	930	2253	465	Extension for reply within third month	
1254	1,450	2254	725	Extension for reply within fourth month	
1255	1,970	2255	985	Extension for reply within fifth month	
1401	320	2401	160	Notice of Appeal	
1402	320	2402	160	Filing a brief in support of an appeal	
1403	280	2403	140	Request for oral hearing	
1451	1,510	1451	1,510	Petition to institute a public use proceeding	
1452	110	2452	55	Petition to revive - unavoidable	
1453	1,300	2453	650	Petition to revive - unintentional	
1501	1,300	2501	650	Utility issue fee (or reissue)	
1502	470	2502	235	Design issue fee	
1503	630	2503	315	Plant issue fee	
1460	130	1460	130	Petitions to the Commissioner	
1807	50	1807	50	Processing fee under 37 CFR 1.17(q)	
1806	180	1806	180	Submission of Information Disclosure Stmt	
8021	40	8021	40	Recording each patent assignment per property (times number of properties)	
1809	750	2809	375	Filing a submission after final rejection (37 CFR 1.129(a))	
1810	750	2810	375	For each additional invention to be examined (37 CFR 1.129(b))	
1801	750	2801	375	Request for Continued Examination (RCE)	
1802	900	1802	900	Request for expedited examination of a design application	

Other fee (specify) _____
*Reduced by Basic Filing Fee Paid

SUBTOTAL (3) ($)

SUBMITTED BY

(Complete (if applicable))

Name (Print/Type)		Registration No. (Attorney/Agent)	Telephone
Signature			Date

WARNING: Information on this form may become public. Credit card information should not be included on this form. Provide credit card information and authorization on PTO-2038.

This collection of information is required by 37 CFR 1.17 and 1.27. The information is required to obtain or retain a benefit by the public which is to file (and by the USPTO to process) an application. Confidentiality is governed by 35 U.S.C. 122 and 37 CFR 1.14. This collection is estimated to take 12 minutes to complete, including gathering, preparing, and submitting the completed application form to the USPTO. Time will vary depending upon the individual case. Any comments on the amount of time you require to complete this form and/or suggestions for reducing this burden, should be sent to the Chief Information Officer, U.S. Patent and Trademark Office, U.S. Department of Commerce, P.O. Box 1450, Alexandria, VA 22313-1450. DO NOT SEND FEES OR COMPLETED FORMS TO THIS ADDRESS. **SEND TO: Commissioner for Patents, P.O. Box 1450, Alexandria, VA 22313-1450.**

If you need assistance in completing the form, call 1-800-PTO-9199 and select option 2.

Illustration 9-2

PTO-2038 (02-2003)
Approved for use through 02/28/2006. OMB 0651-0043
United States Patent and Trademark Office; U.S. DEPARTMENT OF COMMERCE
Under the Paperwork Reduction Act of 1995, no persons are required to respond to a collection of information unless it displays a valid OMB control number.

United States Patent and Trademark Office
Credit Card Payment Form
Please Read Instructions before Completing this Form

Credit Card Information

Credit Card Type: ☐ Visa   ☐ MasterCard   ☐ American Express   ☐ Discover

Credit Card Account #:

Credit Card Expiration Date:

Name as it Appears on Credit Card:

Payment Amount: $ (US Dollars):

Cardholder Signature:	Date:

Refund Policy: The Office may refund a fee paid by mistake or in excess of that required. A change of purpose after the payment of a fee will not entitle a party to a refund of such fee. The office will not refund amounts of $25.00 or less unless a refund is specifically requested, and will not notify the payor of such amounts (37 CFR § 1.26). Refund of a fee paid by credit card will be issued as a credit to the credit card account to which the fee was charged.
Service Charge: There is a $50.00 service charge for processing each payment refused (including a check returned "unpaid") or charged back by a financial institution (37 CFR § 1.21 (m)) .

Credit Card Billing Address

Street Address 1:

Street Address 2:

City:

State/Province:	Zip/Postal Code:

Country:

Daytime Phone #:	Fax #:

Request and Payment Information

Description of Request and Payment Information:

☐ Patent Fee	☐ Patent Maintenance Fee	☐ Trademark Fee	☐ Other Fee
Application No.	Application No.	Application No.	IDON Customer No.
Patent No.	Patent No.	Registration No.	
Attorney Docket No.		Identify or Describe Mark	

If the cardholder includes a credit card number on any form or document other than the Credit Card Payment Form, the United States Patent and Trademark Office will not be liable in the event that the credit card number becomes public knowledge.

Illustration 9-3

PTO/SB/01 (08-03)
Approved for use through 07/31/2006. OMB 0651-0032
U.S. Patent and Trademark Office; U.S. DEPARTMENT OF COMMERCE
Under the Paperwork Reduction Act of 1995, no persons are required to respond to a collection of information unless it contains a valid OMB control number.

DECLARATION FOR UTILITY OR DESIGN PATENT APPLICATION (37 CFR 1.63)	Attorney Docket Number	
	First Named Inventor	
	COMPLETE IF KNOWN	
	Application Number	
	Filing Date	
☐ Declaration Submitted With Initial Filing **OR** ☐ Declaration Submitted after Initial Filing (surcharge (37 CFR 1.16 (e)) required)	Art Unit	
	Examiner Name	

I hereby declare that:

Each inventor's residence, mailing address, and citizenship are as stated below next to their name.

I believe the inventor(s) named below to be the original and first inventor(s) of the subject matter which is claimed and for which a patent is sought on the invention entitled:

(Title of the Invention)

the specification of which

☐ is attached hereto

OR

☐ was filed on (MM/DD/YYYY) [   ] as United States Application Number or PCT International

Application Number [   ] and was amended on (MM/DD/YYYY) [   ] (if applicable).

I hereby state that I have reviewed and understand the contents of the above identified specification, including the claims, as amended by any amendment specifically referred to above.

I acknowledge the duty to disclose information which is material to patentability as defined in 37 CFR 1.56, including for continuation-in-part applications, material information which became available between the filing date of the prior application and the national or PCT international filing date of the continuation-in-part application.

I hereby claim foreign priority benefits under 35 U.S.C. 119(a)-(d) or (f), or 365(b) of any foreign application(s) for patent, inventor's or plant breeder's rights certificate(s), or 365(a) of any PCT international application which designated at least one country other than the United States of America, listed below and have also identified below, by checking the box, any foreign application for patent, inventor's or plant breeder's rights certificate(s), or any PCT international application having a filing date before that of the application on which priority is claimed.

Prior Foreign Application Number(s)	Country	Foreign Filing Date (MM/DD/YYYY)	Priority Not Claimed	Certified Copy Attached? Yes	No
			☐	☐	☐
			☐	☐	☐
			☐	☐	☐
			☐	☐	☐

☐ Additional foreign application numbers are listed on a supplemental priority data sheet PTO/SB/02B attached hereto.

[Page 1 of 2]

This collection of information is required by 35 U.S.C. 115 and 37 CFR 1.63. The information is required to obtain or retain a benefit by the public which is to file (and by the USPTO to process) an application. Confidentiality is governed by 35 U.S.C. 122 and 37 CFR 1.14. This collection is estimated to take 21 minutes to complete, including gathering, preparing, and submitting the completed application form to the USPTO. Time will vary depending upon the individual case. Any comments on the amount of time you require to complete this form and/or suggestions for reducing this burden, should be sent to the Chief Information Officer, U.S. Patent and Trademark Office, U.S. Department of Commerce, P.O. Box 1450, Alexandria, VA 22313-1450. DO NOT SEND FEES OR COMPLETED FORMS TO THIS ADDRESS. **SEND TO: Commissioner for Patents, P.O. Box 1450, Alexandria, VA 22313-1450.**
If you need assistance in completing the form, call 1-800-PTO-9199 and select option 2.

Illustration 9-4a

PTO/SB/01 (06-03)
Approved for use through 07/31/2003. OMB 0651-0032
U.S. Patent and Trademark Office; U.S. DEPARTMENT OF COMMERCE
Under the Paperwork Reduction Act of 1995, no persons are required to respond to a collection of information unless it contains a valid OMB control number.

DECLARATION — Utility or Design Patent Application

Direct all correspondence to: ☐	Customer Number:	**OR** ☐	Correspondence address below

Name

Address

City	State	ZIP

Country	Telephone	Fax

I hereby declare that all statements made herein of my own knowledge are true and that all statements made on information and belief are believed to be true; and further that these statements were made with the knowledge that willful false statements and the like so made are punishable by fine or imprisonment, or both, under 18 U.S.C. 1001 and that such willful false statements may jeopardize the validity of the application or any patent issued thereon.

NAME OF SOLE OR FIRST INVENTOR: ☐ A petition has been filed for this unsigned inventor

Given Name (first and middle [if any])		Family Name or Surname	

Inventor's Signature			Date

Residence: City	State	Country	Citizenship

Mailing Address

City	State	ZIP	Country

NAME OF SECOND INVENTOR: ☐ A petition has been filed for this unsigned inventor

Given Name (first and middle [if any])		Family Name or Surname	

Inventor's Signature			Date

Residence: City	State	Country	Citizenship

Mailing Address

City	State	ZIP	Country

☐ Additional inventors or a legal representative are being named on the _____ supplemental sheet(s) PTO/SB/02A or 02LR attached hereto.

[Page 2 of 2]

Illustration 9-4b

best way to make and use an invention. If the inventor knew of a better way (or "best mode") and failed to disclose it, that failure could result in the loss of patent rights. The specification consists of several sections including:

☐ **title.**

☐ **background of the invention:** This usually includes cross-references to any related applications, references to a microfiche appendix, a statement regarding federally sponsored research or development, the field of the invention, and a discussion of prior art.

☐ **summary of the invention:** This usually includes the objects (what the invention accomplishes) and advantages (why the invention is superior to the prior art) of the invention.

☐ **description of the drawings.**

☐ **detailed description of the invention** and how it works

☐ **abstract:** a concise, one-paragraph summary of the structure, nature, and purpose of the invention, and

☐ **claims.** Of all the elements, claims are often the hardest to draft (and hardest to decipher). One reason is that claims follow strict grammatical requirements: they are sentence fragments, always start with an initial capital letter, and contain one period and no quotation marks or parentheses (except in mathematical or chemical formulas). Claims usually comprise independent and dependent claims. One claim is stated as broadly as possible (the "independent claim") and then followed by successively narrower claims designed to specifically recite possible variations on the invention ("dependent claims"). The independent claim stands by itself while a dependent claim always refers back and incorporates the language of another independent or dependent claim. We provide examples of claims in Chapter 2.

(Most of the elements of the specification are described in detail in Chapter 7, Section D, which explains how to prepare a Provisional Patent Application.) In addition to these documents, the following documents might also be included in the utility patent application:

• **Information Disclosure Statement.** This should be included if you know of any relevant prior art. You don't have to include it with the application; you can file it within three months after you file the application.

• **Petition to Make Special.** Include this if you want to accelerate the examination process by a few months. You can request it only if you meet one of the requirements in the patent law—for example, your invention relates to HIV/ AIDS or cancer research, counters terrorism, or results in significant energy savings, or the applicant's health is poor.

• **Assignment and Cover Sheet.** Include this if you are transferring ownership of the patent. You don't have to provide it with the application; you can file it any time.

- **Disclosure Document Reference Letter.** Include this if a Disclosure Document was filed previously (see Chapter 7).
- **Return Receipt Postcard.** This is optional, but it provides proof that the application was received by the USPTO.

For more on employer ownership of invention and design rights, see *Inventor's Guide to Law and Taxes*, by Stephen Fishman (Nolo).

B. Should You Do It Yourself or Hire a Professional?

Now that you know what goes into the application, you're prepared to make the next decision: should you attempt to do it yourself or should you hire a professional to complete the application?

Many inventors have obtained patents on their own—many using the method David Pressman explains in detail in his book, *Patent It Yourself.* But doing your own patent requires considerable diligence. If you have sufficient funds but don't have the time or writing skills to do it on your own, you may be better off hiring a professional.

Of course, you can do some of the work yourself and hire a professional to do the rest. You can, for example, draft your application, then have an attorney review it, or hire an attorney only if your application runs into problems with a USPTO examiner. Or you can familiarize yourself with the patent drafting rules so that you can save time

Who Applies for the Patent?

A patent application must be filed in the name of the true inventor or inventors. If there is more than one inventor, each becomes an applicant for the patent, and each automatically owns equal shares of the invention and any resulting patents. Inventorship can be different from legal ownership. Often, all or part of the ownership rights to the invention and the patent application must be transferred to someone else, either an individual or a legal entity. For example, some inventors are hired to invent for companies; they may be required to transfer ownership of any inventions they create, as a condition of employment. To make the transfer, the inventor must legally transfer the interest by filing an assignment, either with the patent application or at any time afterward. Some inventors prefer to wait until they have a received a serial number for the application before filing the assignment.

If an assignment has been recorded and the applicant refers to it in the issue fee transmittal form, the PTO will print the patent with the assignee's interest indicated.

Even if the patent doesn't indicate the assignment, the assignment will still be effective if the PTO has recorded it. In May, 2004, the PTO instituted a means of electronically recording patent assignments—ePAS (Electronic Patent Assignment System). You can use this method or the old-fashioned process for recording an assignment—sending a cover letter along with the assignment and the fee.

explaining your invention and preparing your patent.

To determine whether you're the type of person who can successfully tackle your own utility patent application, consider these questions:

- **How are your finances?** For some, the expense of hiring a patent attorney (between $4,000 to $10,000) is the biggest hurdle to filing a utility patent application. If your funds are limited (or if you just can't stand the idea of paying an attorney), consider doing it yourself.

- **How are you fixed for time?** If you are pressed for time, you might want to think twice before drafting your own patent. The process is time consuming—hours of reading to learn how to do it and many more hours to draft and monitor your application. Preparing and prosecuting your application can easily use up 100-200 hours of your time.

- **Are you a writer?** Besides the time, drafting a patent application also requires writing skills, particularly because you must learn the nuances and language of a unique legal process. If you didn't like writing book reports in high school, had trouble composing papers in college, or hate writing memos at work, then you may not be cut out for the precise writing required to prepare your own patent application.

- **Are you a project person?** Are you the person that people turn to when they need a project managed? Are you a can-do person around the house, eager to take on and complete projects? Are you

good at meeting deadlines? (Be honest, here.) If you're good at completing projects, then you've probably got the temperament to do your own patent application. But if your to-do list still has items on it from last month, give some serious thought to hiring a professional.

- **Have you ever been called a control freak?** If you have an overwhelming compulsion to tell people what to do and how to do it, then you may want to control the drafting of your utility patent application. But if you're comfortable delegating tasks, then you may want to work with a professional.

C. What Do the Professionals Say?

We've reviewed the utility patent application process so you should be familiar with the basics of the application package. Below we speak with a few patent professionals to get another perspective on filing utility patent applications.

1. David Pressman, Author of *Patent It Yourself*

David Pressman's *Patent It Yourself* is the best selling patent text in the world. In addition to authoring *Patent It Yourself,* Pressman is the co-author of *Patent Pending in 24 Hours, How to Make Patent Drawings Yourself,* and *Nolo's Patents for Beginners.* He is a patent attorney and electrical engineer, and has worked as a patent examiner at the USPTO, a corporate patent attorney for several companies, and is currently in private practice in San Francisco.

Question: After all these years, why do patent attorneys still disagree with the premise of your book?

Pressman: Many patent attorneys have been programmed in the old school that states that a professional is the only one qualified to handle and prepare legal documents and a layman has not been anointed and is therefore unqualified to understand or prepare any such documents. These patent attorneys many not have seen the work of laypersons who have successfully used *Patent It Yourself*, or they may have seen their work, but have been blind to providing a fair appraisal because of their old-school programming. It is true that most professionals will do a better job than most laypersons, but I strongly believe that any layperson who is willing to follow detailed instructions and "sweat the details" like most pros do will be able to do a competent job. For example, one layperson, Inventor Alexander Weilgart of Oakland, California, with no prior legal training, did his patent application entirely on his own (with the aid of *Patent It Yourself*) and got a patent, # 4,813,710 (1989) that I would put against any professional's. I strongly favor making the law more accessible to all so that it is not just for rich individuals and corporations. Until we can make the law simpler, do-it-yourself legal guides seem to be the best solution to overcoming the "gold rules the law" syndrome.

Question: Some patent attorneys believe that an inventor can draft most of the patent application except the claims. They believe-especially in this post-*Festo* age-that claims drafting should be left to attorneys. How would you respond?

Pressman: *Festo v. Shoketsu* is a U.S. Supreme Court case that restated the rule that if a claim has been amended during prosecution, the doctrine of equivalents cannot be used in litigation to broaden the claim beyond its literal scope (See Chapter 2, Section A). I caution inventors in *Patent It Yourself* to draft as wide a scope of claims as possible when filing, to include all possible ramifications, and to avoid amending or narrowing the claims during prosecution as much as possible. I believe that inventors are capable of following these guidelines.

Question: You have many helpful commandments in your book. When it comes to drafting a patent, can you isolate any one, two, or three that are of primary importance?

Pressman: The most important is undoubtedly to have your specification teach clearly and completely how to make and use the invention in order to avoid a fatal and irremediable incomplete disclosure. Also important are those that state one should draft the main claims as broadly as possible and sell the invention by repeatedly stating its advantages.

Question: Your book has had a great appeal to scientists and engineers. Many of the readers for our book will be artists and entertainers. Do you believe that artists and entertainers will be able to follow the rigors and rules set forth in *Patent It Yourself* with the same facility as scientists? Put another way, do you think artists will have a more difficult time preparing their own application than scientists?

Pressman: *Having edited many applications prepared by users of the book, I find that generally it is the individual, rather than the profession, that determines competence in following the instructions in Patent It Yourself and doing a good job. Some engineers do a magnificent job, while some are very sloppy and fail to heed the instructions or follow the checklists. Many laypersons, such as homemakers, artists, entertainers, retired persons also fall into this dichotomy. I do find, however, that many professors and PhDs do not do a good job at first because they have their own ideas and fail to follow the rules and checklists.*

Question: Do you remember what it was like the first time you had to draft a patent application? Did it seem daunting?

Pressman: No, because I had worked several years at the PTO as an examiner and studied and critiqued many patent applications so I understood the process well. I was eager to do it and enjoyed the process immensely.

Question: Was there an incident or an event that convinced you to write *Patent It Yourself?* What made you decide that patent drafting wasn't just the province of patent attorneys and agents?

Pressman: Yes. I saw and read a book (now out of print) entitled Techniques for *Preparing Your Own Patent Application,*

and found much of it to be inaccurate and incorrect. I was also aware of the well-written Nolo books on doing your own divorce and forming your own corporation, so I thought there was a place for an accurate do-it-yourself patenting guide by a patent attorney.

Question: Starting is always the hardest part. Is there a secret for starting the drafting of a patent application? Do you always start with a specific element like the abstract or the title?

Pressman: No, I always study the invention and the art, and when I understand it well, I come up with my idea of how best to show it, and then have sketches or preliminary drawings done by a drafter. Then I label the parts in the drawings so I don't have to worry about nomenclature. Then I take an outline (Title, Field, Background, etc.) and fill it in. Often I can fill in the prior-art section from my search report.

Question: What's the best advice anyone ever gave you about writing a patent application?

Pressman: Don't look at the whole process, but just the steps. If you've documented it, made a search and commercial evaluation, and are ready to proceed, just concentrate on the first step, the drawings. Once you have good drawings, then label every part with a name and then do the parts of the application one by one. When you finish the spec, do the first main claim in the same step-by-step order (preamble, parts, interconnections, whereby clause). Then do the dependent claims. Don't look at the entire set of claims as a task, just do them step-by-step.

Question: You've worked as a patent examiner. Is it possible that examiners will have an initial negative response to an inventor-prepared application versus an application prepared by an attorney or agent registered to practice before the USPTO?

Pressman: No. Examiners usually take a preliminary look at the formal papers that accompany an application and if they see that the correspondence came from an attorney, they thereby know whether a layperson or an attorney prepared the application. However they also take a preliminary look at the drawings, layout, parts, and abstract of the application, and if they see that these parts are properly done and well laid out, they will have a favorable impression, regardless of who prepared the application. Regardless of their initial impression, examiners must provide proper reasons for any objection or rejection they make in any application, so I don't feel that the initial impression is important. I did hit the roof one time, however. I did an exceptionally good job on one application that the client filed pro se. The examiner did a competent job on the first office action, but inserted a form paragraph that said the applicant may be unfamiliar with patent application procedures and should consider hiring an attorney. In my amendment, although it is not good practice, I blasted the examiner in no uncertain terms, stating that I had prepared the application, I had over 30 years' experience as an examiner and attorney, and had written several books on patent application preparation, and that the present application was a paradigm of a well-prepared application. Fortunately the examiner did not take offense, but actually apologized in the next office action and we got our patent in due course.

Question: The subject of this book is patenting art and entertainment. You play the trumpet, an instrument that's been around at least since the Renaissance. How do you feel about the patenting of musical methods and inventions? Do you think it is possible to come up with novel and nonobvious inventions for centuries-old art forms?

Pressman: I agree with the US Supreme Court's ruling in the *Diamond v. Chakrabarty* (regarding a patented cancer-susceptible mouse) that the government should allow everything possible made by humans to be patented, so long as it is novel and unobvious. If anyone can come up with any novel and unobvious invention in any field, be it a modern area like biotechnology or computers, or an ancient area like buggy whips or lutes, they are entitled to a patent. I have gotten clients patents on simple objects like musical instruments (drums, guitars), condom packages, paper drinking cups, and shower mirrors.

2. Ronald S. Laurie

Ron Laurie is among a handful of Intellectual Property attorneys who has seen it all and can truthfully say "Been there, done that!" He's worked in Silicon Valley for four decades, first as a software engineer and then as an intellectual property attorney. He's developed inspired and imaginative approaches to protecting software, hardware, semiconductors, telecommunications, and new media technologies and was instrumental in implementing reverse engineering and "clean room" design programs for compatible software and chip products—a methodology that minimized legal exposure for copyright and trade secret infringement. He served as litigation counsel to Hewlett Packard in its historic and successful defense of the "look and feel" copyright infringement suit filed by Apple Computer.

Besides his law practice he has taught IP courses at Stanford and Boalt (U.C. Berkeley) law schools and has been an advisor to the USPTO (on business method patents), the U.S. Copyright Office (on software copyright), the National Academy of Science and National Research Council (on software protection), and the World Intellectual Property Organization (WIPO) (on semiconductor chip topography protection). He recently left the Skadden Arps law firm, to co-found Inflexion Point Strategy, LLC, an IP strategy consulting firm.

Since he's an expert on the law and is adept at fashioning intellectual property protection for cutting-edge technology, we were interested in how he approaches the preparation of a patent application. His answers demonstrate that there may be an important strategic advantage in involving a patent professional as early as possible.

Question: You've been working with patents for over three decades. Do you remember the first patent application you prepared?

Laurie: I certainly do. It was for a "quadrature" disk drive head positioning system; it was pretty clever. I wrote and filed a lengthy patent application with claims describing the positioning mechanism in some detail. About two years later I got the first Office Action from the patent office advising me that all of the claims submitted with the application were allowed. I was ecstatic. I called my contact at the client and said, "I've got great news. We got all the claims." And he said, "Oh, we're not using that design anymore. It's obsolete." And I realized then the penalty of patenting narrowly. You need to think beyond the boundaries of the original idea to abstract a high-level description of the fundamental inventive concept—that is, for something that won't go out of date so quickly. That started an evolutionary process for me.

Question: Did anyone ever give you a bit of invaluable advice about drafting or preparing a patent application?

Laurie: When I was just starting out, a senior partner in my first law firm taught me a very important principle. He told me that when a client walks in your office and says they have an invention—what they have in their mind is usually *not* the invention. In their mind is a particular implementation that is almost always narrower than what the invention really is, and it's the primary job of the patent attorney to work with the client to get from the implementation to the invention.

The true "invention" is determined using the principles of patent law—it's the broadest statement or description of some-thing that: (1) was conceived by the client; (2) is the kind of thing protected by patent law, i.e., a useful apparatus, process, chemical composition, etc.; (3) is not found in the "prior art," i.e., is novel and nonobvious with respect to anything that has been done before; and (4) is a natural extension of the particular implementation ("exemplary embodiment") disclosed in the patent application. In addition, the patent application must disclose the best mode of practicing the invention known to the inventor(s) in sufficient detail to permit a person of skill in the art to make use of it "without undue experimentation." These statutory requirements are respectively re-ferred to by patent lawyers as inventorship, statutory subject matter, novelty/non-obviousness, written description, and enablement/best-mode.

Question: So how does the attorney work with the client to discover the real invention?

Laurie: It may help to give you some philo-sophical background about patents because I don't view the patent application prepa-ration process in the "traditional" way.

Question: What's the traditional way?

Laurie: It's a "bottom-up" approach. An inven-tor has developed a concrete embodiment or implementation of a solution to a problem—and he or she walks in to a patent attorney's office and lays it on the desk and says, "This is my invention and I want to patent it." The "bottom-up" patent attorney says, "Okay, we'll file a patent application on that." Whatever "that" is, the attorney will attempt obtain patent protec-tion for it.

Question: What's wrong with that approach?

Laurie: The problem is that, as I mentioned before, the inventor almost never knows what the invention is. In order to draft the application, and more precisely the claims, you have to figure out what the invention really is, and to do that you have to abstract from the specific to the generic. Remember, the inventor comes in with a solution to a problem—that's what inventors do, they solve problems. Employed inventors get paid to solve specific problems given to them by their boss. Independent inventors are different; they solve problems that occur to them, as opposed to problems that are given to them by someone else. But in any case, what the inventor seldom thinks about is other problems that the solution might also solve. Or whether it represents a broader class of solutions?

Question: What do you call this approach?

Laurie: We call it patent strategy, although what we really mean is that the starting point is the development of the claims strategy. It's a top-down, as opposed to a bottom-up, approach. We try to figure out what the broadest expression of the specific solution is. So let's say a client comes in with a software solution to a personal computer user interface design problem. That's all they're thinking about because they work for a PC company and that's all they're paid to think about. What the patent attorney has to do is to get the inventor to think of every possible application of that solution. For example, does the user interface have applications to medical devices, or vehicle control systems, etc.?

Question: How does the client cooperate in this process?

Laurie: Sometimes you really have to press the client to engage in that kind of abstract thinking, because it's not an intuitive process for them. You may ask, "What are the other possible implementations of this solution? Does this have any application in other fields—biotechnology, for example?" Sometimes you have to push hard for this kind of cooperation. It's a kind of birthing process, painful but productive.

We'll typically bring a client in a room with lots of white-board space and an Internet terminal and we'll say what about *this* or what about *that*. Then, we go to the computer and use keyword searches to look for prior art that may preclude patenting what we're considering.

We're always trying to abstract up from the species to the genus and then look for prior art that might force us back down the abstraction scale. It's like throwing up targets—could we claim it this broadly?—and then trying to shoot each one down with prior art. During this process with the client, we work on a broad pseudo-claim, adding or subtracting words until we have something at the highest level of abstraction that doesn't describe anything that's been done before. This is the primary constraint; it can't be in the prior art, or be an obvious variant of something in the prior art.

Question: How does this process apply when you are drafting the claims?

Answer: The objective is to get the broadest claim possible, which means using the fewest number of words. The more words you put in the claims, the easier it is to get the patent but the harder it is to later prove someone is infringing it. That's because in order for a particular device or process to infringe a patent claim, every word (more precisely, every structural or functional "limitation") in the claim (or its equivalent) must be present in the accused device or method. Thus, every word in a claim represents a potential noninfringement argument or an opportunity to "design around" the patent.

After we arrive at a target broadest claim we then build a logic tree of dependent claims below it, where each dependent claim either further elaborates on an element or limitation that is claimed at a higher level or adds another element or limitation to a higher level claim. We try to have as many levels or layers of dependent claims as possible. That's because it's impossible to know about all of the relevant prior art when the application is prepared. Thus, with a multilevel dependent claim strategy, if someone later finds prior art (e.g., in litigation) that invalidates a high-level claim, the more specific claims at the next level down may survive, and hopefully still be infringed.

Question: Is your drafting process also done with an eye on infringement?

Laurie: Absolutely. I was a patent litigator for ten years. And when you're enforcing a patent you see how easy it is for the other side to avoid infringement either by proving that what they're doing is outside the scope of what you have claimed, or by changing the design. The English language is not so precise—that's why medicine uses Latin. When you draft claims you're trying to define the boundaries between your legally protected area and the public domain. In order to define those boundaries you have to use words and the defendant [in an infringement lawsuit] is always going to try and use those words against you.

Question: Doesn't your approach require an extensive knowledge of the technology?

Laurie: Patent lawyers seldom know as much about the technical field as the inventor, but they are trained to go from one technology domain to another and to be a quick study. It's one of the few professions where clients pay you to learn (as long as you can do it quickly). Also, if you work in a larger intellectual property firm you may be able to walk down the hall and talk to somebody who is more knowledgeable in the area. If the field is really obscure or specialized, you might have to bring in a technical expert, or even refer the case to another attorney with the right technical background.

Question: From what you're saying, it seems like you would consider it inappropriate for an inventor to prepare his own patent application.

Laurie: Yes and no. The process of getting patent protection has both strategic and mechanical aspects. The mechanical portion involves meeting the Patent Office requirement of providing an "enabling" disclosure of an exemplary embodiment (sometimes referred to as a "preferred" embodiment) of the invention. The portion of the patent application that contains this material is called the "detailed description" or "specification." To do this, the most important qualifications are a working knowledge of the technology and good technical writing skills. Patent attorney involvement in the drafting of the detailed description is important to avoid any statements that may limit the scope of the claims in later litigation, but the lion's share of the work here is really technical writing, and doesn't require legal training.

The strategic part of the process is the drafting of the claims as described earlier, and this is where good patent lawyer skills are critical. But the inventor is best suited to write the detailed description. No one knows the technical details of the invention like the inventor. So that's a perfect role for the inventor—to describe the "best mode" of practicing the invention (of which he or she is aware at the time the application is filed).

This assumes that the inventor is available to write the detailed description. This can be an issue in a corporate environment where the engineers, scientists, programmers, etc. are hired to create products and the section or project leader typically assigns a higher priority to R&D milestones or product shipment deadlines than to filing patent applications. In other cases, it also may not work if English is a second language for the inventor.

If the inventor can't play the lead role in the specification drafting process, it has to be done by patent counsel, or in some cases by an outside technical consultant.

We try to split responsibility for the strategic and mechanical aspects of the process by assigning the drafting of the specification to the inventor whenever possible, or to a patent prosecution specialist when the inventor is not available. Fortunately, there are a lot of very good patent specification drafters working in small and solo practices with relatively low hourly billing rates as compared with patent attorneys in larger firms. Regardless of how, and to whom, the work is allocated, the most important thing is to get the sequence right, i.e., do the claims strategy first to develop the broadest possible set of claims and then write the detailed description to provide "support" for those claims, rather than writing the detailed description first in the hope that by the time you're finished you will have figured out what the invention is.

D. Working With a Patent Attorney

As far as inventors are concerned, there are two kinds of attorneys: those who are licensed to practice before the USPTO (patent attorneys) and those who are not. You should consult a patent attorney for assistance performing patent searching, drafting a provisional or regular patent application, responding to patent examiners, and dealing with the USPTO. (An attorney does not have to be licensed to practice before the USPTO in order to enforce your patent in a court case.) We recommend that you also use a patent attorney to prepare or analyze patent-related agreements on your behalf—for example, to prepare invention assignments, license agreements, or co-inventorship agreements.

1. Finding a Patent Attorney

The best way to get a referral to a good patent lawyer is to talk to other people who have actually used a particular lawyer's services. The worst way is to comb through advertisements or unscreened lists of lawyers provided by a local bar association (or the phone company).

Local bar associations often maintain and advertise lawyer referral services. However, a lawyer can usually get on this list simply by volunteering. Very little (if any) screening is done to find out whether the lawyers are any good. Similarly, advertisements in the Yellow Pages, in newspapers, on television, or online say nothing meaningful about a lawyer's skills or manner—just that he could afford to pay for the ad. In many states, lawyers can advertise any specialization they choose—even if they have never handled a case in that area of law.

If you are having difficulty locating an attorney knowledgeable about inventions and patent law, check out the American Intellectual Property Law Association (AIPLA), at www

.aipla.org, or the Intellectual Property Law Association of the American Bar Association, at www.abanet.org. The USPTO website (www.uspto.gov) also maintains a list of attorneys and patent agents licensed to practice before the USPTO.

Issued patents always list the inventor's attorney. If you notice, while searching through prior art, that many of the patents in your field were prepared by the same attorney, you may want to consider contacting that attorney. The lawyer is likely to be familiar with the field and the prior art.

2. Keeping Fees Down

Patent and intellectual property attorneys generally charge $200 to $400 per hour, and preparing and filing an application can cost anywhere from $4,000 to $10,000. To save yourself a lot of money and grief, follow these tips:

- **Keep it short.** If you are paying your attorney on an hourly basis, keep your conversations short—the meter is always running. Avoid making several calls a day; instead, consolidate your questions and ask them all in one conversation.

- **Get a fee agreement.** Always get a written fee agreement when dealing with an attorney. Read it and make sure you understand it. Your fee agreement should give you the right to an itemized billing statement that details the work done and time spent.

- **Watch out for hidden expenses.** Find out what expenses you will have to pay. Hopefully you can avoid an attorney that bills for services like word processing. (This means you will be paying the secretary's salary.) Also beware of exorbitant fax and copying charges.

- **Remember, you can always fire your lawyer.** (You're still obligated to pay outstanding bills, though.) If you don't respect and trust your attorney's professional abilities, you should find a new attorney. But switching attorneys is a nuisance, and you may lose time and money. ■

Appendix A

How the USPTO Handles
Patent Applications

*I*magine a board game called "Get a Patent." Each player starts with an invention, rolls the dice, and moves around the board until they land on "File an Application." After that, the play becomes more complicated, as players fend off objections from USPTO examiners and overcome patent-defeating obstacles, including discovery of relevant prior art, technical errors in the application, delays at the USPTO, and so on. In this game, you're going to need money, perseverance, and maybe even a lawyer in order to get to the final square—"Letters Patent Granted."

In the real world, this "game" of guiding a patent application through the USPTO is officially known as patent prosecution. Patent prosecution is not for the bureaucratically challenged. The laborious, time-consuming process of overcoming examiner objections is explained in detail in *Patent It Yourself,* by David Pressman (Nolo)—as well as in several weighty patent treatises. In this chapter, we explain what you might expect during patent prosecution by looking at a couple of file wrappers—the collection of documents (including correspondence and other paperwork) that the USPTO maintains for each issued patent.

Each file wrapper contains all of the paperwork that flows between the patent applicant (or the applicant's lawyer) and the USPTO. Once the patent issues, the file wrapper is made available to the public so that others can see exactly how the USPTO processed the application. (You can get a file wrapper for any issued patent or published application at the USPTO website: at www.uspto.gov.

Click "Patents," then, under "eBusiness," click "Buy Copies.") The USPTO charges approximately $200 for a file wrapper like the one shown in Section B.

This appendix reviews two file wrappers— one for a utility patent and one for a design patent. These documents are relatively straightforward—the USPTO pretty much accepted the patent applications as they were filed with little dispute. In other cases, especially for utility patents, the patent examiner will ask the applicant to narrow or change the patent claims to distinguish the invention from prior art found by the applicant or the examiner.

When Is your Patent "Pending"?

Once the USPTO mails you the official filing receipt, the patent application is officially pending. At this point, the invention and any descriptive literature can be labeled either as "patent pending" or "patent applied for" (both expressions mean the same thing). (An invention can also be labeled patent pending once a provisional patent application is filed— see Chapter 7, Section D). It's a criminal offense to use the words "patent applied for" or "patent pending" in any advertising when there's no active regular or provisional patent application on file for the item.

In Section A, we provide a brief overview of patent prosecution. Section B reviews the file wrapper for a utility patent, the Mosaic Collage (U.S. Pat. 6,273,979), and Section C covers the file wrapper for the Praying Angel design patent (U.S. Pat. D449249). Because of the size of these file wrappers, we have not printed all the contents in this book. Instead, we reproduce a few selected pages.

 Examiners and applicants rely on three resources during patent prosecution:

- Patent statutes. The patent laws passed by Congress are found in Title 35 of the United States Code (35 USC).
- *Patent Rules of Practice.* The *Patent Rules of Practice* are administrative regulations interpreting the patent laws. You can find them in Volume 37 of the Code of Federal Regulations (37 CFR § 1).
- *Manual of Patent Examining Procedure* (MPEP). The MPEP is often referred to as the "examiner's bible," because it covers almost any situation that might come up during patent prosecution. It contains the USPTO's Rules of Practice and the patent statutes.

You can find these resources at the USPTO's website, www.uspto.gov. They are also available on the CASSIS CD-ROMs, which you can find at special Patent Trademark Deposit Libraries (also known as PTDLs). To locate the PTDL nearest you, check the USPTO website.

A. Patent Prosecution

Every applicant's goal during patent prosecution is to obtain a Notice of Allowance, a statement from a USPTO examiner that the application meets the legal requirements of patentability. There are usually four steps

between filing your application and receiving your notice:

- **The USPTO receives and catalogues the patent application.** Within one to three months after you submit the application, the USPTO will send you an official filing receipt that includes the filing date, an eight-digit serial number, and more detailed information about the patent (such as the title of the patent application, the examining group to which the application has been assigned, and the number of claims). If you enclosed a return post card with your application, then you will receive that first, stamped with the serial number and filing date.
- **A USPTO examiner examines and initially rejects or allows the claims of the application.** Correspondence from the patent examiner to an applicant is commonly referred to as "office actions" (sometimes called "official letters" or "OA"). The first office action may raise various objections to the application—for example, the examiner may reject claims, report relevant prior art, or point out defects in the specification or drawing. The first office action will specify the deadline (usually three months) for filing a response (known as an "amendment").
- **The applicant responds to the rejection.** Your response (known as an "amendment") should include all of the information necessary to counter or respond to the examiner's rejection. (In some cases, if the changes are minor, the examiner will prepare this amendment after getting your approval by telephone.) The

amendment(s) usually include an analysis of the rejections made, references cited by the examiner, a discussion of prior-art references with relative arguments and distinctions, a request for reconsideration of the examiner's position, and/or a summary of how the claims have been changed.

⚠ You can't add new material in an amendment or response. An applicant can never add new matter to a pending application (PTO Rule 118). New matter is any technical information, including dimensions, materials, and so on, that was not present in the application as originally filed.

- **The examiner reviews the amendment and either issues a Notice of Allowance or makes a final rejection of the application.** If the amendment convinces the examiner that the application meets the requirements of patentability, you will receive a Notice of Allowance. If the examiner is not satisfied with your response, you will receive a second and "final" office action within two to six months after you filed the first amendment. Although this notice is supposed to end the prosecution stage, a "final action" is rarely final. You can ask the examiner to reconsider, agree to the amendments suggested by the examiner, file a Continuation or Request for Continued Examination (documents that starts a process for further review by the examiner), or

appeal to the Board of Appeals and Patent Interferences, a tribunal of judges within the USPTO.

Patent Extensions: When the USPTO Takes Too Long

If the USPTO takes too long to review your patent, you may be entitled to a longer patent term—that is, your patent will remain in effect for a longer period of time, to make up for the USPTO's delay. Under 35 USC § 154(b), the term of a patent will be extended for as long as necessary to compensate for:

- any delay caused by the USPTO's failure to examine a new application within 14 months from filing
- any delay caused by the USPTO's failure to take any of the following actions within four months:
  1. reply to an amendment or an appeal brief
  2. issue an allowance or office action after a decision on appeal, or
  3. issue a patent after the issue fee is paid and any required drawings are filed
- any delay caused by the USPTO's failure to issue a patent within three years from filing, unless the delay was due to the applicant filing a continuation or divisional application, or buying a delay to reply to an Office Action, or
- any delay due to secrecy orders, appeals, or interferences.

Keep others from patenting your invention—even if you don't get a patent.
Some applicants decide to abandon their patent application, but also want to prevent anyone else from getting a valid patent on the same invention. You can accomplish this by converting the application to a Statutory Invention Registration (SIR). The SIR precludes anyone else from obtaining a patent on the invention, except for someone who filed before the applicant.

B. The Mosaic Collage File Wrapper: U.S. Pat. 6,273,979

In August 2001, the USPTO issued U.S. Pat. 6,273,979 for the technique of mosaic collage. In the patent, the inventor provides some background regarding collage and mosaic techniques. She writes, "A collage is a technique of composing a work of art by pasting on a single surface various materials not normally associated with one another, as newspaper clippings, parts of photographs, theater tickets and fragments of an envelope. A mosaic is a picture or decoration made of small, usually colored pieces of inlaid stone, glass, etc. The present invention combines the techniques of both in forming a work of art or decoration.

In other words, the inventor has patented a method of combining two art forms, mosaics and collages.

The first claim in the patent reads as follows:

I claim: 1. A method for making a combination mosaic and collage work, comprising the steps of: dry mounting a museum board on a foam backing; preparing and executing a sketch drawing on the museum board; fixing whole photographic pictures with taped backing to various sheets of paper; copying the sheets with photographs attached on a copier machine; cutting copies of the sheets with photographs into different shapes; attaching the cut shapes onto the sketched drawing; copying sheets of material on a copier machine onto copied sheets of varying color and texture; cutting the copied sheets into different shapes; attaching the copied sheets of different shapes onto the sketched drawing; dry mounting said cut copied sheets and photographs on said museum board to form an assembly; and applying varnish to the assembly.

Let's review the file wrapper that documents this invention's journey from patent application through Notice of Allowance. Due to space limitations, we cannot include copies of all the file-wrapper documents so we have included a relevant selection on the following pages.

Page 1 is an indexing document form that contains general information about the history of the patent application, including when the patent issued (August 14, 2001), the patent number, the date the Notice of Allowance was mailed, the number of claims, and so forth.

Page 2 is a log listing documents the examiner sends or receives. Patent examiners sometimes don't list every document. Only three documents are indicated here, including the applicant's amendment and the formal drawings.

Page 3 indexes which claims were rejected, allowed, and so on. In this case, all of the claims were allowed.

Prior Art and Mosaic Collage

As we explained in Chapter 2, there can be a big difference between what might be patented and what should be patented. If you haven't made sure that there isn't any disqualifying prior art for your invention, approval by the USPTO—even for the most well-written claims—may prove worthless.

In our example, the USPTO has determined that the inventor's concept for a combination of collage and mosaic is both novel and non-obvious. Because both mosaics and collages have existed for centuries and both use small planar objects to compose an image, however, the mosaic collage—at least at the time when this patent was filed in 1999—seems like a natural, obvious combination.

We're not here to second-guess the USPTO, but in Warren Farnworth's *Approaches to Collage,* (BT Batsford, Ltd., 1976), the author documents (in Figure 46 of the book) what appears to be a mosaic collage. Perhaps we're wrong and this prior art does not affect the validity of the Mosaic Collage patent. Nevertheless, an inventor is obligated to inform the USPTO of any existing prior art references when filing a patent application—and this reference (which wasn't very hard for us to locate) was not mentioned in the application or by the examiner.

In fact, this patent does not provide any prior art, which seems odd, considering that both mosaic and collage techniques have been used for centuries. A reader of this patent might fairly surmise that the USPTO was not equipped to fully investigate this patent. As we indicated, if you want a strong patent that will sustain scrutiny, you should do a thorough patent search yourself before you apply for your patent. Chapter 6 provides information on prior art searching.

JC564 U.S. PTO
09/440454
11/24/99

156 63
Class Subclass
ISSUE CLASSIFICATION

PATENT NUMBER

6273979

6273979

U.S. **UTILITY** Patent Application

O.I.P.E.

SCANNED

Q.A.

PATENT DATE

AUG 14 2001

CLASS	SUBCLASS	ART UNIT	EXAMINER
428	63		Aftergut

TITLE OF INVENTION:

APPLICANT(S):

ISSUING CLASSIFICATION

ORIGINAL		CROSS REFERENCE(S)					
CLASS	SUBCLASS	CLASS	SUBCLASS (ONE SUBCLASS PER BLOCK)				
156	63	156	263	267	297		

INTERNATIONAL CLASSIFICATION

		428	39				
B32B	31/00	434	96				
B44C	1/16						

☐ Continued on Issue Slip Inside File Jacket

TERMINAL DISCLAIMER	DRAWINGS			CLAIMS ALLOWED	
	Sheets Drwg.	Figs. Drwg.	Print Fig.	Total Claims	Print Claim for O.G.
	6	6	6	10	1

☐ The term of this patent subsequent to _____ (date) has been disclaimed.

(Assistant Examiner)   (Date)

NOTICE OF ALLOWANCE MAILED

☐ The term of this patent shall not extend beyond the expiration date of U.S Patent No. _____

JEFF H. AFTERGUT
PRIMARY EXAMINER
GROUP 1300

4-3-01

Jeff H Aftergut 4/3/01
(Primary Examiner)   (Date)

ISSUE FEE

Amount Due	Date Paid
$620.00	5/18/01

☐ The terminal ____ months of this patent have been disclaimed.

Hensley 4-11-01
(Legal Instruments Examiner)   (Date)

ISSUE BATCH NUMBER

E47

WARNING:

The information disclosed herein may be restricted. Unauthorized disclosure may be prohibited by the United States Code Title 35, Sections 122, 181 and 368. Possession outside the U.S. Patent & Trademark Office is restricted to authorized employees and contractors only.

Form PTO-436A
(Rev. 6/99)

FILED WITH: ☐ DISK (CRF) ☐ FICHE ☐ CD-ROM

(Attached in pocket on right inside flap)

Formal Drawings (____ shts) set ____

ISSUE FEE IN FILE

(FACE)

ISSUE SLIP STAPLE AREA (for additional cross references)

POSITION	INITIALS	ID NO.	DATE
			12/07/94
FEE DETERMINATION			7, 12-14-99
O.I.P.E. CLASSIFIER			
FORMALITY REVIEW		71476	1/12/00
RESPONSE FORMALITY REVIEW			

INDEX OF CLAIMS

✓ .... Rejected		N .... Non-elected
= .... Allowed		I .... Interference
− (Through numeral)... Canceled		A .... Appeal
÷ .... Restricted		O .... Objected

Claim		Date	Claim		Date	Claim		Date
Final	Original		Final	Original		Final	Original	
1	1		51			101		
2	2		52			102		
3	3		53			103		
4	4		54			104		
5	5		55			105		
6	6		56			106		
7	7		57			107		
8	8		58			108		
9	9		59			109		
10	10		60			110		
	11		61			111		
	12		62			112		
	13		63			113		
	14		64			114		
	15		65			115		
	16		66			116		
	17		67			117		
	18		68			118		
	19		69			119		
	20		70			120		
	21		71			121		
	22		72			122		
	23		73			123		
	24		74			124		
	25		75			125		
	26		76			126		
	27		77			127		
	28		78			128		
	29		79			129		
	30		80			130		
	31		81			131		
	32		82			132		
	33		83			133		
	34		84			134		
	35		85			135		
	36		86			136		
	37		87			137		
	38		88			138		
	39		89			139		
	40		90			140		
	41		91			141		
	42		92			142		
	43		93			143		
	44		94			144		
	45		95			145		
	46		96			146		
	47		97			147		
	48		98			148		
	49		99			149		
	50		100			150		

If more than 150 claims or 10 actions
staple additional sheet here

(LEFT INSIDE)

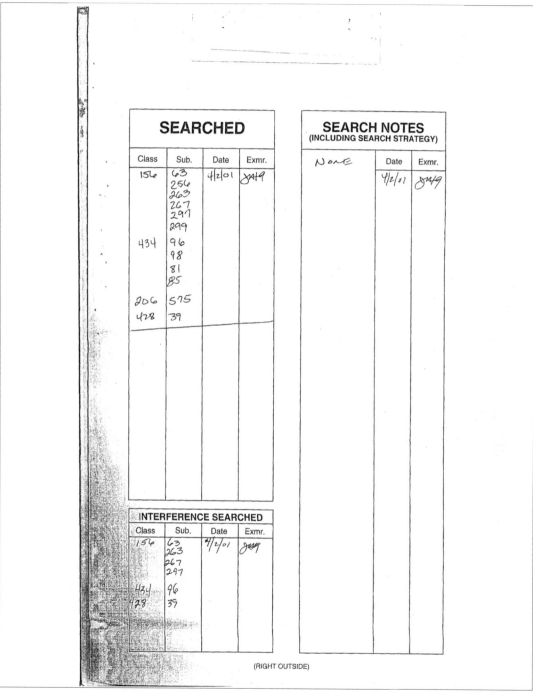

SEARCHED

Class	Sub.	Date	Exmr.
156	63	4/2/01	JM9
	256		
	263		
	267		
	297		
	299		
434	96		
	98		
	81		
	85		
206	575		
428	39		

SEARCH NOTES
(INCLUDING SEARCH STRATEGY)

None	Date	Exmr.
	4/2/01	JM9

INTERFERENCE SEARCHED

Class	Sub.	Date	Exmr.
156	63	4/2/01	JM9
	263		
	267		
	297		
434	96		
428	39		

(RIGHT OUTSIDE)

The Mosaic Collage File Wrapper: U.S. Pat. 6,273,979   Page 4

I claim:

1.   A method for making a combination mosaic and collage
work, comprising the steps of:

> dry mounting a museum board on a foam backing;
>
> preparing and executing a sketch drawing on the museum
> > board;
>
> fixing whole photographic pictures with taped backing
> > to various sheets of paper;
>
> copying the sheets with photographs attached on a copier
> > machine;
>
> cutting copies of the sheets with photographs into
> > different shapes;
>
> attaching the cut shapes onto the sketched drawing;
>
> copying sheets of material on a copier machine onto
> > copied sheets of varying color and texture/;
>
> cutting the copied sheets into different shapes;
>
> attaching the copied sheets different shapes onto the
> > sketched drawing;

a

dry mounting said ~~work~~ *cut copied sheets and photographs* on said museum board; *to form an assembly* and

applying varnish to the ~~work~~ *assembly*.

2. The method recited in claim 1, further comprising the step of:

changing sizes of the sheets with photographs attached while copying.

3. The method recited in claim 2, further comprising the step of:

changing sizes of the sheets of material while copying.

4. The method recited in claim 3, further comprising the steps of:

making multiple copies of one particular image;

cutting the multiple copies of said particular image into a variety of shapes; and

attaching the variety of image shapes onto and around the sketched drawing.

8

5.   The method recited in claim 4, further comprising the step of:

    framing the work with a plexiglass.

6.   A method for making a combination mosaic and collage work, comprising the steps of:

    preparing and executing a sketch drawing on a piece of
        sealed wood having a prepared surface;

    fixing whole photographic pictures with taped backing
        to various sheets of paper;

    copying the sheets with photographs attached on a copier
        machine;

    cutting copies of the sheets with photographs into
        different shapes;

    attaching the cut shapes onto the sketched drawing;

    copying sheets of material on a copier machine onto
        copied sheets of varying color and texture/;

    cutting the copied sheets into different shapes;

    attaching the copied sheets different shapes onto the
        sketched drawing;

9

a

a

cut copied sheets and photographs *piece of sealed wood*

dry mounting said ~~work~~ on said ~~museum board~~ *to form an assembly* and

applying varnish to the *assembly* ~~work~~.

7. The method recited in claim 6, further comprising the step of:

changing sizes of the sheets with photographs attached while copying.

8. The method recited in claim 7, further comprising the step of:

changing sizes of the sheets of material while copying.

9. The method recited in claim 8, further comprising the steps of:

making multiple copies of one particular image;

cutting the multiple copies of said particular image into a variety of shapes; and

attaching the variety of image shapes onto and around the sketched drawing.

10

10.   The method recited in claim 9, further comprising the step of:

imbuing said work with a plastic-polymer.

11

	Application No.	Applicant(s)
Notice of Allowability	09/448,454	LASTORIA, ESTER E.
	Examiner	Art Unit
	Jeff H. Aftergut	1733

-- The MAILING DATE of this communication appears on the cover sheet with the correspondence address--
All claims being allowable, PROSECUTION ON THE MERITS IS (OR REMAINS) CLOSED in this application. If not included herewith (or previously mailed), a Notice of Allowance and Issue Fee Due or other appropriate communication will be mailed in due course. **THIS NOTICE OF ALLOWABILITY IS NOT A GRANT OF PATENT RIGHTS.** This application is subject to withdrawal from issue at the initiative of the Office or upon petition by the applicant. See 37 CFR 1.313 and MPEP 1308.

1. ☒ This communication is responsive to *application filed 11-24-99*.
2. ☒ The allowed claim(s) is/are *1-10*.
3. ☐ The drawings filed on _____ are acceptable as formal drawings.
4. ☐ Acknowledgment is made of a claim for foreign priority under 35 U.S.C. § 119(a)-(d) or (f).
  a) ☐ All   b) ☐ Some*   c) ☐ None   of the:
    1. ☐ Certified copies of the priority documents have been received.
    2. ☐ Certified copies of the priority documents have been received in Application No. _____ .
    3. ☐ Copies of the certified copies of the priority documents have been received in this national stage application from the International Bureau (PCT Rule 17.2(a)).
  * Certified copies not received: _____ .
5. ☐ Acknowledgement is made of a claim for domestic priority under 35 U.S.C. § 119(e).

Applicant has THREE MONTHS FROM THE "MAILING DATE" of this communication to file a reply complying with the requirements noted below. Failure to timely comply will result in ABANDONMENT of this application. **THIS THREE-MONTH PERIOD IS NOT EXTENDABLE FOR SUBMITTING NEW FORMAL DRAWINGS, OR A SUBSTITUTE OATH OR DECLARATION.** This three-month period for complying with the REQUIREMENT FOR THE DEPOSIT OF BIOLOGICAL MATERIAL is extendable under 37 CFR 1.136(a).

6. ☐ Note the attached EXAMINER'S AMENDMENT or NOTICE OF INFORMAL APPLICATION (PTO-152) which gives reason(s) why the oath or declaration is deficient. A SUBSTITUTE OATH OR DECLARATION IS REQUIRED.

7. ☒ Applicant MUST submit NEW FORMAL DRAWINGS
  (a) ☒ including changes required by the Notice of Draftsperson's Patent Drawing Review(PTO-948) attached
    1) ☒ hereto or 2) ☐ to Paper No. ____.
  (b) ☐ including changes required by the proposed drawing correction filed _____, which has been approved by the examiner.
  (c) ☐ including changes required by the attached Examiner's Amendment / Comment or in the Office action of Paper No. _____.

  Identifying indicia such as the application number (see 37 CFR 1.84(c)) should be written on the drawings. The drawings should be filed as a separate paper with a transmittal letter addressed to the Official Draftsperson.

8. ☐ Note the attached Examiner's comment regarding REQUIREMENT FOR THE DEPOSIT OF BIOLOGICAL MATERIAL.

Any reply to this letter should include, in the upper right hand corner, the APPLICATION NUMBER (SERIES CODE / SERIAL NUMBER). If applicant has received a Notice of Allowance and Issue Fee Due, the ISSUE BATCH NUMBER and DATE of the NOTICE OF ALLOWANCE should also be included.

Attachment(s)

1 ☒ Notice of References Cited (PTO-892)
3 ☒ Notice of Draftsperson's Patent Drawing Review (PTO-948)
5 ☒ Information Disclosure Statements (PTO-1449), Paper No. *2*.
7 ☐ Examiner's Comment Regarding Requirement for Deposit of Biological Material

2 ☐ Notice of Informal Patent Application (PTO-152)
4 ☐ Interview Summary (PTO-413), Paper No.____ .
6 ☒ Examiner's Amendment/Comment
8 ☒ Examiner's Statement of Reasons for Allowance
9 ☐ Other

Jeff H. Aftergut
Primary Examiner
Art Unit: 1733

U.S. Patent and Trademark Office
PTO-37 (Rev. 01-01) | Notice of Allowability | Part of Paper No. 3

Application/Control Number: 09/448,454

Art Unit: 1733

3/9

Page 2

4-3-01

1.   An examiner's amendment to the record appears below. Should the changes and/or additions be unacceptable to applicant, an amendment may be filed as provided by 37 CFR 1.312. To ensure consideration of such an amendment, it MUST be submitted no later than the payment of the issue fee.

Authorization for this examiner's amendment was given in a telephone interview with John McGonagle on 4-2-01.

The application has been amended as follows:

In the claims:

In claim 1, line 14, "." has been changed to --;--.

In claim 1, line 18, "work" has been changed to --cut copied sheets and photographs--.

In claim 1, line 18, after "board" the language --to form an assembly-- has been added.

In claim 1, line 19, "work" has been changed to --assembly--.

In claim 6, line 13, "." has been changed to --;--.

In claim 6, line 17, "work" has been changed to --cut copied sheets and photographs--.

In claim 6, line 17, "museum board" has been changed to --piece of sealed wood---

In claim 6, line 17, before the ";" the language --to form an assembly-- has been added.

Application/Control Number: 09/448,454   Page 3
Art Unit: 1733

In claim 6, line 18, "work" has been changed to --assembly--.

2.   The following is an examiner's statement of reasons for allowance: None of the prior art

of record taught the formation of a combination of a mosaic and collage work which included the

steps of sketching a drawing upon a substrate and dry mounting a plurality of cut copied sheets

and photographs (note that the prior art failed to teach that one would have copied photographs

and cut the same as well as cut sheets of material of varying color and texture and cut the copies)

to form the work. The reference to Pilgrim, Jr. taught decorating a bottle by attaching a plurality

of cut colored pieces to a bottle, however the colored pieces were not cut from copies. Grant

taught a process of making a picture from cut pieces of material with various colors wherein the

colored pieces were cut and adhesively attached to a backing.

Any comments considered necessary by applicant must be submitted no later than the

payment of the issue fee and, to avoid processing delays, should preferably accompany the issue

fee. Such submissions should be clearly labeled "Comments on Statement of Reasons for

Allowance."

Any inquiry concerning this communication or earlier communications from the

examiner should be directed to Jeff H. Aftergut whose telephone number is 703-308-2069. The

examiner can normally be reached on Monday-Friday 6:30-3:00pm.

If attempts to reach the examiner by telephone are unsuccessful, the examiner's

supervisor, Michael W. Ball can be reached on 703-308-2058. The fax phone numbers for the

organization where this application or proceeding is assigned are 703-305-3599 for regular

communications and 703-305-7718 for After Final communications.

Application/Control Number: 09/448,454   Page 4
Art Unit: 1733

Any inquiry of a general nature or relating to the status of this application or proceeding

should be directed to the receptionist whose telephone number is 703-308-0661.

Jeff H. Affergut
Primary Examiner
Art Unit 1733

JHA
April 2, 2001

		Application/Control No. 09/448,454	Applicant(s)/Patent Under Reexamination LASTORIA, ESTER E.	
Notice of References Cited		Examiner Jeff H. Aftergut	Art Unit 1733	Page 1 of 1

U.S. PATENT DOCUMENTS

*		Document Number Country Code-Number-Kind Code	Date MM-YYYY	Name	Classification	
*	A	US-5106305-	04-1992	Grant	434	96
*	B	US-4940153-	07-1990	Pilgrim, Jr.	156	63
	C	US- -				
	D	US- -				
	E	US- -				
	F	US- -				
	G	US- -				
	H	US- -				
	I	US- -				
	J	US- -				
	K	US- -				
	L	US- -				
	M	US- -				

FOREIGN PATENT DOCUMENTS

*		Document Number Country Code-Number-Kind Code	Date MM-YYYY	Country	Name	Classification
	N	- -				
	O	- -				
	P	- -				
	Q	- -				
	R	- -				
	S	- -				
	T	- -				

NON-PATENT DOCUMENTS

*		Include as applicable: Author, Title Date, Publisher, Edition or Volume, Pertinent Pages)
	U	
	V	
	W	
	X	

*A copy of this reference is not being furnished with this Office action. (See MPEP § 707.05(a).)
Dates in MM-YYYY format are publication dates. Classifications may be US or foreign.

U.S. Patent and Trademark Office
PTO-892 (Rev. 01-2001)   Notice of References Cited   Part of Paper No. 3

Form PTO 948 (Rev. 8-98)   U.S. DEPARTMENT OF COMMERCE - Patent and Trademark Office   Application No. 09/448,454

NOTICE OF DRAFTSPERSON'S
PATENT DRAWING REVIEW

The drawing(s) filed (insert date) 11/24/99 are:
A. ☐ approved by the Draftsperson under 37 CFR 1.84 or 1.152.
B. ☑ objected to by the Draftsperson under 37 CFR 1.84 or 1.152 for the reasons indicated below. The Examiner will require
submission of new, corrected drawings when necessary. Corrected drawing must be sumitted according to the instructions on the back of this notice.

1. DRAWINGS. 37 CFR 1.84(a): Acceptable categories of drawings:
Black ink. Color.
____ Color drawings are not acceptable until petiton is granted.
Fig(s) _____
____ Pencil and non black ink not permitted. Fig(s) _____
2. PHOTOGRAPHS. 37 CFR 1.84 (b)
____ 1 full-tone set is required. Fig(s) _____
____ Photographs not properly mounted (must use brystol board or photographic double-weight paper). Fig(s) _____
____ Poor quality (half-tone). Fig(s) _____
3. TYPE OF PAPER. 37 CFR 1.84(e)
____ Paper not flexible, strong, white, and durable.
Fig(s) _____
____ Erasures, alterations, overwritings, interlineations, folds, copy machine marks not accepted. Fig(s) _____
____ Mylar, velum paper is not acceptable (too thin).
Fig(s) _____
4. SIZE OF PAPER. 37 CFR 1.84(f): Acceptable sizes:
____ 21.0 cm by 29.7 cm (DIN size A4)
____ 21.6 cm by 27.9 cm (8 1/2 x 11 inches)
____ All drawing sheets not the same size.
Sheet(s) _____
____ Drawings sheets not an acceptable size. Fig(s) _____
5. MARGINS. 37 CFR 1.84(g): Acceptable margins:
Top 2.5 cm Left 2.5cm Right 1.5 cm Bottom 1.0 cm
SIZE: A4 Size
Top 2.5 cm Left 2.5 cm Right 1.5 cm Bottom 1.0 cm,
SIZE: 8 1/2 x 11
Margins not acceptable. Fig(s) _____
____ Top (T) ____ Left (L)
____ Right (R) ____ Bottom (B)
6. VIEWS. 37 CFR 1.84(h)
REMINDER: Specification may require revision to correspond to drawing changes.
Partial views. 37 CFR 1.84(h)(2)
____ Brackets needed to show figure as one entity.
Fig(s) _____
____ Views not labeled separately or properly.
Fig(s) _____
____ Enlarged view not labeled separetely or properly.
Fig(s) _____
7. SECTIONAL VIEWS. 37 CFR 1.84 (h)(3)
____ Hatching not indicated for sectional portions of an object.
Fig(s) _____
____ Sectional designation should be noted with Arabic or Roman numbers. Fig(s) _____

8. ARRANGEMENT OF VIEWS. 37 CFR 1.84(i)
____ Words do not appear on a horizontal, left-to-right fashion when page is either upright or turned so that the top becomes the right side, except for graphs. Fig(s) _____
9. SCALE. 37 CFR 1.84(k)
____ Scale not large enough to show mechanism without crowding when drawing is reduced in size to two-thirds in reproduction. Fig(s) _____
10. CHARACTER OF LINES, NUMBERS, & LETTERS. 37 CFR 1.84(i)
✓ Lines, numbers & letters not uniformly thick and well defined, clean, durable, and black (poor line quality). Fig(s) 1-6
11. SHADING. 37 CFR 1.84(m)
____ Solid black areas pale. Fig(s) _____
____ Solid black shading not permitted. Fig(s) _____
____ Shade lines, pale, rough and blurred. Fig(s) _____
12. NUMBERS, LETTERS, & REFERENCE CHARACTERS. 37 CFR 1.84(p)
____ Numbers and reference characters not plain and legible. Fig(s) _____
____ Figure legends are poor. Fig(s) _____
____ Numbers and reference characters not oriented in the same direction as the view. 37 CFR 1.84(p)(1) Fig(s) _____
____ English alphabet not used. 37 CFR 1.84(p)(2) Figs _____
____ Numbers, letters and reference characters must be at least .32 cm (1/8 inch) in height. 37 CFR 1.84(p)(3) Fig(s) _____
13. LEAD LINES. 37 CFR 1.84(q)
____ Lead lines cross each other. Fig(s) _____
____ Lead lines missing. Fig(s) _____
14. NUMBERING OF SHEETS OF DRAWINGS. 37 CFR 1.84(t)
____ Sheets not numbered consecutively, and in Arabic numerals beginning with number 1. Sheet(s) _____
15. NUMBERING OF VIEWS. 37 CFR 1.84(u)
____ Views not numbered consecutively, and in Arabic numerals, beginning with number 1. Fig(s) _____
16. CORRECTIONS. 37 CFR 1.84(w)
____ Corrections not made from prior PTO-948 dated _____
17. DESIGN DRAWINGS. 37 CFR 1.152
____ Surface shading shown not appropriate. Fig(s) _____
____ Solid black shading not used for color contrast. Fig(s) _____

COMMENTS

REVIEWER Draftsman Son Lam   DATE 04/02/01   TELEPHONE NO. _____
(703,000-0000)

ATTACHMENT TO PAPER NO. _____

Interview Summary	Application No.	Applicant(s)
	09/448,454	LASTORIA, ESTER E.
	Examiner	Art Unit
	Jeff H. Aftergut	1733

All participants (applicant, applicant's representative, PTO personnel):

(1) *Jeff H. Aftergut.*   (3)_____ .

(2) *John McGonagle.*   (4)_____ .

Date of Interview: *02 April 2001* .

Type: a)☒ Telephonic   b)☐ Video Conference
       c)☐ Personal [copy given to: 1)☐ applicant   2)☐ applicant's representative]

Exhibit shown or demonstration conducted: d)☐ Yes   e)☒ No.
    If Yes, brief description:

Claim(s) discussed: *1 and 6* .

Identification of prior art discussed: *None* .

Agreement with respect to the claims f)☒ was reached. g)☐ was not reached. h)☐ N/A.

Substance of Interview including description of the general nature of what was agreed to if an agreement was reached, or any other comments: *Discussed a need to remove the period in the middle of both claims 1 and 6. Additionally noted that there was no proper antecedent basis for "the work" in the claim Also in claim 6 there was no antecedent basis for "said museum board". Applicant's rep. agreed to correct all of these problems by examiner's amendment* .

(A fuller description, if necessary, and a copy of the amendments which the examiner agreed would render the claims allowable, if available, must be attached. Also, where no copy of the amendments that would render the claims allowable is available, a summary thereof must be attached.)

    i)☒ It is not necessary for applicant to provide a separate record of the substance of the interview(if box is checked).

Unless the paragraph above has been checked, THE FORMAL WRITTEN REPLY TO THE LAST OFFICE ACTION MUST INCLUDE THE SUBSTANCE OF THE INTERVIEW. (See MPEP Section 713.04). If a reply to the last Office action has already been filed, APPLICANT IS GIVEN ONE MONTH FROM THIS INTERVIEW DATE TO FILE A STATEMENT OF THE SUBSTANCE OF THE INTERVIEW. See Summary of Record of Interview requirements on reverse side or on attached sheet.

Examiner Note: You must sign this form unless it is an Attachment to a signed Office action.

Examiner's signature, if required

U.S. Patent and Trademark Office
PTO-413 (Rev. 03- 98)   Interview Summary   Paper No. 3.

UNITED STATES DEPARTMENT OF COMMERCE
Patent and Trademark Office

NOTICE OF ALLOWANCE AND ISSUE FEE DUE

IM52/0403

JOHN P MCGONAGLE
LAW OFFICES OF JOHN P MCGONAGLE
800 HINGHAM STREET 2N
ROCKLAND MA 02370

APPLICATION NO.	FILING DATE	TOTAL CLAIMS	EXAMINER AND GROUP ART UNIT		DATE MAILED
09/448,454	11/24/99	010	AFTERGUT, J	1733	04/03/01

First Named Applicant	LASTORIA,		35 USC 154(b) term ext. =		0 Days.

TITLE OF INVENTION MOSAIC COLLAGE

ATTY'S DOCKET NO.		CLASS-SUBCLASS	BATCH NO.	APPLN. TYPE	SMALL ENTITY	FEE DUE	DATE DUE
1	6976	156-063.000	E47	UTILITY	YES	$620.00	07/03/01

**THE APPLICATION IDENTIFIED ABOVE HAS BEEN EXAMINED AND IS ALLOWED FOR ISSUANCE AS A PATENT.
PROSECUTION ON THE MERITS IS CLOSED.**

**THE ISSUE FEE MUST BE PAID WITHIN <u>THREE MONTHS</u> FROM THE MAILING DATE OF THIS NOTICE OR THIS
APPLICATION SHALL BE REGARDED AS ABANDONED. <u>THIS STATUTORY PERIOD CANNOT BE EXTENDED.</u>**

HOW TO RESPOND TO THIS NOTICE:

I. Review the SMALL ENTITY status shown above.
If the SMALL ENTITY is shown as YES, verify your
current SMALL ENTITY status:

   A. If the status is changed, pay twice the amount of the
      FEE DUE shown above and notify the Patent and
      Trademark Office of the change in status, or
   B. If the status is the same, pay the FEE DUE shown
      above.

If the SMALL ENTITY is shown as NO:

   A. Pay FEE DUE shown above, or

   B. File verified statement of Small Entity Status before, or with,
      payment of 1/2 the FEE DUE shown above.

II. Part B-Issue Fee Transmittal should be completed and returned to the Patent and Trademark Office (PTO) with your
   ISSUE FEE. Even if the ISSUE FEE has already been paid by charge to deposit account, Part B Issue Fee Transmittal
   should be completed and returned. If you are charging the ISSUE FEE to your deposit account, section "4b" of Part
   B-Issue Fee Transmittal should be completed and an extra copy of the form should be submitted.

III. All communications regarding this application must give application number and batch number.
   Please direct all communications prior to issuance to Box ISSUE FEE unless advised to the contrary.

IMPORTANT REMINDER: *Utility patents issuing on applications filed on or after Dec. 12, 1980 may require payment of
maintenance fees. It is patentee's responsibility to ensure timely payment of maintenance
fees when due.*
      PATENT AND TRADEMARK OFFICE COPY

PTOL-85 (REV. 10-96) Approved for use through 06/30/99. (0651-0033)

Page 4 is a report of how the patent examiner searched for prior art. In this case, the examiner searched four classes and 12 subclasses for relevant prior art.

Pages 5 through 34 are copies of the application documents, including the text of the patent application, drawings, a declaration and power of attorney, a transmittal form, and a document reflecting whether the applicant will seek foreign patent rights.

Page 35 is a document acknowledging receipt of the $380 filing fee.

Pages 36 through 41 are correspondence from the examiner to the applicant, including a cover letter, a Notice of Allowability (in which the patent examiner informs the applicant that the patent application will be granted, but some corrections have to be made). Also included is a proposed amendment to the application. Apparently, the examiner talked to the applicant's attorney on the telephone and, as a result of that call, the examiner prepared an amendment with minor changes to the language of the claims. The Notice of Allowability also includes (in paragraph number two) an explanation of why the examiner felt that the patent was novel. Page 41 is an index of the references cited by the examiner in his Notice.

Page 42 is a Notice of Draftperson's Patent Drafting Review, in which a USPTO draftsperson tells the applicant what is wrong with the patent application's drawings. In this case, the changes are minor, regarding lines and margins.

Pages 43 is a summary of the telephone interview discussed on page 38.

Page 44 is a Notice Of Allowance and Issue Fee Due, where the Patent Office informs the applicant that a design patent will issue once the issue fees are paid.

Page 45 is a document explaining the rules for the interview summarized on Page 43.

Pages 46 is a cover letter from the applicant's lawyer providing revised formal drawings.

Pages 47 to 52 are the revised drawings.

Page 53 to 55 are the Issue Fee Transmittal (indicating the requested fees are being submitted to the USPTO), a listing of the number of claims, and a form used to calculate the fee based upon the number of claims.

Page 56 through 64 show the final patent and drawings as issued by the USPTO.

C. Design Patent Prosecution: The Praying Angel File Wrapper: (D449249)

Design patent prosecution is much simpler than regular patent prosecution. Once you file your application, you will rarely be required to do anything more than make elementary changes to the application or design. Usually, the examiner tells the applicant exactly what to do to obtain a Notice of Allowance.

Below, we examine the file wrapper for a design patent for a statue of a praying angel. (Due to space limitations, we cannot include copies of all the file-wrapper documents so we have included a relevant selection on the following pages.) The design patent application was filed December 13, 2000, and the patent issued on October 16, 2001. The inventors were Shalom Zadok and Itchak Tarkay.

J-930 U.S. PTO 29/134053 12/13/00

D11 162 Class / Subclass / ISSUE CLASSIFICATION

PATENT NUMBER

D449249

D449249

U.S. DESIGN Patent Application

O.I.P.E.

M·H SCANNED Q.A.

PATENT DATE

OCT 1 6 2001

CLASS	SUBCLASS	ART UNIT	EXAMINER
D11	~~127~~ 162	2912	Simone

TITLE OF INVENTION:

APPLICANT(S):

ISSUE FEE IN FILE

ISSUING CLASSIFICATION

ORIGINAL		CROSS REFERENCE(S)				
CLASS	SUBCLASS	CLASS	SUBCLASS (ONE SUBCLASS PER BLOCK)			
D11	162					

INTERNATIONAL CLASSIFICATION

		11/01					

☐ Continued on Issue Slip Inside File Jacket

☐ TERMINAL DISCLAIMER	DRAWINGS			NOTICE OF ALLOWANCE MAILED
	Sheets Drwg.	Figs. Drwg.	Print Fig.	
	5	7	1	

☐ The term of this patent subsequent to _____ (date) has been disclaimed.

(Assistant Examiner) (Date)

5/15/01

ISSUE FEE

☐ The term of this patent shall not extend beyond the expiration date of U.S Patent No. _____

DOMINIC SIMONE
PRIMARY EXAMINER
GROUP 2900
(Primary Examiner) (Date)

Amount Due	Date Paid
440.00	8/20/01

ISSUE BATCH NUMBER

X67

☐ The terminal ____ months of this patent have been disclaimed.

(Legal Instruments Examiner) (Date) 5-17-01

WARNING:
The information disclosed herein may be restricted. Unauthorized disclosure may be prohibited by the United States Code Title 35, Sections 122, 181 and 368. Possession outside the U.S. Patent & Trademark Office is restricted to authorized employees and contractors only.

Form PTO-450
(Rev. 6/99)

DESIGN

29134053

Jc930 U.S. PTO
29/134053

12/13/00

APPROVED FOR LICENSE ☐

INITIALS _____

Date Entered or Counted	CONTENTS	Date Received (Incl. C. of M.) or Date Mailed
	1. Application ✓ _____ papers.	
	2. _____	1-18-01
	3. _____ fee	3-21-01
4|19|01	4. Priority Document	3.21.01
5-15=	5. N. of Allowability	5/15/0
	6. N. of Allowance	5/15/01
	7. Change of Address	6/08/01
	8. _____	
	9. _____	
	10. _____	
	11. _____	
	12. _____	
	13. _____	
	14. _____	
	15. _____	
	16. _____	
	17. _____	
	18. _____	
	19. _____	
	20. _____	
	21. _____	
	22. _____	
	23. _____	
	24. _____	
	25. _____	
	26. _____	
	27. _____	
	28. _____	
	29. _____	
	30. _____	
	31. _____	
	32. _____	

(LEFT OUTSIDE)

The Praying Angel File Wrapper: U.S. Pat. D449249 Page 2

ISSUE SLIP STAPLE AREA (for additional cross references)

POSITION	INITIALS	ID NO.	DATE
FEE DETERMINATION			
O.I.P.E. CLASSIFIER			
FORMALITY REVIEW			
RESPONSE FORMALITY REVIEW			

SEARCHED

Class	Sub.	Date	Exmr.
D11	121		
	128		
	160		
	162	5/8/01	ℬ
D21	626	5/8/01	ℬ
D99	21	5/8/01	ℬ

SEARCH NOTES
(INCLUDING SEARCH STRATEGY)

	Date	Exmr.
3/10	4/14/01	ℬ
Xmas Angel	5/8/01	ℬ
Garden Ornaments (Ex. Room)	5/8/01	ℬ

(LEFT INSIDE)

The Praying Angel File Wrapper: U.S. Pat. D449249

29/134053 U.S. PTO 12/13/00

ISSUE CLASSIFICATION
Class D11 162 Subclass

PATENT NUMBER

D449249

D449249

U.S. DESIGN Patent Application

O.I.P.E.	PATENT DATE
SCANNED	OCT 1 6 2001
Q.A.	

CLASS	SUBCLASS 162	ART UNIT	EXAMINER

TITLE OF INVENTION:

APPLICANT(S):

ISSUING CLASSIFICATION

ORIGINAL			CROSS REFERENCE(S)		
CLASS	SUBCLASS	CLASS	SUBCLASS (ONE SUBCLASS PER BLOCK)		
D11	163				
INTERNATIONAL CLASSIFICATION					
11/01					

☐ Continued on Issue Slip Inside File Jacket

☐TERMINAL ☐DISCLAIMER	DRAWINGS			NOTICE OF ALLOWANCE MAILED
	Sheets Drwg.	Figs. Drwg.	Print Fig.	
	5	7	1	5 / 15/01

☐ The term of this patent subsequent to _____ (date) has been disclaimed.	
	(Assistant Examiner) (Date)

ISSUE FEE NM

Amount Due	Date Paid
440.00	8/20/01

☐ The term of this patent shall not extend beyond the expiration date of U.S Patent No. _____

Dominic Simone
DOMINIC SIMONE
PRIMARY EXAMINER
GROUP 2900
(Primary Examiner) (Date)

ISSUE BATCH NUMBER
X67

☐ The terminal _____ months of this patent have been disclaimed.

_____ 5-17-01
(Legal Instruments Examiner) (Date)

WARNING:
The information disclosed herein may be restricted. Unauthorized disclosure may be prohibited by the United States Code Title 35, Sections 122, 181 and 368. Possession outside the U.S. Patent & Trademark Office is restricted to authorized employees and contractors only.

Form PTO-450
(Rev. 6/99)

(FACE)

Page 1 of 1

UNITED STATES PATENT AND TRADEMARK OFFICE

COMMISSIONER FOR PATENTS
UNITED STATES PATENT AND TRADEMARK OFFICE
WASHINGTON, D.C. 20231
www.uspto.gov

Bib Data Sheet

CONFIRMATION NO. 4521

SERIAL NUMBER 29/134,053	FILING DATE 12/13/2000 RULE	CLASS D11	GROUP ART UNIT 2900	ATTORNEY DOCKET NO. 3429-8 Design

APPLICANTS

Shalom Zadok, Holon, ISRAEL;
Itchak Tarkay, Holon, ISRAEL;

** CONTINUING DATA ***************************

** FOREIGN APPLICATIONS *********************
ISRAEL 34249 10/06/2000

IF REQUIRED, FOREIGN FILING LICENSE
GRANTED ** 01/17/2001   ** SMALL ENTITY **

Foreign Priority claimed ☐ yes ☑ no		STATE OR COUNTRY ISRAEL	SHEETS DRAWING 5	TOTAL CLAIMS 1	INDEPENDENT CLAIMS 1
35 USC 119 (a-d) conditions met ☐ yes ☐ no ☐ Met after Allowance					
Verified and Acknowledged Examiner's Signature Initials					

ADDRESS

Brown Raysman Millstein Felder & Steiner LLP
~~120 West 45th Street~~
~~New York, NY 10036~~

900 Third Avenue
New York, New York 10022-4728

TITLE

Sculpture

FILING FEE RECEIVED 225	FEES: Authority has been given in Paper No. _____ to charge/credit DEPOSIT ACCOUNT No. _____ for following:	☐ All Fees
		☐ 1.16 Fees (Filing)
		☐ 1.17 Fees (Processing Ext. of time)
		☐ 1.18 Fees (Issue)
		☐ Other _____
		☐ Credit

SPECIFICATION

BE IT KNOWN that we, SHALOM ZADOK and ITCHAK TARKAY have invented a new, original, and ornamental design for a SCULPTURE of which the following is the specification, reference being had to the accompanying drawings forming a part hereof.

FIG. 1 is a perspective view showing a sculpture in accordance with our new design;

FIG. 2 is a front view thereof;

FIG. 3 is a rear view thereof;

FIG. 4 is a left side view thereof;

FIG. 5 is a right side view thereof;

FIG. 6 is a top view thereof; and

FIG. 7 is a bottom view thereof.

WE CLAIM:

The ornamental design for a SCULPTURE, as shown and described.

BRMFS1 229971v1

'₂5

FIG.1
PERSPECTIVE VIEW

7

2.25

FIG.2
FRONT VIEW

375

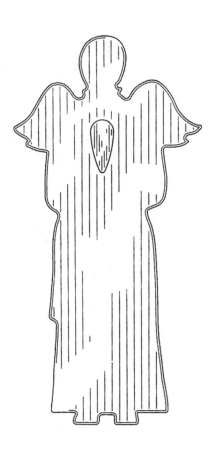

FIG.3
REAR VIEW

4/25

FIG.4
LEFT SIDE VIEW

FIG.5
RIGHT SIDE VIEW

5₂5

FIG.6
TOP VIEW

FIG.7
BOTTOM VIEW

Page 1 of 1

 UNITED STATES PATENT AND TRADEMARK OFFICE

COMMISSIONER FOR PATENTS
UNITED STATES PATENT AND TRADEMARK OFFICE
WASHINGTON, D.C. 20231
www.uspto.gov

APPLICATION NUMBER	FILING/RECEIPT DATE	FIRST NAMED APPLICANT	ATTORNEY DOCKET NUMBER
29/134,053	12/13/2000	Shalom Zadok	3429-8 Design

CONFIRMATION NO. 4521

FORMALITIES LETTER

Brown Raysman Millstein Felder & Steiner LLP
120 West 45th Street
New York, NY 10036

OC000000005686136

Date Mailed: 01/18/2001

NOTICE TO FILE MISSING PARTS OF NONPROVISIONAL APPLICATION

FILED UNDER 37 CFR 1.53(b)

Filing Date Granted

An application number and filing date have been accorded to this application. The item(s) indicated below, however, are missing. Applicant is given TWO MONTHS from the date of this Notice within which to file all required items and pay any fees required below to avoid abandonment. Extensions of time may be obtained by filing a petition accompanied by the extension fee under the provisions of 37 CFR 1.136(a).

- The statutory basic filing fee is missing.
  Applicant must submit $ 320 to complete the basic filing fee and/or file a small entity statement claiming such status (37 CFR 1.27).
- The oath or declaration is unsigned.
- To avoid abandonment, a late filing fee or oath or declaration surcharge as set forth in 37 CFR 1.16(e) of $130 for a non-small entity, must be submitted with the missing items identified in this letter.

- **The balance due by applicant is $ 450.**

A copy of this notice MUST be returned with the reply.

Customer Service Center
Initial Patent Examination Division (703) 308-1202
PART 3 - OFFICE COPY

2230
0360

GAU 2900
2912
T3   3429/8 Design

IN THE UNITED STATES PATENT AND TRADEMARK OFFICE

In re Application of	:	Shalom Zadok et al.	Examiner: To be assigned
Application. No.	:	29/134,053	Group Art Unit: 2900
Filed	:	December 13, 2000	
Title	:	SCULPTURE	

RECEIVED

APR 1 7 2001

TECH CENTER 1600/29

Assistant Commissioner for Patents
Washington, D.C. 20231

CLAIM OF PRIORITY

Priority is being claimed from Israeli Design Patent Application No. 34249 filed on October

6, 2000. A certified copy of the priority document is submitted herewith.

Respectfully submitted,

Date: March 16, 2001

Seth H. Ostrow, Reg. No. 37,410
BROWN RAYSMAN MILLSTEIN
FELDER & STEINER LLP
120 West Forty-Fifth Street
New York, New York 10036
Tele: (212) 944-1515
Fax : (212) 840-2429

OIPE
MAR 2 1 2001
PATENT & TRADEMARK OFFICE

RECT

APR 1 7 *2001*

TECH CEN... *1600/2900*

מדינת ישראל

This is to certify that the
annexed are true copies of the
representation as filed with
application No.
for registration of a design
to be applied to:

34249

זאת לתעודה כי המסמך
הרצוף בזה הינו העתק
נאמן של הדמות כפי
שהופקדה
עם הבקשה מספר
לרישום מדגם   מתייחס
ל:

SCULPTURE

פסל

made on	06/10/2000		שהוגשה ביום
by			ע"יי
SHALOM ZADOK			שלום צדוק
			רח' קראוזה 17
HOLON	58278	58278	חולון
Israel			ישראל
ITCHAK TARKAY			יצחק טרקאי
			רח' נורדאו 11
HOLON 58278		58278	חולון
Israel			ישראל

This, 18/12/2000 ,היום

משה ש. גולדברג

משה ש. גולדברג

Moshe S. goldberg

רשם הפטנטים

Commissioner of Patents

		Applicant/Patent	Application/Control No.	
Notice of References Cited		halom ZADOK And Itchak TARKA	29/134,053	
		Examiner	Art Unit	
		Dominic Simone	2912	Page 1 of 1

U.S. PATENT DOCUMENTS

*		Document Number Country Code-Number-Kind Code	Date MM-YYYY[1]	Name	Classification[2]	
X	A	D13,727	3/1883	Muldoon	D99	22
X	B	D304,347	10/1989	Murtagh	D11	128 X
X	C	D312,058	11/1990	Vermillion	D11	128
X	D	D347,405	5/1994	Corson et al.	D11	160
X	E	D371,987	7/1996	Chiu	D11	160
X	F	D407,041	3/1999	Bloemer Gerth	D11	128
	G					
	H					
	I					
	J					
	K					
	L					
	M					

FOREIGN PATENT DOCUMENTS

*		Document Number Country Code-Number-Kind Code	Date MM-YYYY[1]	Country	Name	Classification[2]
	N					
	O					
	P					
	Q					
	R					
	S					
	T					

NON-PATENT DOCUMENTS

*		Include, as applicable: Author, Title, Date, Publisher, Edition or Volume, Pertinent Pages
	U	
	V	
	W	
	X	

* A copy of this reference is not being furnished with this Office action. See MPEP § 707.05(a).   [1] Dates in MM-YYYY format are publication dates.   [2] Classifications may be U.S. or foreign.

U. S. Patent and Trademark Office
PTO-892 (Rev. 01-2001)   **Notice of References Cited**   Part of Paper No. 5

Tarkay (an attorney and artist) is well-known in intellectual property circles for convincing an American court to allow him to protect the style of his imagery as "trade-dress" (see Chapter 4, Section D2), a fleeting application of trademark law that has not since been duplicated.

Page 1 is a form that provides basic information about the patent application: How it is classified by the USPTO, the name of the patent examiner, when the applicants were notified that their patent was accepted, and the date the patent was made public.

In this case, the form indicates that the angel statue was assigned to Design Class D11, Subclass 162. The Art Unit designation (2912) refers to the group of examiners at the Patent Office who handle patents in this class. This form is prepared by the Patent Office.

Page 2 is a directory of the contents of the file wrapper, a list of the documents exchanged by the applicant and the USPTO. (Note: these directories don't always list every document.)

Page 3 is a report of how the patent examiner searched for prior art relating to angel statues. Typically, examiners start their search by looking at previously issued U.S. patents by classification category. In this case, the examiner searched six categories, as listed in the "Searched" table.

Examiners also search nonpatent resources. In this case, the examiner searched through a publication, *Xmas Digest*, and a collection of ornaments kept at the Patent Office.

Page 4 documents the final "issuing classification" for the design: Class D11, Subclass 162.

Page 5 is a form containing statistical data regarding the invention.

Page 6 lists the text of the patent application for the angel statue (and illustrates the simplicity of such texts).

Pages 7, 8, and 9 include a Declaration and Power of Attorney form, in which the inventors state who they are, mention any foreign patent applications related to this patent application, and grant power of attorney to some lawyers. (If you are an American filing the design patent application on your own, you won't need such a lengthy declaration.)

Pages 10 through 14 are the illustrations submitted along with the patent specification, seven figures distributed across five pages.

Pages 15 to 19 are a duplicate set of illustrations. Examiners sometimes make extra copies of figures to use while they are examining the application.

Page 20 is a copy of the cover letter sent by the law firm for the initial patent application.

Page 21 is a copy of a letter that the USPTO sent to the applicants, informing them of a few correctable deficiencies in their submission. In this case, they didn't pay the filing fee and didn't have the inventors sign the declaration. To correct these mistakes, they will have to pay a late filing fee. This letter, called a "Notice to File Missing Parts of Nonprovisional Application," gives the applicant two months to respond. Technical errors like this cost applicants money and delay the examination process.

Page 22 is a cover letter sent by the lawyers regarding an enclosed declaration and check.

Pages 23 through 25 include the original declaration with the signatures of the two inventors.

Page 26 is a copy of page 21, which the applicant had to send back to the Patent Office.

Page 27 is a priority claim document, in which the patent applicants notify the Patent Office that the original version of this design patent was filed in another country at an earlier time. Most countries are signatories to global patent treaties that allow people to file patents in other countries while retaining the filing date of their original patent application.

Pages 28 and 29 are copies of some of the documents filed with the original Israeli patent application. Again, if you are an American, you won't have to file these papers.

Page 30 is a Notice of Allowability, in which the patent examiner informs the applicants that their patent application will be granted, but they might have to make some corrections. In this case, the patent applicants did not meet all of the Patent Office requirements for drawings.

Page 31 is a Notice of References Cited, a list of patent and nonpatent prior art that the examiner looked at while examining the patent application. (To save the examiner time, and to improve your chances of acquiring a strong design patent, spend some time searching the patent and nonpatent prior art, and submit the results of your search along with your patent application.)

Page 32 is a Notice of Draftperson's Patent Drafting Review, in which a USPTO draftsperson tells the applicants what is wrong with their patent application drawings. In this case, the application erroneously included text descriptions of point of view in the drawing.

Page 33 is a Notice of Allowance and Issue Fee Due, which the Patent Office uses to inform the applicants that the design patent will issue once the issue fees are paid.

Pages 34 and 35 are a letter from the lawyers informing the Patent Office that they have moved to a new address.

Pages 36 to 41 are a cover letter and re-submission of the drawings, this time without the text descriptions of perspective.

Pages 42 and 43 are USPTO records showing that the issue fee was paid.

Page 44 is a letter from the itinerant patent attorneys, once again informing the Patent Office that they have moved their offices.

Page 45 is a copy of the envelope that the lawyers used to send the issue fee to the Patent Office.

If you are applying for a design patent and there are few existing designs that are similar to your design, your exchange with the USPTO will probably look a lot like this one (absent the documents on foreign registration, for most applicants).

Additional Application Issues

A number of additional issues may arise during patent prosecution, including interferences, divisional applications, reissue applications, substitute applications, and double patenting. Below is a short explanation of each:

- **Interferences.** An interference is a costly, complex USPTO proceeding to determine who will get a patent when two or more applicants are claiming the same invention. In other words, it is a method of sorting out priority of inventorship. Approximately 2% of applications run into interferences.

- **Divisional Applications.** If a patent application contains more than one invention, the USPTO will require you to "restrict" it to just one of the inventions. That's because the application fee entitles an applicant to have only one invention examined. The only solution that protects several inventions originally filed in one application is to file a divisional application, officially described as "a later application for a distinct or independent invention, carved out of a pending application and disclosing and claiming only subject matter disclosed in the earlier or parent application" (MPEP 201.06). As you might imagine, this can get pretty complicated.

- **Reissue Applications.** A reissue application is an attempt to correct information in an issued patent. It is usually filed when a patent owner believes the claims are not broad enough, the claims are too broad (usually because the applicant discovered a prior-art reference that overlaps with the claims), or there are significant errors in the specification. There is some risk when you file a reissue application, because all of the claims in the original patent will be examined and can be rejected.

- **Substitute Applications.** If you abandon your patent application, you can file a substitute application that essentially duplicates the abandoned application. (See MPEP 201.09.) The disadvantage of a substitute application is that you don't get to claim the filing date of the previously abandoned patent application.

- **Double Patenting.** If a patent issues and the patent owner files a second application containing the same invention ("double patenting"), the second application will be rejected. If the second application resulted in a patent, that patent will be invalidated. Two applications contain the same invention when either the two inventions are literally the same or the second invention is an obvious modification of the first invention.

Art & Entertainment Classifications

In order to help with your USPTO searching, we have isolated most of the art and entertainment-related patent classifications. This will help you begin your search by patent class instead of keyword. Classifications preceded by the letter "D" are for design patents.

A

Accordion
  Musical instrument,
    84/376 R
      Design, D17/3+
Acoustics, 181
  Building construction,
    52/144+
Acridone Dye, 8/662
Advertising
  Aerial, 40/212+
  Calendars, 40/107
  Card support, D06/512
  Coupons, electronic
    redemption, 705/14
  Design, D20/10+
  Display cards, 40/12401+
  Mirror or reflector devices,
    359/838+
  Printed matter, 283/56

Show boxes and cards,
    D20/40
Sign exhibiting, 40
Skywriting, 40/213
Vehicle body, 296/21
Afghan Blanket, D06/603
Amusement Devices, 472
  Design, D21/811+
  Elevator, 472/131
    Roundabout, 472/2
  Exercising devices, 482
  Games, 473
  Houses, 472/136
    Illusionary, 472/74
  Mechanical guns &
    projectors, 124
  Mirrors and reflectors,
    359/838+
  Nonprojectile game, 463
  Projectile games, 473

Railway, 104/53+
    Car in wheel, 104/77
  Roundabout stationary,
    472/1+
  Roundabout transported,
    472/3
  Trip illusions, 472/59+
  Water guns, 222/78+
Anaglyphs, 359/464+
Animation, 345/473+
Apparel, 2
  Adornment, attachable, D11
  Apparatus, 223
    Boot and shoe making, 12
    Knitting, 66
    Patterns, 33/2 R+
    Sewing, 112
    Weaving, 139
  Blouse, shirt, D02/840+
    Design, D02/896+

C

Filter, 359/885+
   Photographic, chemically
     defined, 430/6+
Flowers by absorption of
   dye, 427/4
Food, 426/540+
   Preserving or modifying
     color, 426/262
Fresh flowers, 47/58.1 CF
Glass heat developed,
   65/111+
Lanterns, 362/166+
   Signal, 362/168
Luminous, inorganic,
   252/301.6 R+
Luminous, organic,
   252/301.16
Mineral oil, 208/12
Musical instrument
   accessory, 84/464 R
Photography, see
   photography, 430/357+
     Separation record-making,
     430/356
Cornet, 84/388+
   Design, D17/11
   Mouthpieces, 84/398+
   Mutes, 84/400
   Tremolos, 84/401
Costume, D02/741
Crayon, 401/49+
Crepe Paper, 428/153+
Crystal
   Composition, inorganic
     luminescent, 252/6+
   Composition, organic
     luminescent, 252/301.16

Filter, 333/187+
   In sample holder, 378/79
   Liquid crystal composition,
     252/299.01+
   Liquid optical filter, 349/1+
   Liquid stock material,
     428/1.1
   Metalworking, making,
     29/DIG 17
   Microphones, 381/173
   Pickups, 369/144
   Piezoelectric, 310/311+
   Scintillation, 250/458.1
   Single-crystal, oriented-crystal,
   Epitaxy
     Apparatus other than
       coating, 117/200+
     Coating apparatus, 118
     Processes of growth, 117
Curved Work Forming Means
   Glass molding, 65/286+
   Metal bending, 72/380
   Milling, 409/64+
   Pattern, curvilinear draw,
     164/215+
   Planing, 409/309+
   Plate-cutting, 82/72+
   Wood-shaping guide,
     144/152+

D

Daguerreotypy, 396/438
Davenports, i.e., Sofa Beds,
   5/12.1+
Decoration
   Bow rosette, pompon,
     428/4+

Collapsible, 428/12
Displays and exhibitors,
   40/406+
   With special effects,
     40/427+
Feathers and plumes, 428/6
Festoon, 428/10
   Collapsible, 428/9
Filamentary, 428/542.6
Flora, artificial, 428/17+
Lamp housing, 362/362+
Lights, 362/227+
   X-art collection, 362/806*
Party type, 428/7+
Pole, cap, 52/301
Roof finial or cresting, 52/57
Sheet-form, 428/542.6
Trimming for clothing, 2/244
Trimming for hat, 2/175.3
Trimstrip for building,
   52/716.1+
Desserts, 426/573
Dioramas, 472/57+
Dolls, 446/268+
   Aquatic, 446/156+
   Assembling and
     disassembling, 29/805
   Design, D21/621
   Eating, drinking, nursing,
     446/304+
   Sleeping, 446/345+
   Talking, crying, 446/297+
     Wheeled, 446/270+
   Wheeled, 446/269+
     Inflatable, 446/226
Dome, 362/479
   Arcuate design, D25/19

Index

Remember:

Little publishers have big ears.
We really listen to you.

Take 2 Minutes & Give Us Your 2 cents

Your comments make a big difference in the development and revision of Nolo books and software. Please take a few minutes and register your Nolo product—and your comments—with us. Not only will your input make a difference, you'll receive special offers available only to registered owners of Nolo products on our newest books and software. Register now by:

PHONE
1-800-728-3555

FAX
1-800-645-0895

EMAIL
cs@nolo.com

or **MAIL** us
this registration card

_ _ _ _ _ _ _ _ _ _ _ _ fold here _ _ _ _ _ _ _ _ _ _ _ _ _

Registration Card

NAME _____ DATE _____

ADDRESS _____

_____

CITY _____ STATE _____ ZIP _____

PHONE _____ EMAIL _____

WHERE DID YOU HEAR ABOUT THIS PRODUCT? _____

WHERE DID YOU PURCHASE THIS PRODUCT? _____

DID YOU CONSULT A LAWYER? (PLEASE CIRCLE ONE)   YES   NO   NOT APPLICABLE

DID YOU FIND THIS BOOK HELPFUL?   (VERY)   5   4   3   2   1   (NOT AT ALL)

COMMENTS _____

_____

_____

WAS IT EASY TO USE?   (VERY EASY)   5   4   3   2   1   (VERY DIFFICULT)

We occasionally make our mailing list available to carefully selected companies whose products may be of interest to you.

❏ If you do not wish to receive mailings from these companies, please check this box.

❏ You can quote me in future Nolo promotional materials.
  Daytime phone number _____.

PATAE 1.0

Nolo
in the
NEWS

"Nolo helps lay people perform legal tasks without the aid—or fees—of lawyers."

—USA TODAY

Nolo books are ..."written in plain language, free of legal mumbo jumbo, and spiced with witty personal observations."

—ASSOCIATED PRESS

"...Nolo publications...guide people simply through the how, when, where and why of law."

—WASHINGTON POST

"Increasingly, people who are not lawyers are performing tasks usually regarded as legal work... And consumers, using books like Nolo's, do routine legal work themselves."

—NEW YORK TIMES

"...All of [Nolo's] books are easy-to-understand, are updated regularly, provide pull-out forms...and are often quite moving in their sense of compassion for the struggles of the lay reader."

—SAN FRANCISCO CHRONICLE

fold here

- -

Place
stamp here

Nolo
950 Parker Street
Berkeley, CA 94710-9867

Attn: PATAE 1.0